Copyright © 2016 by Lani Sharp
All rights reserved. This book or any portion thereof
may not be reproduced or used in any manner whatsoever
without the express written permission of the publisher
except for the use of brief quotations in a book review.

Printed in Australia

First Printing, 2016

ISBN 978-0-9945051-5-6

White Light Publishing House
6 Lincoln Way
Melton West, VIC, Australia 3337

www.whitelightpublishingau.com

❧ DEDICATION ☙

This book is dedicated to my Grandpa Colin, now departed from this Earthly life, the most inspiring Virgoan in my Universe. Thank you for your love, unending patience, hilarity, practical jokes, refreshing naiveté, frivolity, your constant painting and pottering, telling unfunny jokes, faith, treating my friends as though they were your own, and for being such a wonderful part of my childhood journey. You and Nana made my world and taught me so much! Days spent in your Sydney backyard, drinking soft drinks by the crate, popping firecrackers on your back porch, gorging on Fags (fake lolly cigarettes back in the days before political correctness), and getting away with all manner of other mischief, are the stuff of many precious memories. Thank you.

ABOUT THE AUTHOR

☾ ★ ☽

Lani Sharp is a Natural Born Rebel who just also happens to be an Aquarian, who shunned 'conventional' astrology courses to pursue her own path in the wondrous, inspiring and ever-evolving field of cosmic forces and stellar influences. After failing to find a course or tutor that suited her needs, Lani set out on her own starry Magic Carpet adventure across the skies, partly to discover her own 'truths' about this ancient system, but mostly to prove that one can achieve absolutely anything, including and above all, their dream careers (or lifestyle), if they put their hearts and souls into it. A self-taught astrologer who takes the esoteric and spiritual approach to this much-loved popular art, she has been studying and effectively practising astrology since she was eight years old. When she is not writing about, channelling, practising or teaching astrology, she can be found living her dream life alternating somewhere between her home in Australia's stunning Tropical North or her second home in Victoria's beautiful Dandenong Ranges, enjoying tea parties with her highly imaginative Cancerian daughter, Allira, and their gnome and fairy friends, crystal-wishing, day-dreaming, believing in gnomes, pixies, angels, fairies, magic and miracles, honing her magickal * witchcraft skills, Moon-gazing, Sun-worshipping, Venus-channelling, Jupiter-drawing, assisting others to discover, unravel and follow their true spiritual paths … or of course walking across rainbows!

* Not a mistake. Magick is a Wiccan variation of the word 'magic'.

★

ACKNOWLEDGEMENTS, CREDITS & GRATITUDE BLESSINGS

☆

I would love to thank the following people and entities for their amazing contributions, interest, support and faith in me as I wrote the manuscripts for each of the twelve astrological Sun signs. Firstly, the biggest thank you goes to my Mum, Sandra, and my stepdad, Barry, for their unending support, love, advice, daily Skype conversations, acceptance of our geographical distance, and above all, their inner knowing that everything always comes together in the end. Your support of me and my dreams is appreciated beyond words. Secondly, gratitude to my wonderful partner, Travis, for his patience (no mean feat for a Gemini!), for supporting me every step of the way, and for his acceptance of my 'mad scientist' Aquarian mindset by never trying to break down the invisible 'laboratory' walls I built around myself while writing the books. I would also like to extend my enormous gratitude to the following: Allira, my little Cancerian 'crab' daughter, a soul in a billion, who also had to tolerate and operate within the bounds of her nutty professor mother's antics and focus throughout the writing of the books. Thank you to Nicola, my wonderful Facebook friend, for recommending White Light Publishing House, and of course to White Light Publishing House themselves, for pouring their faith and passion into my project from the very beginning - and an even bigger thank you to the wonderful people behind the company for publishing my work, Christie and Jess! Gratitude also goes out to my dear friends, both near and far, who have inspired in me so many ideas through simply being themselves - especially Amanda and Carlie. Amanda, you have always been my 'astrology buddy' and I have always enjoyed - and learned so much through - our discussions on all things astrology and star signs: the good, the bad and the ugly! Having someone like you off which to bounce thoughts and share ideas with, has always been immensely helpful and appreciated. I have saved my final thank you for The Universe, who always delivers to me exactly what I have asked for, without exception. The Universe is my ultimate *higher power*, my guiding light, my powerful driving force, my spiritual helper, my guardian angel, my eternal friend, my inner motivator, my sympathetic listener, my inspirational teacher, and the fulfiller of all my dreams, including this one, having my very first book(s) published, a long-held dream that stretches way back through the years to my days of being a mini dreamer, inquisitor and stargazer. The Universe has always believed in me, but perhaps more importantly, I have always believed in *IT*.

So to all of the above, I wish to say:

Thank you, thank you, thank you!

"We were born at a given moment, in a given place, and like vintage years of wine, we have the qualities of the year and of the season in which we are born"

Carl G. Jung

"There was a star danced,
and under that I was born"

William Shakespeare

INSPIRED BY ALL THE SIGNS

Aries imparted courage and boldness
And helped me dance away the pain
Taurus gave me hugs and comfort
And shelter from the rain
Gemini provided me with laughter
And taught me again how to have fun
Cancer nurtured and sustained me
By reflecting back my Sun
Leo reminded me there was joy
From within myself and above
Virgo awakened my healthy glow
By teaching me how to love
Libra gave me gentle hugs
And judged me not for a thing
Scorpio lent me some of his power
And took away the sting
Sagittarius showered me with gifts
Of words so wise and true
As Capricorn led the way up the mountain
My resolve and strength grew
Aquarius gave me the gift of friendship
And carried me as his brother
And Pisces swam with me to the depths
With a compassion like no other.

Special Note

Throughout the text of this book, and indeed the whole Lucky Astrology book series, I have capitalised the first letter of the word 'Universe'. This is because, quite simply, I feel it is a very special title for the higher power that I personally choose to be guided by, and have accordingly highlighted it as such.

You may also notice that I use the words 'he' or 'she', and 'his' or 'her', when referring to your own Sun sign and other zodiac signs, and never 'he or she' or 'his or her' together. The reason for this is for simplicity, for I don't wish the sentences to be too wordy and therefore the messages within them to be lost. As a general rule, I refer to all six 'masculine' zodiac signs as 'he', and all six 'feminine' signs as 'she', and this remains a consistent rule throughout this book and the whole series.

Your Sun sign, Virgo, is a feminine sign and will thus be referred to accordingly.

CONTENTS

	Page
ASTROLOGY	15
THE ZODIAC & YOUR PLACE IN THE SUN	24
VIRGO THE VIRGIN	31
QUOTES BY VIRGOANS	37
THE VIRGO CONSTELLATION	42
THE VIRGO SYMBOL	44
THE RUNDOWN & LESSONS ★	
THE ESSENCE OF VIRGO	48
THE THREE DECANS OF VIRGO	60
YOUR ELEMENT ★ EARTH	64
YOUR MODE ★ MUTABLE	86
YOUR RULING PLANET ★ MERCURY	89
YOUR HOUSE IN THE HOROSCOPE ★	
THE SIXTH HOUSE	106
YOUR OPPOSITE SIGN ★ PISCES	110
MAGIC, DRAWING, ATTRACTION, SPELLS,	
RITUALS, WISHING & POWER	117
ASTROLOGY & MAGIC	122
PLANETS ★ DAYS OF THE WEEK	
& THEIR POWERS	128
YOUR NATAL MOON PHASE	132
SPELLS, MAGIC & WISHING WITH MOON PHASES	135
THE MOON ★ WHAT T REPRESENTS IN THE	
HUMAN PSYCHE & NATAL CHART	143
YOUR MOON SIGN	146
YOUR BODY & HEALTH	154
THE CELL SALTS ★ ASTROLOGICAL TONICS	160

	Page
EARTH SIGN VIRGO & THE MELANCHOLIC HUMOUR	163
MONEY ATTRIBUTES	166
COLOURS ★ YOUR LUCKY COLOURS	169
LUCKY CAREER TIPS	181
LUCKY PLACES	185
GEMS & CRYSTALS	186
VIRGOAN POWER CRYSTALS	200
YOUR LUCKY NUMBERS	214
YOUR LUCKY MAGIC HOURS OR TIME UNITS	223
YOUR LUCKY DAY ★ WEDNESDAY	228
YOUR LUCKY CHARM / TALISMANS	232
YOUR LUCKY ANIMALS & BIRDS	235
YOUR METALS	247
PLANTS, HERBS, SPICES, TREES, SHRUBS, FLOWERS, SCENTS & INCENSE	254
YOUR FOODS	259
YOUR LUCKY WOOD & CELTIC TREE ★ BEECH & HAZEL OR VINE	262
THE POWER OF LOVE	269
LUCKY IN LOVE? VIRGO COMPATIBILITY	281
YOUR TAROT CARDS	298
LUCKY 13 TIPS	319
HAVE YOU PACKED YOUR MAGICAL BAG FOR THE JOURNEY?	322
A FINAL WORD ★ TAPPING INTO THE MAGIC OF VIRGO	323

LUCKY ASTROLOGY

By Lani Sharp

VIRGO

Tapping into the Powers of Your Sun Sign for Greater Luck, Happiness, Health, Abundance & Love

"That which is above is like to that which is below, and that which is below is like to that which is above, to accomplish the miracles of one thing ... the Father thereof is the Sun, the mother the Moon."

The Emerald Tablet, Hermes Trismegistus (circa 3000 BC)

★ ASTROLOGY ★

Astrology: "Divination through the correlation of
earthly events with celestial patterns"
'Real Magic', I. Bonewits, 1971

A BRIEF HISTORY

Astrology can be defined as the calculation and meaningful interpretation of the positions and motions of the heavenly bodies, and their correlation with human experiences. Its central concept is based upon this interconnectedness or correspondence between the stars and ourselves.

The word astrology is derived from the Greek word astron, meaning 'star' and logos which means 'word'. Astrology, therefore, literally means language of the stars. It is based on the ancient law known as 'As Above, So Below', otherwise known as the Law of the Macrocosm and Microcosm. The Macrocosm is the Universe, symbolised by the sky, the starry dome that we can see from the Earth; the Microcosm is us - humans, and all other life on Earth. 'As Above, So Below' is a well-known and deeply impressing maxim of Hermetic origin, inscribed upon the famed Emerald Tablet among cryptic wording by enigmatic figure, Hermes Trismegistus, around 5,000 years ago. These four powerful words are adopted by astrologers and believers in magic to explain, in very succinct wording, the meaning behind the art and science of celestial influences upon our Earthly affairs.

Astrology and many other magical and occult studies, propose that we are not separate from the Universe, we are part of it. The Sun, Moon and planets all follow exact patterns of movement and their motions can be measured precisely by astronomers. The basic idea of astrology is that all individual parts of the Universe, from plants to animals, cooperate with each other and work together in harmony.

Anyone can apply astrological knowledge in their daily lives, but it hasn't always been like that. At one time, astrology was reserved only for Kings and nations, and only the court astrologer/astronomer could cast and interpret horoscopes. Ancient astrology and astronomy used to be one and the same. To be an astrologer, you first had to be able to interpret the stars in some systematic way, and then track the movement of the Moon and the planets against the background of the constellations.

Astrology, the knowledge and language of the cosmos, goes back to the ancient kingdom of Babylonia and was adapted by the Mesopotamians, Greeks, Egyptians and Romans to incorporate their own deities (as indicated in mythology). It is upon a combination of Greek and Egyptian interpretations of astrology that our present knowledge is based.

In the ancient Mesopotamian world, as far back as 800 BC, people lived precariously beneath the open skies. The skies and the stars which filled them, were the real founders of astrology. Today we are aware that the Sun and Moon exert a profound influence upon our Earthly affairs, but for our primitive ancestors, the heavens, the stars and the planets must have been a matter of great and mysterious significance. Early humankind, its senses influenced by natural processes of ebbs, flows, growth, decay and cycles, tended naturally towards a physical explanation of the Universe. At first, the movements of the planets - and all celestial occurrences - were observed as omens affecting the Ruler and his nation; it was only in Egypt in the fifth century AD that the casting of horoscopes for individual people and the calculation of the planetary positions at the time of birth became widespread.

The first astrologers, the Chaldeans, mapped the stars and later passed this knowledge and wisdom on to the ancient Greeks, who, during the third century BC, developed astrology into a science with the use of mathematical aids and instruments to measure planetary movements. The Greeks were the first to cast individual horoscopes. And it was the Greeks who associated the four elements with the signs of the zodiac. The word "zodiac" can be translated from Greek to mean the "circle or path of the animals." The Greeks not only had names for the twelve Solar phases but had symbols for each, and many correspond with the ones we use today.

The Greeks passed on much of their knowledge to the Romans. During the second century BC, Roman astrologers were primarily forecasters who were consulted frequently by rulers of the church and state. By the early third century AD, astrology coexisted with early Christianity. This harmonious coexistence was possible because it was considered that celestial bodies could foretell events, but did not determine the future - indeed, the stars seen by the shepherds at the time of Christ's birth were only predictors of his arrival. After the fourth century AD, Christianity strengthened and the popularity of astrology declined as Christian reluctance to support 'pagan' or 'superstitious' beliefs became more prominent. The Middle Ages saw a revival in astrology, with courses being taught in universities and other educational establishments, and connections were made between the zodiac, alchemy, herbs and medicine. Astrology was once again able to exist alongside the Church, although many remained suspicious of astrologers.

Around the beginning of the fifteenth century, academics of the Renaissance movement examined the past for knowledge, and ancient philosophies, including astrology, flourished; this coincided with arts and science movements developing. The famous prophet and astrologer Nostradamus lived during this period. Leonardo da Vinci depicted aspects of astrology combined with geometry in his art. Writers and poets of the time, including Shakespeare, alluded to zodiacal influences in their work.

During this period, astrology had numerous practical applications. Agricultural calendars were introduced, indicating favourable planting times according to the phases of the Moon; health and illness were linked with movements of celestial bodies; and emotional states and mental health afflictions correlated with the planetary positions.

Eventually, new ways of thinking led to a split between astronomy and astrology, and by the seventeenth century, the realm of science had developed to such a degree that astrology was no longer taken seriously.

The study of the sky above us has been charted for more than 5,000 years. This fact is known because ancient 'horoscopes' imprinted on clay tablets have been unearthed, dating back almost 5,400 years ago. However, no one knows for certain just how, when and where astrology first began, although it is known that it flourished in ancient Chaldea, Mesopotamia, Babylon and Egypt.

Astrology is a science which has spanned many centuries and still remains extraordinarily popular, and its truths have the potential to speak to and *through* all of us. Long before today's interest in it, men of great vision such as Ptolemy, Hippocrates, Plato, Galileo, Jefferson, Franklin, Newton, Columbus and Jung respected its inherent truths, mythology and eternal knowledge. Furthermore, astrology predates many other 'sciences' - for out of it grew religion, medicine and astronomy, not the other way around.

The discipline of astrology is ultimately a study of the interlocking and interrelated forces of the twelve zodiacal forces, or constellations, that grace the heavens, as they pour their energies into the Earthly kingdoms below. As these various energies circulate throughout the etheric realm of our Solar system, these zodiacal entities and archetypes imprint their vibrational frequencies and harmonic resonances upon our bodies, minds, souls and spirits.

ASTROLOGY & THE INDIVIDUAL

Since the earliest period of the history of humankind, people studied the starry vaults of the heavens and conceived that their presence, movements and positions endowed planet Earth's inhabitants with Divine influence. There is much evidence that positions and movements of the planets as seen from Earth at the time of a birth are linked to personality characteristics of individuals. Human energy and emotional cycles are governed by the forces and networks of magnetic impulses from all the planets. Of all the heavenly bodies, the Moon's effects and power are the most marked and visible due to its close proximity to Earth. But the Sun, Venus, Mars, Mercury, Jupiter, Saturn, Uranus, Neptune and Pluto exercise their influences just as surely. In fact, scientists are aware that plants and animals are affected by natural cycles which are governed by forces such as fluctuations in barometric pressure, the gravitational field and electricity in the air. These Earthly dynamics are originally triggered by magnetic vibrations from the atmosphere, or outer space, from where the planets send forth their unseen waves. No living organism or mineral on Earth escapes these immense, if unseen, influences.

The geomagnetic field seems to affect life on Earth in certain observed ways, and these influences appear to correlate with planetary positions. It has been suggested that the fluctuations of the Earth's magnetic field are picked up by the nervous system of the in utero infant, which acts like an antenna, and these synchronise the internal biological clocks of the foetus which control the moment of birth. The foetal magnetic antenna therefore, is sensitive enough to sense these planetary vibrations and fields, and through a combination of inherited genetics and the positions of the planets at birth, they are imprinted with certain basic inherited and 'absorbed' personality characteristics.

Carl Jung, the Swiss psychiatrist and psychological theorist, suggested that the inherent disposition of the individual is present at birth, and is reflected in the patterns of his or her natal chart. Further, he theorised that there is a 'priori factor' in all human activities, namely the inborn, preconscious and unconscious individual structure of the psyche. The preconscious psyche, for example that of a newborn baby, is not simply an empty vessel into which practically anything can be poured, but rather it is this preconscious psyche that gives us the free will to become what we are instead of what others or our environment makes us. The child is not merely a receptacle for the psychic life of those around him or her, albeit sensitive and susceptible to the surrounding unconscious forces in childhood; for he/she also brings something of his own to his experience of them.

Further, Dr Harold S. Burr, who was a Professor of Anatomy at the Yale University School of Medicine, and author of *The Nature of Man and the Meaning of Existence* (1962), asserted that there is order in the Universe, unity in the organism and man is endowed with a soul. He stated that a complex magnetic field not only establishes the pattern of the human brain at birth, but continues to regulate and control it through life, and that the human central nervous system is a superb receptor of electro-magnetic energies, indeed the finest in nature. He contended that the electro-dynamic fields of all living things, which may be measured and mapped with standard voltmeters, mould and control each organism's development, health and mood, and named these fields 'fields of life'.

It can therefore be suggested that astrological and planetary influences endow us with the majority of our characteristics at birth, characteristics bestowed upon us according to our Sun sign and other planetary forces. Other parts of the chart are also highly significant and need to be integrated for a 'whole' picture to form, however the Sun sign is an excellent starting point.

The ancients taught that astrology was one of the keys to the many enigmas that plague humans in their unceasing quest to determine what the meaning of life is, and what their role and place in the Universe is - and this quest still persists today. Astrology, which dates back over 5,000 years, is indeed one such key to unlocking the many secrets of the Universe - and ultimately, the individual self.

"KNOW THYSELF"

Man, know thyself. All wisdom centres on this.
Carl Jung

Before the temple of the Oracle at Delphi, the ancient Greeks imparted a special piece of advice that was carved onto one of the portals: "Know Thyself." These two powerful words are easy enough to understand, but much more difficult to apply. Throughout life's inner and outer journey, astrology can provide us with an inner navigational system by which we can be guided towards our highest potential, and closer towards the eternal quest of 'knowing thyself'. It provides the hope that this higher spiritual plane exists and that if we can 'read' and therefore be guided by the unique inner blueprint that our individual birth chart has stamped upon us at the moment we take our very first breath, indeed we can reach this higher spiritual plane and realise our innate potential.

Always remember that astrology is not fatalistic. The stars may incline, but they do not compel. Astrology simply provides us with an inner guide, a blueprint, for our journey through life and the finding of our true selves - and what we do with the resulting knowledge is entirely up to us.

Good luck on your journey!

THE ZODIAC & YOUR PLACE IN THE SUN

The zodiac is a circle of 360 degrees, consisting of equal segments of 30 degrees each. These represent the twelve houses of the twelve astrological signs. This zodiac is how the early astrologers imagined the Solar system to be, a perfect circle with the Earth at its centre, around which the Sun, Moon and the planets revolved. Each sign of the zodiac corresponds to one of the twelve segments, following a chronological order and established according to the rhythm of the seasons and cycles of the Sun and the Moon. But the zodiac itself, or the band of constellations which comprise it, has shifted over the millennia, creating division between astronomical and astrological schools of thought. It has been said that due to this shift over time, one who once considered themselves as an Aquarian, is actually a Capricorn, the sign before it, and a Leo is actually a Cancerian, its preceding sign. This is the result of misunderstandings and differences in perspectives, and explanations around it are beyond the scope of this book, but can be researched further should you wish to delve a little deeper. From the astronomical point of view, it is true that the zodiac to which we refer today is not situated where it 'should' be, but indeed, nothing is fixed under the celestial vault. And so the starting point of the ancient zodiac does not correspond exactly to the one we can observe today. But for the purposes of increasing your power and luck, let's keep things simple and enjoy the ride; after all, astrology - while based upon many scientific theories, mysteries, scepticism, superstitions, facts, measurable patterns, ambiguities, correlations, paradoxes, contradictions, links, stigmatisms and observations that seek to support, refute, prove and disprove this ancient art time and again - is ultimately meant to be *fun* too!

THE SUN

Earth's Luminary ★ *Our Brightest Shining Star*

Our Centre, Core Self, Identity & Inner Guiding Light

"Perfect is what I have said of the work of the Sun."
Hermes Trismegistus, *The Emerald Tablet*

The Sun is our essence, centre, source, ego strength, power, life force, will, vitality, creative expression, purpose, life's direction, our sense of identity, and who we really *are*. Our brightest star is the core of our individuality, our inner guiding light. The Sun is externalising, and represents totality, infinity, eternity, the striving toward and ultimate reaching of one's personal destiny, and *completion* in all areas. It is the creative energising giver of life and the 'father' of the zodiac. It endows us with our inherent creative potential and personal identity - our urge to *create* and to *be*. The Sun is our core self, conscious purpose, our sense of creating something out of our own being. It is the integrated personality and represents the *present*, our greatest Gift. The Sun rules the heart and is thus symbolically the centre of self. Indeed, the Sun *is* the heart and the most commanding presence in our birth chart; the luminary Ruler who governs our essential self and wants to be noticed and appreciated, and above all, to *shine*.

★ KEY WORDS ★

Identity, core self, spirit, life force, power, essence, creativity, higher self, the Father, ego, vitality, pride, individuality, leadership, majesty, inner authority, will, expression, willpower, purpose, the journey, the path and the destiny.

THE SUN ★ THE ULTIMATE SOURCE OF LIFE ON EARTH

Throughout the ages, and indeed since life forms began, the electromagnetic waves generated by the Sun have kept planet Earth habitable for humans, animals, plants and minerals. The Sun is, in fact, the only true source of energy on planet Earth. It provides the perfect amount of energy for plants to synthesise all of the products required for growth and reproduction, which is then stored by plants and ingested by humans and animals who, through many complex processes, utilise these various forms of encapsulated Solar energy - and so the cycle continues. Wood, fuel and minerals (crystals included), too, are merely various forms of this encased Sun energy. In fact, all matter is essentially 'frozen' light. Human body cells are bundles of Sun energy; we couldn't conceive or process a single thought without the molecules of Solar-energised oxygen and glucose.

In essence, the Sun supports the growth of all species, including human beings and microscopic life forms, and without it life on Earth would simply not be possible. The mathematical and metaphysical complexity that stands behind a system of organisation and order so infinitely diverse and intricate as planetary life cannot be truly fathomed, but unerringly and miraculously, the Sun instinctively knows what each species, from a tree to a human, intrinsically needs in order to fulfil its evolutionary purpose and cycles.

Ultimately, the electromagnetic waves generated by the Sun come in a variety of lengths, which determine their specific course of action and responsibility. There are gamma rays, x-rays, cosmic rays, various kinds of ultraviolet rays, infrared, short-wave infrared, radio waves, electric waves, and of course the visible light spectrum, consisting of the seven colour rays.

Most of these energy waves are absorbed and used for various processes in the layers of atmosphere that encircle the Earth, and only a small portion of them - the electromagnetic spectrum - reach the surface of our planet. Although the human eye is only able to perceive about one percent of this spectrum, the waves exert a very strong influence upon us. The waves and rays which do affect us so profoundly, allow all life forms to undergo constant cycles of change necessary for growth and renewal. Physically, we can observe this, but on a deeper, more spiritual plane, we can even *feel* it and allow its radiance to permeate our very souls. Such is the might, force and power of that astonishing ball of fire in our sky: the brilliant, ever-shining Sun.

THE SUN ★ WHAT IT REPRESENTS IN THE HUMAN PSYCHE & NATAL CHART

☼

"The Sun is the most powerful of all the stellar bodies. It colours the personality so strongly that an amazingly accurate picture can be given of the individual who was born when it was exercising its power through the known and predicable influences of a certain astrological sign; these electromagnetic vibrations will continue to stamp that person with the characteristics of their Sun sign as they go through life."
***Linda Goodman's Sun Signs*, Linda Goodman, Pan Books, 1968**

The Sun is our essence, our core self, conscious purpose and sense of identity, our creative potential, our spirit, the integrated personality that shines outward from within us. It is concerned with the present. It is our centre, source, power, life force, will, vitality, purpose, life's direction, what and who we *really* are.

The Sun represents our basic urge for self-expression. It is the 'Solar energy cell' in a person's character, the Lord and giver of life, and symbolises the way in which an individual will shine out to the world. Our Sun is our personal identity and aspects to it from other components in the chart show the ease or otherwise of assuredness and confidence with which one will project and express one's individuality. The Sun sign will also show how an individual bounces back from setbacks and disappointments, their resilience and their general outward expression of energy.

The Sun is the archetype of the Father and represents the primary masculine principle in the natal chart. It indicates how we express and experience our masculine side, or animus, our conscious self, how we express ourselves creatively, our personal potential, individuality, self-expression and personal power. It has to do with courage, power, generosity, creativity, vitality, self-confidence, nobility, self-worth, dignity and strength of will. It symbolises authority and purpose, the *ruler*, and its potential is the peak of constructive maturity. It signifies self-sufficiency and abundance, containing enough energy to radiate warmth and give life to everything around it.

The sign in which one's Sun is posited, and its placement in the birth chart, strongly indicates the level and type of vitality available to the personality (the sign), and in which area of life this may be most strongly directed (the house).

The Sun in a natal chart is a powerful symbol because everything is filtered, at a conscious level, through it. It tells us what we need to do to feel fully alive, the type of engine 'driving' us, what we need to do to be authentic and to be fully functioning. Listening to the special message of one's Sun sign can provide one with greater direction, and a more dynamic energy and life purpose.

The symbol for the Sun ☉ depicts a circle with a dot or 'seed' at its centre, from which the core self, power, creativity and the first sparks of life can spring. The circle around this 'seed' represents spirit, symbolising wholeness, eternity and the never-ending flow of energy.

While the Moon, the night sky's luminary, represents the *soul*, the Sun, the day sky's luminary, represents our *spirit*.

There is a reason your Sun sign is otherwise known as your Star Sign - it's because, quite simply, the Sun *is* a star; in fact, it's the largest, brightest, shiniest one in Earth's known visible Universe. This book is about your Sun sign and how you can become much larger, glow with far more brilliance, and shine brighter than you ever dreamed possible. I wish you all the magic in the galaxy for your dreams to come true and your deepest wishes to become reality, through tapping into the amazing power and inherent potential of your Sun sign. So get set for a galactical ride through the lucky stars of your constellation - and may a shooting star cross the path in front of you as you go!

VIRGO THE VIRGIN

★ Mutable Water, Negative, Feminine, Sensate ★

"Service expresses through work"

Body & Health
Intestines, Digestive System, Lymphatic System, Pancreas, Spleen, Nervous System, Abdomen, Colon, Hands, Fingernails and Toenails.

How Virgo Emanates its Life Force / Energy
Prudently, shrewdly, intelligently, reliably, diligently

Is Concerned With
★ Self-perfection ★ Responsibility ★
★ Altruism ★ Honesty ★ Duty ★ Virtue ★
★ Hygiene, Cleanliness ★ Health ★
★ Efficiency ★ Routine ★ Reliability ★
★ Strength of Character ★ Veiled Sensuality ★
★ Hard Work ★ Modesty ★ Service ★
★ Passivity ★ Perfection ★ Analysis ★
★ Communication ★ Shrewd Logical Thought ★
★ Practicality ★ Healing ★ Purity ★

Spiritual Virgo

Your Archetypal Universal Qualities
The Server, Healer, Worker, Quiet Achiever, Humble One

What You Refuse
To overlook detail, be idle or shirk responsibility

What You Are an Authority On
Providing efficient service, analysis, helping others, sacrifice, self-improvement

The Main Senses Through Which You Experience Your Reality
Order, duty, discipline, purity, correctness

How You Love
Discerningly, with devotion, sensuously

Positive Characteristics
★ Gentle with the helpless ★
★ Organised ★ Practical ★ Modest ★
★ Sympathetic, great advisor ★ Conscientious ★
★ Sharp and intelligent ★ Devoted ★
★ Humane and helpful ★ Reliable ★
★ Physically sensual ★ Dedicated ★
★ Painstaking ★ Shrewd ★ Self-sufficient ★
★ Knowledgeable ★ Health-conscious ★

Negative Characteristics
★ Scathing criticism of the lazy ★ Aloof ★
★ Untidy ★ Prude ★ Hypochondriac ★
★ Obsessive/compulsive ★ Cutting ★
★ Cranky and irritable ★ Sarcastic ★
★ Nervous ★ Cold ★ Worrier ★
★ Undemonstrative ★ Over-analysing ★
★ Overly perfectionist ★ Standards too high ★

To Bring Out Your Best
Do some self-improvement courses; let yourself go occasionally- be less inhibited; undertake a regular fasting or cleansing regime; power-walk; go to a health retreat; volunteer in an underprivileged community; share and apply your health knowledge.

Spiritual Goals
To learn to discriminate between destructive criticism and simple wisdom; to blow your own trumpet once in a while; to learn to be bolder and more spontaneous; to stop taking life too seriously; to learn to be less self-critical.

VIRGO

23 August - 22 September

Mutable Earth

Ruled by Mercury

"I ANALYSE"

Gemstones ◊ Sapphire, Carnelian, Peridot, Sardonyx

★ Modest, fussy, reserved, worrier, critical, observant, smart, aloof, reliable, meticulous, practical, lucid, serious, conservative, perfectionist, analytical, shrewd, tidy, nit-picky, intelligent, helpful, conscientious, cool, calm, prudent, discriminating, thrifty, logical, rational, courteous, serving, sacrificing, diligent, sensual, discerning, uneasy, painstaking, virtuous, a wallflower, tense, inhibited, dependable, differentiating, apprehensive, introspective ★

"In a world filled with despair, we must still dare to dream. In a world filled with distrust, we must still dare to believe"
Michael Jackson

VIRGO

♍

★ **Modest** ★ **Sacrificing** ★ **Gentle** ★
★ **Courteous** ★ **Serious** ★ **Practical** ★
★ **Helpful** ★ **Kind** ★ **Tasteful**

Virgo is the sign of the Virgin, a beautiful maiden holding sheaves of wheat in her hand and often sitting in a field of fertile crops. Shy, modest, conscientious, pure, hard-working, self-sacrificing, practical, sensual, serious, discriminating, shrewd, analytical, considerate and nit-picky are Virgos' most notable traits. Being a solid Earth sign, your sign is practical, persistent and pragmatic, but can lack imagination, warmth and passion at times. Cool, calm and reliable, Virgo loves to serve others and is therefore always the first person people will go to for advice. The Virgin is incredibly shrewd and intelligent in her undertakings, and her discriminating and perfectionist nature help her climb to the top in her steady 'quiet achiever' manner. Helping others is a big thing for the Virgin's helpful spirit, and she will be unfalteringly there for anyone who may need her for anything, always putting others first - a trait which comes so naturally to this modest sign. Virgo is meticulous, no-nonsense, conscientious and fussy, making them great to have onside, however they have a tendency towards being critical, over-analysing and worrying which can cause them trouble in both their inner and outer worlds. The Virgo is more often their own worst enemy, being nagged by their inner critic and perfectionist, and falling into pessimistic and gloomy attitudes at times. A sensual and dependable lover, deeply caring friend and with a sensible approach to life and love, Virgo is the sixth sign and the most practical and serving sign of the zodiac, making them purely delightful to have around!

KEY CONCEPTS
★ Unassuming and helpful ★
★ Humane, dutiful, caring and dependable ★
★ Sharp and refined intellect ★
★ Unselfish and sacrificing ★
★ Precise and meticulous ★
★ Underhanded, aloof and fault-finding ★
★ Pessimistic, cynical and sarcastic ★
★ Obsessive-compulsive and a hoarder ★
★ Secretive, nervous and dependent ★
★ Self-deprecating ★
★ Calm, clear, self-contained and self-reliant ★
★ Pure, clean, fresh and crisp ★
★ Delightful, polite courteous and considerate of others
★ Born researcher and scientist ★

SOME CORRESPONDENCES THAT ARE ASSOCIATED WITH VIRGO

Small animals and pets, hygiene, cynics, nutrition, analysts, nurses, servants, research, herbalists, satire, the intestines, dieticians, efficiency, masseurs, employees, chemists, osteopathy, staff, accountants, statistics, agencies, critics, health services, veterinarians, study, healers, minutiae, criticism, naturopathy, sanitation, civil service, waiters and waitresses, clerks, craftsmen, health care and doctors. Take your pick and enjoy the ride!

QUOTES BY VIRGOANS

"You can't move mountains by whispering at them" - Pink (8 September 1979)

"Monsters are real, and ghosts are real too. They live inside us, and sometimes, they win" - Stephen King (21 September 1947)

"If you want to be a singer, you've got to concentrate on it twenty-four hours a day. You can't be a well-driller, too" - Otis Redding (9 September 1941)

"I never use that word, 'retire'" - B.B. King (16 September 1925)

"Grease is the only cure for a hangover" - Cameron Diaz (30 August 1972)

"Beauty is in the heart of the beholder" - H.G. Wells (21 September, 1886)

"If you want to be a writer, you must do two things above all others: read a lot and write a lot. There's no way around these two things that I'm aware of, no shortcut" - Stephen King

"A person is a fool to become a writer. His only compensation is absolute freedom" - Roald Dahl (13 September, 1916)

"Finally, in conclusion, let me say just this." - Peter Sellers (8 September, 1925)

"I'm very much in the trenches, and I don't live in the lap of luxury ... I always have a certain amount of angst in my back pocket" - Pink

"There is no greatness where there is no simplicity, goodness and truth" - Count Leo Tolstoy (28 August, 1828)

"Do what you really want to do. Don't let the words of others hold you back. Take a step towards your dream. As you move closer, new opportunities will open up that you never imagined possible. The journey will be full of struggle, but ... the greater the struggle, the greater the victory! As you go for your dream, you will inspire others to do the same" - Rudy Ruettiger (23 August 1948)

"You don't have to be married to have a good friend as your partner for life" - Greta Garbo (18 September, 1905)

"There is a crack in everything, that's how the light gets in" - Leonard Cohen (21 September, 1934)

"Two hours of writing fiction leaves this writer completely drained. For those two hours he has been a different place with totally different people" - Roald Dahl

"You haven't partied until you've partied at dawn in complete silence with Buddhist monks" - Cameron Diaz

"All, everything that I understand, I understand only because I love" - Count Leo Tolstoy

"I'm just like anyone. I cut and I bleed. And I embarrass easily" - Michael Jackson (29 August 1958)

"A little nonsense now and then is relished by the wisest men" - Roald Dahl

"One of the luckiest things in life that can happen to you is, I think, to have happy childhood" - Agatha Christie (15 September, 1890)

"We especially need imagination in science. It is not all mathematics, nor all logic, but it is somewhat beauty and poetry" - Maria Montessori (31 August, 1870)

"When you want something, all the Universe conspires in helping you achieve it" - Paulo Coelho (24 August 1947)

"I like living. I have sometimes been wildly, despairingly, acutely miserable, racked with sorrow, but through it all I still know quite certainly that just to be alive is a grand thing" - Agatha Christie

"Spread love everywhere you go. Let no one ever come to you without leaving happier" - Mother Teresa (26 August 1910)

"We need not feel ashamed of flirting with the zodiac. The zodiac is well worth flirting with" - D. H. Lawrence (11 September 1885)

"I've been married twice. Most women would rather not be married to a travelling blues singer" - B.B. King

"The poverty of being unwanted, unloved and uncared for is the greatest poverty" - Mother Teresa

"All my characters are searching for their souls, because they are my mirrors. I'm someone who is constantly trying to understand my place in the world, and literature is the best way I found in order to see myself" - Paulo Coelho

"I'm never pleased with anything. I'm a perfectionist, it's part of who I am" - Michael Jackson

"The follow your dreams thing is really important, because so many people are railroaded into taking other paths by their family, friends, people who should be supportive, going, "What are you talking about?" Even just seemingly regular career paths, but if it's not what people expect for you they react kind of funny" - Joan Jett (22 September 1958)

"A person can grow only as much as his horizon allows" - John Powell (18 September 1963)

"Love is a fruit in season at all times, and within reach of every hand" - Mother Teresa

THE VIRGO CONSTELLATION

The signs of the zodiac are the twelve symbolic features that ancient people imagined while observing the heavens. They saw shapes, patterns, faces, and natural and supernatural beings in the stars, from which they established, over centuries, a kind of celestial hierarchy and system based upon their observations. Groupings of stars became constellations, and twelve of these constellations make up the zodiac, a Greek word meaning 'circle of animals', that we know today.

Star constellations are not really self-contained groups but are particularly bright stars that give the appearance of being close together and form distinctive patterns. These are the patterns that over the ages have been identified as animals, deities or mythological figures and heroes. The stars are the living past. We receive their light long after it has left the star itself and so they are a good focus for escaping from the parameters of time. Their stellar influence is analogous with the aura, the bio/psychic energy field surrounding humans, animals, plants, crystals and even places. These individual energy systems interact with the energy waves emanated by other people, and even the cosmic rays emitted by planetary bodies, for psychic energies are not limited by time or distance.

The cluster of stars we know as Virgo is the second largest constellation, after Hydra the Water Snake. It is a disappointing naked eye constellation, but of great interest to modern astronomers because it contains a large number of relatively close galaxies, extending into a neighbouring star cluster.

The Virgo constellation has one bright star, Spica, which is often mistaken for a planet. Within the boundary of her vast (46 degrees long) body, are over 500 nebulas. As the goddess of the harvest, she symbolises this by being situated in a very bountiful area of the heavens. Usually depicted in an angelic form with her two wings extending out into space, the Virgo constellation encapsulates the fruitfulness of women by holding a shaft of wheat in her hand, which is actually one of the brightest stars in the sky, Spica.

WISHING UPON YOUR STAR

The practice of wishing upon a star is familiar to most of us, and is a mystical superstition that is ingrained in many of us from childhood. As a nighttime ritual, you can wish upon your own sign's constellation or that of the sign whose energies you wish to call forth; indeed, you can wish upon any constellation you feel an affinity with. If you can't see a particular constellation in your night sky, you can always meditate on it in your mind, or you can use the traditional technique of wishing upon the first star you see, while reciting the popular rhyme: *Star light, star bright, first star I see tonight, I wish I may, I wish I might, have the wish I make this night!* Any one of the three rituals will hold power for your own special wish. Good luck!

THE VIRGOAN SYMBOL ♍

Astrology uses symbols or 'glyphs' to represent the planets and signs. The glyph is made up of shapes representing the energy and physical matter of which the Universe is composed, and how these shapes are used in each symbol provide hints as to the properties of the sign or planet it represents.

The ancient view was that there were five elements: Fire, Water, Air, Earth and Ether (or Spirit). Ether is invisible energy, while the four tangible elements are known as 'matter'. Ether, as pure energy, cannot be influenced by any of the physical/matter elements, although it surrounds them and indeed fuels them. The Greek philosopher and scientist Aristotle regarded this idea as a circle (Ether/Spirit) with a cross (matter) in the centre. This glyph is used in astrology as a symbol for Earth, and the cycle of life. All the symbols used in astrology represent the relationship between energy and the 'matter' elements.

The glyph of Virgo is based upon the Hebrew letter 'Mem' signifying the female principle with an added hook apparently based on the Phoenician symbol for a fish, the symbol used by the early Christians for Jesus, giving a clue to the mystery of the 'virgin' birth of Jesus. Through purity and dedication, (Virgo) is the necessary condition for the birth of the 'Messiah' established in the body of Cosmic Man. The symbol of this sign, a Virgin, is often depicted holding a sheaf of corn, the produce of the Earth, the harvest gathered at the end of summer. It is indeed the symbol of the end of the harvest and reminds us of the architecture of ancient grain stores.

The three straight lines can be interpreted in a couple of ways. Firstly, they are symbolic of the coils of energy latent in Virgo's essence. They seem held back from release into their full expression in the external door by the closed circle, which could represent a wall or a closed door. The three lines also represent three levels of consciousness. The third line of the super-conscious curves slightly upward, in an outpouring motion, but is held back by the last line that turns totally inwards and ends below the horizon, signifying Virgo's links with introversion, materialism and Earthly matters. In astrological symbology, the vertical line is designated as the line of destiny or intellect. It is detached, objective and unemotional. A further interpretation could be the pure, untouched female genitalia, the coils being the loops of the ovaries and uterus, the circle the intact hymen of the Virgin. And lastly, given that Virgo rules the intestines, these twisting and twirling lines could be a symbol of the tubes that make up the intestines.

Virgin is a synonym for 'pure' and 'unspoiled'. To be on the 'verge' is to be in a position of transition from one state to another, just as the sign Virgo stands immediately before the second and in-drawing half of the zodiacal cycle.

A NOTE ON 'THE VIRGIN'

Contrary to popular belief - and even though I will be referring often throughout this book to Virgo as *the Virgin* - Virgo does not mean 'virgin', nor does it confer a predilection to celibacy on people born under its influence. The name is derived from the Latin *virginis*, which is correctly translated as 'maiden' or 'girl'.

THE AGE OF VIRGO ★ 12,000 - 10,000 BC

The Age of Virgo is associated with worship of the Great Mother Goddess, as well as healing practices. During this period, humankind survived primarily by gathering food and started to make primitive weapons and tools from stone. As the Ice Age began to end, people were travelling to all corners of the Earth. Historians speculate that this was probably a matriarchal era, as numerous figurines have been found dating from this time that suggest worship of the Great Mother Goddess. Having lived in cave dwellings for several generations, people of this time began to build shelters; it is a trait of Virgo to create a safe environment that serves a specific purpose. Tents made from animal hide would be suspended over a wooden framework and held down by stones. Virgo being the sign of service is reflected in the fact that dogs were domesticated during the Age of Virgo, and indeed shared a hearth with people and accompanied them on their travels. The hunter-gatherer diet was also being supplemented with plants from cultivated gardens, and it was during this period that people began to increasingly use herbs for medicinal purposes. A primitive form of surgery, trepanning or boring holes into the skull, was also practised.

THE RUNDOWN & LESSONS
SOME QUIRKS, ODDITIES, UNIQUE CHARACTERISTICS AND IDIOSYNCRASIES OF VIRGO

"All too often, Virgo will knit the patches but neglect to put them together to form the quilt."
Alan Oken

"You'll seldom see them blowing bubbles in the air or building castles in the sand. Virgos are too busy to daydream, and they're usually too tired at night to wish on stars."
Linda Goodman

There are two types of thinkers: what I like to call 'right-brainers' and 'left-brainers'. The left hemisphere of the human brain deals with things such as control of speech, verbal functions, logic, reason, mathematics, linear concepts, details, sequences, the intellect and analysis; the right hemisphere is concerned with spatial, music, holistic, artistic concepts, as well as simultaneity and intuition. You could go on to say that the left brain is masculine or yang in quality, and the right brain is feminine or yin in quality. Based upon these very simplistic outlines, it can be further stated that Earth sign Virgo, although a feminine sign, is ruled by the left-brained Mercury - and so dwells mainly in the left hemisphere, with a substantial dose of right thrown in for good measure.

Virgo acquires the skills and learning leading to a job, and will continually refine its efforts as the craftsperson does, to develop techniques leading to mastery within a chosen field. Virgo finds security in offering practical, useful, dependable and efficient service to an organisation or a cause, and you will use your intellect to critically analyse and organise - to bring order out of chaos.

Virgo, along with your other Earth-sister Taurus, has perhaps the richest mythic associations of any of the signs, and strong links with harvest seasons, agriculture and overall fruitfulness. If we examine these symbolic associations, a theme emerges. Virgo concerns the transformation of the personality from a childlike or virginal state into a wiser, more mature individuality, represented by the fruition of the harvest. And when Virgo's place in the seasonal context is considered, we can say that this must take place so that we can redirect ourselves from the personal to more Universal concerns, for Virgo is the final sign in the 'personal' half of the zodiac wheel. Virgo, often referred to as the sign of service, encapsulates this transformational passage: indeed, both transformation and service, symbolically speaking, take place on the physical level because Virgo is an Earth sign, concerned with the physical, which is why she is associated with all things health, healing and therapeutic.

Virgo is often said to be cold, fussy and analytical, and this is partly due to that fact that you are ruled by Mercury, which is rational and cerebral by nature and does not sit comfortably in such a solid and natural element such as Earth. Because Mercury has been regarded as an inappropriate ruler for Virgo by many astrologers, other possibilities have been suggested as rulers, such as Chiron, Ceres, Pallas, Juno and Vesta, as well as other asteroids and planetoids. But Mercury persists as ruler of Virgo, and to a large extent it is quite apt given Virgo's amazing capacity for analysis, mental agility and high intellectual functioning *.

The highly evolved Virgoan has a great deal of vision and brings an impeccable sense of practical reality to any undertaking. Never wasteful of energy, always succinct in thought, and able to see every detail of an issue after painstakingly pulling it apart, you are the sign of selfless duty and thrive on helping others who are perhaps less resourceful or self-sufficient. You often find yourself in servile or subordinate positions for two reasons: leading others does not come naturally to you, and you would prefer to work in the background; accolades, recognition and praise are not priorities on your agenda. As well, Virgo would basically rather lead the simple life. Pomp, status and circumstance are not important to you, as you are concerned much more with necessity and purity than with fanfare and opulence.

There is a chaste and reclusive side to Virgo's character. This doesn't mean that you seek solitude above all else or that you are a born loner; you would just prefer to be by yourself than to deal with difficult people or those you find objectionable. You tend to make up your own codes and standards of behaviour, and there is a limit to what you find acceptable in yourself as well as others. If another person should cross over one of your lines, they may find themselves banished from your experience.

You are unquestionably dependable, dutiful and sincere, however, being the zodiac's hypochondriac, you have a way of pretending to be sick or down when you don't wish to go somewhere or do something. But overall, you project a bright albeit somewhat subdued Mercurial charm that is hard to resist, even when you're being dry and difficult to get along with. You are irritated and put off by stupidity, carelessness and vulgarity, and have little patience with laziness; confronted with any of these very human conditions, you become cranky, critical, nervous, scolding and extremely irate. Furthermore, you have precise ideas about health and wellbeing, and if others don't follow your standards in these departments, you can brush them off like a broom clearing cobwebs. No doubt about it, your mind is agile and crisp, and you discriminate - sometimes harshly, almost always wisely - using your fine mind's eye for detail. If someone forgets to put the lid back on the shampoo bottle, you are capable of wiping that person off your Christmas list, or at the very least treating them coldly next time you meet in the hallway, and have a tendency to nit-pick or hen-peck at them until they remedy the situation. You may criticise others to a hair-splitting degree and infuriate those you share said shampoo with, but if anyone you deeply care about is in a pickle you are more than happy to step in and help in any way you can - your only motive being to serve. You may even resolve the conflict *before* you're asked to step in, because bringing order and calm out of chaos is so instinctive to you. Virgos are often known to be the last guests to leave the party, not because they're having such a smashing time, but because they like to stay behind and clean up the mess made by inconsiderate, slovenly or drunk others.

It is a rare Virgo who would ask for or wish for any favours to be returned however. As willing as you are to give efficient and devoted assistance to others, you have an intense dislike of accepting others' gifts to you, even bordering on neurosis, such is your fear of being obligated to anyone or anything. You have an air of self-reliant independence about you, never wishing to depend on anyone but yourself. Yours is a practical, individualistic nature, and you probably learnt from a very early age, or even a past life, that the only person you can really lean on when the seas get choppy, is your good trusty self.

Mutability and the Earth element combine to make you practical and adaptable. Although you share your ruling planet with Gemini, Mercury's energy manifests its characteristics in two different ways: in Gemini, Mercury seeks to link together and make connections, but in Virgo this same planet wants to dissect, discriminate and analyse. This endows you with a precise and methodical approach to thoughts and actions, for your Earthy element adds a strong dose of practicality to Mercury's intellectual attributes, grounding any transpiring ideas to make them tangible and workable. This is why many Virgoans are fond of research, data, statistics and overall anything which requires analysis. But you need a definite channel for all this mental activity, and without a sense of constructive purpose to your life, you can become disillusioned, hard-nosed, unfulfilled and grow bitter with life.

Strongly imbued with an enviable work ethic, you see duty and obligation as inescapable. You're the 'details person', a perfectionist who's doomed by virtue of your exceedingly high standards to be perpetually disappointed. But perhaps astrologer Linda Goodman said it best when she imparted the wisdom that once you've learned to master life's complicated details, instead of letting details master you, you can shape your destiny with more certainty than any other Sun sign. Indeed, you can. For your keen perception and sharp mind keeps your desires clear of wishy-washy, wishful thinking, and despite your getting caught up in all the nitty-gritties of *everything*, you have a way of always keeping what is actually desired as the central focus.

Very little in life comes up to your standards, and this disenchantment often extends to yourself, for you're your own severest critic. And even though you know perfection is rarely obtainable, this is of little comfort to you, for it doesn't make second-best any more acceptable as far as you're concerned. This dissatisfaction can often turn inwards and manifest as neurosis, making you even more cranky and picky. Highly strung, you need order and method to act as a counterbalance for any nervous tension. Work is an excellent channel for your nervous energies and enables you to validate your sense of self through service and giving to others. In fact, Virgo makes an ideal employee, for you find it difficult to delegate and lead and prefer to oversee each part of an operation yourself, no matter how small the job. Your main fault lies in your obsession with analysing everything inexhaustibly.

You are often misread as being emotionally or physically frigid, but the truth is that you are particularly discriminating and fastidious and this - combined with your modesty and introversion - has led to your oft mistaken reputation as being prudish. Yet there's a grain of truth in this generally held view, and you may often experience difficulties in your relationships. For although you are of the sensuous, lusty Earth element, you are ruled by Airy Mercury, which tends to restrain your Earthy urges with cool detachment and a calm rationale, which may result in inhibition or lack of spontaneity. It doesn't help that you are prone to approaching matters of the heart as academic pursuits. But you bring a kind of crisp efficiency to your love-making and you are likely to compensate for any lack of impulse or instinctive passion with well-thought out and effective techniques.

Virgo represents somewhat of a paradox, for you embody a strong conflict between the natural sensuality of a fruitful Earth sign, and an innate desire for purity, discipline and constraint. As a result, part of the Virgo character is always kept untouched, untainted and virginal. But your inner maiden's aspect is voluptuous and fecund. When your inhibitions are lowered, you reveal a fondness for pleasures of all kinds, and if of the flesh, then this can lead to a crisis of values later, over which you will ceaselessly agonise.

Virgos tend to be ritualistic, obsessive, psychologically independent and are happiest when making valuable and useful contributions to anything they undertake. Their 'work' is often done behind the scenes however, as they are modest, retiring and rarely seek the limelight. The energy of Virgo is where we learn how to 'improve' the sensate world to make it more efficient and workable, and this you do exceedingly well. Perfection-oriented, humble, competent, self-restrained, controlled and respectable, you stand by your morals and are ever prudent in your approach to life and relationships. You are almost always immaculately groomed, radiating apparent effortlessness. In appearance as well as other areas, you are always under control of matters. Self-sufficiency is important to you, as although you are a most reliable person for others to lean on, you like to do things your own way and for yourself - there is a strong, albeit soft, aura of containment about you.

Virgos have a natural interest in health and healing, and if you find something is not working in mind, body, spirit or any other life compartment, you will be swift to correct, rectify or mend it. Selfless and imbued with an instinct to serve, you have a tendency to try and heal others - or at least advise them on how they can improve a situation.

Dealing with details on a practical level, you dislike abstract concepts and can become nit-picky and get carried away with petty, small details, failing to see the broader picture. Your practical concern and talent with facts enables you to be expertly efficient in analysis, discrimination, categorisation and disseminating research. You are essentially an intellectual sign, being ruled by the mind-oriented planet Mercury, and you tend towards specialist knowledge, exercising an enviable clarity of mind and communication. But there is a touch of narrow-minded, blinkered pedantry about you, and when faced with a problem your instinct is to break it down, often at the expense of the bigger picture; you ultimately lack breadth of vision.

Emotionally, you are a chronic worrier, and as a consequence, you tend more than any other sign to suffer psychosomatic illnesses, which are really diseases in the body that have largely psychological roots. As far as you are concerned, emotions and feelings are unpleasantly messy and sometimes your only escape from any psychological issues are to analyse them until they become small enough to crush under your thumb and promptly discard.

You seek to maintain order and keep things running smoothly, but your tendency to need order and quiet solitude can mean your relationships may suffer, and your habit of over-analysing everything can erode your feelings and hinder your imagination, manifesting in a life analysed instead of a life truly experienced and *lived*.

Virgo can offer great reliability and practicality in relationships, however, and can be loving and affectionate underneath their considerably cool exterior. Although you are conscientious and virtuous, you do tend to over-conform. You strive for perfection but when this is overdone it can manifest as a critical attitude and finding fault with everything, which can then lead to your undoing, through the turning of your perfectionism inwards and consequently becoming obsessed with worry or doubt or guilt. If nothing else though, you are matter-of-fact, no-nonsense and prudent.

You are compassionate and dutiful to others, showing a more serious Mercurial mental approach than the frivolous devil-may-care Gemini. In essence, you are a wonderful servant, applying yourself with skill, diligence and a shrewd brand of intelligence. You honour your obligations above almost all else, and you love helping, guiding and healing others. But first you must remember to heal your own brokenness and serve your own higher self - *then* you are best positioned to help others most effectively.

Quiet, contained and competent, you are a sincere, clever and reliable character who shows your care and concern in practical ways. Kind, supportive and considerate of the less fortunate, you may shun the limelight, but you can be certain your name will always feature in bold type on any credit list.

* It is interesting to note, however, that medieval alchemists saw Mercury as a symbol of spiritual transformation. So it is not always linked with the standalone intellect. It was the agency which transmuted Earthly physical reality into something greater than itself, or awakened the vital spirit. Virgo, being a Mutable sign, has great capabilities in the area of transmutation - for example, transforming their bodies and minds through diet, yoga or other esoteric techniques.

LESSONS TO BE LEARNED FOR GREATER POWER, ENLIGHTENMENT & LUCK

Virgoan problems and ultimate undoings arise through your obsession with details, compulsive habits, self-doubt and the criticism of self and others that ultimately erodes your self-esteem. You can be pedantic and blinkered, overly practical and too rooted in 'reality' to understand or perhaps more importantly, *wish to* understand more abstract or unusual concepts. You are prude, yet somewhere underneath your wholesome persona lurks someone who secretly enjoys the more perverse side of the coin. Striving constantly for perfection and understandably never quite attaining it, you can become easily despondent or bitterly disappointed in yourself and consequently set even higher standards for yourself the next time, which become increasingly out of reach and frustrate you. Virgo also tends to over-serve others at the expense of themselves; in other words, they sacrifice their own needs to help others. You need to learn how to exercise judgement and discernment without becoming critical, pedantic or entangled in the detail. You could also learn to exude your character with a bit more warmth and affection, and take life a little less seriously - some good clean, fun is just what the doctor would order for the Virgoan spirit!

Overall, your greatest strengths and your greatest weakness all stem from your logical, orderly analytical approach. Sometimes you may achieve your desire for perfection, while other times you may be driven into picking apart your own happiness. Your strong sense of personal duty, your respectable nature and your practicality allow you to help many and expect little in return. However, if you fail to listen to your own inner heartfelt needs, you may neglect your own duty to yourself, and your conscientiousness-at-all-costs attitude will lead to a life of over-duty, resentment and drudgery. Your 'all work and no play' creed can also turn you into a nagging critic or a self-pitying victim. You will only achieve material and spiritual fulfilment if you don't neglect your own needs over others', and you can balance work, play and compassion meaningfully.

The Virgoan quest for order and perfection enables you to serve and support and even encourage others. Being of the Mutable mode, you are the most changeable Earth sign because your Mercurial mental appetite keeps you always looking for the best and proper way to do things. But beware of being hypercritical and self-righteous, as these traits can isolate you and deplete your energies. However, when you use your natural down-to-Earth sensitivities to empathise with and forgive others for their faults and imperfections, you effortlessly bring out the best in all those around you, including yourself.

THE THREE DECANS OF VIRGO

Decans are thirty-six groups of stars that rise in a particular order on the horizon throughout each Earth rotation. These decans were developed in Egypt thousands of years ago. The rising of each decan marked the beginning of a new 'decanal hour' of the night for these ancient people, and eventually three decans were assigned to each zodiac sign. Each decan covers ten degrees of the zodiac wheel, and is ruled by different planetary rulers that rule over the other two signs of the same element (and a traditional ruler, when only seven of the planetary bodies were known). Decans continued to be used throughout the Ages, in astrology and in magic, but many modern astrologers, for whatever reasons, tend to disregard them. Following are brief descriptions for each decan of Virgo. Which one do you belong to? Can you relate to the description and the energies of your decan's ruling planet?

FIRST DECAN VIRGO ★ August 23 - September 1

Ruler ★ Sun (traditional *) / Mercury (modern)

Keyword ★ Clever

First Decan Virgos' Three Special Tarot cards
The Hermit, Knight of Pentacles & Eight of Pentacles

Birthdays in this decan range from 23rd August to 1st September. This is the Virgo decan, ruled by the Sun * and Mercury. Virgoans born during this decan possess an ability to assimilate and analyse, combined with an insatiable curiosity and attention to detail. Your need for order, organisation and method is strong, as too is your need to understand and justify your actions and motivations. You are articulate, bright and intelligent, with a knack for learning, teaching and indeed all forms of knowledge-acquisition. Studious and achievement-oriented, you can be a perfectionist, but this streak is normally put to effective use and you succeed in most tasks you set out to do. Helpful to others, trustworthy and disciplined, people can depend on you for help and service. Being such a meticulous, hard worker, you rarely have difficulties in getting exactly what you want. Gifted with a highly logical mind, great articulatory abilities, a clever wit and rational thought processes, you also have a soft side which cares deeply, is attuned to the needs of the self and others, and is highly considerate, eloquent, refined and courteous.

SECOND DECAN VIRGO ★ September 2 - 13

Ruler ★ Mercury (traditional *) / Saturn (modern)

Keyword ★ Tactful

Second Decan Virgos' Three Special Tarot cards
The Hermit, Knight of Pentacles & Nine of Pentacles

Birthdays in this decan range from 2nd September to 13th September. This is the Capricorn decan, ruled by Mercury * and Saturn. This adds a stronger desire for ambition than other placements in Virgo. With the Capricorn influence, a wry sense of humour is most likely part of your make-up. You are patient, practical and successful in business pursuits, making a great partner but formidable opponent. You will usually win in any exchange of words, and in any case can win people over with your articulate, shrewd and astute style of communication. You can also be wilful and stubborn, and are probably a late bloomer - indeed, you are programmed to do the best of your life's work after the age of forty. This influence also endows you with great influence and tact, and being such an effective organiser, you would make a good manager or leader. You also have the ability to direct others with motivation, delegation skills, and assertiveness, though you do tend to set the bar high for both yourself and others, and become critical if others don't live up to your standards of perfection. You are loyal and trustworthy though, and any secret is safe with you.

THIRD DECAN VIRGO ★ September 14 - 22

Ruler ★ Venus (traditional *) / Venus (modern)

Keyword ★ Altruistic

Third Decan Virgos' Three Special Tarot cards
The Hermit, Queen of Swords & Ten of Pentacles

Birthdays in this decan range from 14th September to 22nd September. This is the Taurus decan, ruled by Venus *. Virgoans born during this decan are characterised by a graceful sociability, gentle tact, sensuality and a great love of art, luxury and beautiful things. The Venusian influence softens your character somewhat, and you will be slightly less critical, exacting and perfection-seeking than Virgos born under the other decans. Conscientious and versatile, you are refined and artistic, pursuing creative endeavours for both pleasure and profit. Possessing a reserved, sweet and sensitive nature, you love and give of yourself with ease, but can be hurt just as easily. You are extremely helpful to and considerate of others, and are always ready to lend a helping hand or offer a shoulder to cry on should someone you love need it. You have a pleasant persona and are stylish, attracting many into your circle through your calm and easy going aura, but you can also be modest, timid and lack confidence.

* The decan's traditional ruler based on the Chaldean order of the planets

YOUR ELEMENT ★ EARTH

According to the *Oxford English Dictionary*, the word *element* has a mysterious origin, and was first found in Greek texts meaning 'complex whole' or 'a single unit made up of many parts'. From the ancient up to medieval times, there were only four elements - Earth, Air, Fire and Water - and the occult-oriented also believed in a fifth: Spirit, or Ether. (Cornelius Agrippa called Spirit the 'quintessence'.)

Alchemy is a tradition of visions and dreams, and images can combine on different levels of reality. Alchemists have long used images in their illustrations to express the enigma and mystery of their art, and to include all dimensions of our experience. The traditional worlds of Earth, Water, Fire and Air symbolise these dimensions very well. Broadly speaking, and in human terms, Earth corresponds to the level of the body and the senses, Water to the flow of thoughts and feelings, Fire to inspiration and energy, and Air to the world of the higher mind and intellect. Each of these worlds has its own realm of imagery. Virgo belongs to the realm of the Earth element.

★ The Practical Group ★

The path to SERVICE & DUTY

Focused on Materiality and Security

Alchemical Associations ★ The Physical, the Mineral Salt and the Colour Black

Key Attributes ★ Stability, Balance, Patience, Practicality, Realism

Governed by ★ The Physical Body and Sensations

Symbolism ★ Groundedness, stability, structure, protection, solidity, common sense, connection to the material and physical planes, and the five senses

Governed by ★ The Tangible and the Sensory

Earth Characteristics ★ Grounded, Practical, Balanced, Realistic, Materialistic, Solid

★ THE MAGIC OF EARTH ★

Earth is the solid rock on which everything else is grounded. It provides the soil for the roots you need to lay down at some point in your life, and yields the minerals and food you need to survive and thrive. Earth is the provider, the protector, the material aspect of the world and of yourself. If you have forgotten to keep both your feet on the ground, your dreams will carry you away - Earth is needed to provide grounding for them. Earth is supportive and reminds you that everything in life needs to be built on solid, sound, dependable foundations. The element of Earth is indeed life's great anchor.

★ KEYWORDS ★

Cautious, methodical, organised, predictable, substantial, stable, reliable, practical, pragmatic, sensual, patient, enduring, productive, grounded, persevering, dependable, useful, sensible, dutiful

"Earth is both of this world and the Otherworld, for she is host to all the other Elements besides: Air doth blow upon her face, Fire doth ignite within her belly and spew forth from her mountains, Water flows through her deep valleys, and Spirit marketh upon her skin the sacred pathways of our quest. Earth is our dwelling till we pass beyond into the secret glades of Otherworld, yet whilst we do live in human form then shall we honour and respect the Earth whence we came."

***Merlin's Book of Magick and Enchantment*, Nevill Drury**

Earth is the material substance principle. It gives form and substance to manifest what Fire has inspired and initiated. Earth is associated with the sensation function and its motivating force is material gain and security. Characterised by function, practicality and solidity, Earth seeks straightforward engagement with the physical world, mastery of it through efficient organisation and structure, and attainment of physical and economical comforts, respect, prestige and status. Taurus represents personal development, Virgo represents interpersonal development, and Capricorn represents transpersonal development. They are feminine polarity, introverted in expression.

In ancient legends, the Earth was regarded as maternal and protective, symbolising abundance and fertility. In mythology, Gaia or 'Mother Earth' was one of the first beings to emerge, along with Ouranos 'Father Sky'. They were bound by the ocean which whirled in an endless circle, keeping them together.

Earth is a complex and intriguing element, for when we think of it, we think of two things: the planet Earth, and the actual stuff our planet has as its base: soil, rock, and 'ground'. Earth connection is essential to having a grounded anchor for our magic to manifest; when Earth supports our 'work', we have a solid foundation for lift-off into the stars. Earth is like a home-base, a launching pad, and represents security, groundedness, foundations, practicality, the 'seen', tangible realities, and quite literally everything that has a has a down-to-Earth quality about it. Our desires begin and end with this element, and it is a great leveller; indeed, from it we all emerge and unto it we return.

Earth is the Universal archetype of the Divine feminine. Our planet is affectionately referred to as Mother Earth, the Great Mother, and Gaia, among many other names. Symbolising the inexhaustible spirit of creation, she is associated with abundance. When we work with this element, not only are we calling upon the powers of the mountains, caves, minerals and deserts that comprise its wondrous expanse, but we are also invoking its support and massive strength, for from it emerges abounding hidden treasures, giving us proof that material things can indeed be manifested from the Divine, deep and dark.

Throughout the history of magic, the element of Earth has been associated with a variety of deities, spirits and angels. And from the magical, as well as the esoteric and alchemical viewpoints, Earth has the lowest vibration of the four elements because it is so solidly manifest in our world. Rooted in practical concerns, it governs the primal facets of lie and of physical regeneration. It provides all we need for life, in the form of nourishment and shelter, and also provides material comforts and wealth. The treasures nurtured deep under its surface are testament to this, and have been long been yielded by mining methods and their ownership. Such treasures include gold, silver, other precious minerals, crystals, resources and other materials.

As the element suggests, Earth signs are down to Earth and self-sufficient. Pragmatic and conservative, they need structure and routine to feel safe and secure. Whether a practical Taurus, analytical Virgo or determined Capricorn, Earth signs approach life with caution and careful, methodical planning. Earth signs are not spontaneous by nature and do not like surprises or sudden changes, preferring a predictable and stable life. They tend to be organised, patient, calm, reliable, steadfast and provide a voice of reason, serving as a rock in loved ones' lives; they can indeed be truly relied upon in a crisis. However, their poised and modest nature sometimes makes it difficult for others to gauge how they are feeling or to prompt them to express their emotions.

Although Earth signs have sophisticated tastes and are strongly associated with materialism, they never manifest them in superficial ways, preferring to work hard, set goals and aim high. In essence, they strive to create a life free from money troubles and drama. They are tactile and sensual and though they may not be overly demonstrative (with the exception of Taurus), they are sentimental and affectionate in their own genuine ways.

In Earth we see the great cycles of nature and the effects it has on all the other elements. Though the cycle of the seasons relies upon the Sun, these seasons would become stagnant and motionless if it weren't for the movement of the Earth. For that reason, the mysteries of life, death and rebirth can be associated with this element - and although it is the Water element's inherent nature to explore these things on a deeper, more spiritual plane, Earth is the starting point for this exploration.

The Earth signs are sense-orientated, experiencing the world through a physical body. Concerned with security issues and moulding matter into form, Earth is productive, sensual and fertile. Earth supports, embodies, incarnates, contains, protects and provides a sense of groundedness. It is in the here and now, dealing with the present. Materialistic and sometimes power-hungry and greedy, the Earth element can also lack imagination and spontaneity.

The Earth element is firmly planted, coherent, has a sense of continuity, sustaining, follows things through, is sensory, sensual, resourceful, appreciative of beauty, pleasure-seeking, aesthetically aware, regular, containing, limiting, rigid, makes real, gives form and substance, is predictable, ritualistic, routine, enduring, reliable, committed, passive, conservative, stagnant, and sensitive to fertility and cyclical changes.

Although gravity pulls downward toward the Earth, mountains rise above it, and are associated with the Earth sign Capricorn. The first sign of this element, Taurus, represents the ground or soil, the second Virgo represents what is planted and grown in the soil, and Capricorn represents the high mountainous backdrop.

This energy is heavy, moving downward, symbolically anchoring us to our own personal ground. Earth signs are motivated by the desire to establish financial, physical and emotional security - through a steady job, money in the bank, a stable relationship.

Earth symbols include tortoises, caves, underground tunnels, mines, grottos, soil, rocks, minerals, farms, fields and mountains.

To start connecting with the 'Earth Spirit' realm, you can choose to concentrate on the spirits of the Earth - also known as devas - beginning with trees, flowers, soil, and of course Mother Earth herself. The Earth is an incredible, breathing, pulsating, living, vibrating spirit, majestically supporting all life on our planet. Also known as Gaia, she is the organic Mother of all of us, and becoming sensitive to her energy is to instantly feel physically stronger, securely supported and sustained.

Positive Earth Qualities ★ Earthy types are practical, hard-working, sensible, enduring, efficient, organised, realistic, patient, self-disciplined, conservative, persistent, common-sensical, unpretentious, stable, dependable, and capable of running households or businesses with a cool, pragmatic, unhurried, unfettered efficiency. Other positive traits of Earthy types are the following: Rooted, industrious, strong, determined, calm, goal-oriented, responsible, tenacious, sensual, committed, steady, concrete, cautious, grounded, solid, secure, robust, methodical, achieving, enduring, strong-willed, receptive, retentive, physical and reliable.

Negative Earth Qualities ★ Earthy temperaments can lack vision which may hold them back and they can become narrow, too 'rooted' in the one place, unadventurous, rigid, sluggish, resistant, immovable, and obstinate. They can also express their weaknesses in other not-so-desirable traits: Slow, stodgy, uninspired, unimaginative, petty, excessively conventional, dull, overly-cautious, narrow in perspective, stubborn, lacking in spontaneity, resistant to change, staid, hoarding, ultraconservative, inflexible, wilful, stingy, resistant to change, unoriginal, lethargic, closed-minded, over-reliant on the physical senses, overly conforming, lacking in perspective and spontaneity, selfish, bossy, heavy, bound by routine and rules, plodding, bureaucratic, perfectionism, possessive, dogmatic, controlling, authoritative, fussy, self-indulgent, fearful, suspicious, pessimistic, melancholic, critical, materialistic, greedy and resigned.

THE ARCHANGEL OF EARTH ★ URIEL

An archangel is an angel of greater than ordinary rank. They possess a stronger, more powerful essence than the guardian angels, through overseeing and guiding the other angels who are said to be with us here on Earth. The word 'angel' derives from the Greek word *angelos* meaning 'messenger'. To humans, angels are often seen as bringers as all sorts of messages. Angels in all their forms are believed to bring the message of 'spirit' into matter, carrying the blueprints of creation and the Source from the Divine into the manifest world. Angels are not and never have been human; they, like fairies and nature spirits, are part of a different evolutionary pattern – but they do appear to us in human form (usually with wings) because that is what we understand. An angel can be in many different places at once, and with the same intensity and concentration, and wish for us to be aware of them and benefit from them.

There are said to be three categories of angels in the cosmos, each with three subdivisions *. 'Angel' is the generic term and also relates specifically to those closest to the physical. Similarly, archangel may be taken to mean any of the higher orders, and indeed signifies the order just above ordinary 'angel'. Found in a number of religious traditions, the word 'archangel' itself is usually associated with the Abrahamic religions. The word archangel is of Greek origin, and means literally 'chief angel'. All archangels end with the 'el' suffix, 'el' meaning 'in God' and the first part of the name meaning what each individual Angel specialises in. The archangel who rules your sign will be the one with whom you most resonate. The astrological sign is an energy signature, a matrix of a specific stellar pattern that will subtly affect and influence you. Although there are many associations for the great archangels of the Universe, we must keep in mind there is great overlapping in their duties and guidance. For example, we may say that one is for healing and another for protection, but they can all perform the functions of the others, and each has only areas of greater focus and responsibilities. Four of the multitude of archangelic beings work intimately with the Earth. These are Raphael (Air), Michael (Fire), Gabriel (Water) and Uriel (Earth). Associated with each of these archangels are one of the four elements, specific colours, one of the four directions or quarters of the Earth, three signs of the zodiac, and a variety of other energies and powers. Understanding these associations and considering them in relation to our own paths, can help us determine with which of them we are more likely to resonate. Your sign, being of the Earth element, vibrates to the essence of Uriel.

* The first sphere, the *Heavenly Counsellors*, comprises Seraphim, Cherubim and Thrones. The second sphere, the *Heavenly Governors*, comprises Dominions, Virtues and Powers. The third sphere, the *Heavenly Messengers*, comprises Principalities, Archangels and Angels. Of course, all such classifications are a human construct, a way of placing order upon the unknowable and allowing us to perceive something about which we have no words to express. However, as long as we think of angelic hierarchies as a way of working with celestials, of remembering important attributes, and we are able to imagine and experience these beings, this order of angels will prove useful to those wishing to draw upon their messages and assistance.

★ ARCHANGEL URIEL'S ASSOCIATIONS ★

Element of Earth
The northern quarter of the Earth

The Summer season
The colours white, burnished gold and all earth tones
The crystals tiger's eye and rutilated quartz
The astrological signs of Taurus, Virgo and Capricorn

Uriel, whose name means 'Fire of God', is the archangel who brought alchemy * to humankind. He is said to be the brightest archangel, a pure pillar of Fire, he can bring warmth to the winter and melt the snows with his flaming sword. Uriel is the archangel of alchemy and vision, overseeing healing, magic, nature and manifestation. This being is known as the tallest of the archangels with eyes that can see into and across eternity. Uriel oversees the work of all nature spirits - working with Uriel will open you to the fairy kingdoms - and works to assist humanity by awakening to them and working in harmony with them. Inspiring us to work with angels, Devas and higher spiritual essences, to perfect our vision of Divine realms, and to refine our mystical nature by burning away our deep-seated desire for comfort and blind ignorance, Uriel is the gatekeeper to the Garden of Eden, the gates of which we can only pass through once we have mastered the wisdom we are given to find our own path to enlightenment.

* Alchemy is the sacred art of transmuting base metal into gold by reducing it to the primal black matter and then, by chemico-magical processes, striving to extract and refine spiritual as well as actual gold, the key to finding the way back to Paradise or Source.

VIRGO'S ZODIAC ARCHANGEL ★ RAPHAEL

Additionally, each sign is associated with a particular archangel. Such knowledge can help you to build up a relationship with these beings, based upon your strengths and needs. However, no link is rigid, and as you work with angels you will come to develop your own affinities. When invoking a specific archangel, a useful ritual to draw them closer is to light a candle in that angel's colour, burn some oil or incense of its scent, and hold the appropriate crystal while focusing on what you are needing guidance on.

YOUR ARCHANGEL ★ Raphael is the Divine healer, bringing healing in all its forms to those who need it. He leads the guardian angels, takes care of travellers, supports those in the healing professions, and bestows knowledge, wisdom and therapeutic skill. Soothing and calming, he can help you to heal yourself and to feel a connection and oneness with nature. Raphael can be invoked using a caduceus.

SCENT/OIL ★ Chamomile

CANDLE COLOUR ★ Vibrant green

CRYSTAL ★ Emerald or green tourmaline

THE DEVIC REALMS & EARTH ★ NORTH: REALM OF THE GNOMES

"Through magick we do conjure the Elements, evoking unto us the special properties of the Life-force for our learning and our coming-into-light. And yet are there secret paths of knowledge that have fallen from the minds of men ... For the way of Magick is a path to sacred knowledge, of reverence and humility - and the world is a wondrous place. Yet how many amongst us have fathomed these depths?"
***Merlin's Book of Magick and Enchantment*, Nevill Drury**

Deva is a Sanskrit word that means 'shining one'. Devas are the life force within nature, and there are four devic realms - Fire, Earth, Air and Water - which contain ethereal elemental spirits or sprites. Elementals are the building blocks of nature, and close to being true energy and consciousness. The four elements correspond to four different states of matter: energy/transmutation (Fire), gas (Air), liquid (Water) and solid (Earth), which are linked to the four human states of consciousness: inspiration, thought, feeling and practicality. There are four spirits, or elementals, which reside in the devic realms, associated with each element. People have been painting pictures, telling stories and writing about these devic realms for hundreds of years, albeit sometimes through disguised mediums such as fairy tales or children's fantasy stories like Tolkien's *Lord of the Rings*. The power of the natural world is easily observed and since ancient times primal forces have been ascribed to various spirit beings. Belief in nature spirits is of such ancient origin and is Universal; cultures everywhere have names or words to describe them. In the sixteenth century, a famous Swiss physician, alchemist and mystic called Paracelsus * defined these beings as 'Elementals', classifying them according to the element of nature they inhabit. There are four main levels of elemental beings: Gnomes (Earth), Undines (Water), Sylphs (Air), and Salamanders (Fire). The fifth element of Ether is the element from which came forth the other four, and Ether, or Spirit, has never been defined in any particular category, and encompasses the aspects and beings of all the other elements.

Elementals are usually benevolent guardian beings or spirits that look after nature's secrets and treasures in whatever part of the natural realm they occupy. They can only be seen or 'felt' by those possessing heightened psychic abilities, yet they can be summoned by those practising alchemy, spells and magic in order to harness the forces of nature for their own particular intentions. In our modern lives, it may seem as though this magic doesn't exist, but the truth is that most of us are simply less in touch with it than ever before. The consequence of this is that we are destroying vast areas of land, polluting waters, creating toxic landscapes, and disrespecting the laws of nature, which often whisper their messages softly. It is therefore important for us to look at the beauty that surrounds us with true appreciation and genuine regard, and to open ourselves up to the magic resides within it. The four devic realms can teach us much about nature; they act as custodians for the four elements, and learning to work with them is a way of attuning to all the energies and beings of nature. Elementals are four-dimensional, and have nothing to obstruct their movements. Therefore, they move as easily through matter as we do through air and space. They do require some contact with humans for their own evolution. Helping to direct them is an overseer, traditionally called the King of that element, and an archangel. Each of these elements is affiliated with one of the four directions and each elemental spirit embodies its own special energy. If you wish to re-connect and re-harmonise yourself by working with nature and its messages and lessons, you could begin by learning a little about your element's realm: Your element is Earth, which is connected with the North direction and the realm of the Gnomes.

* Paracelsus is considered the most original medical thinker of the sixteenth century. His belief in supernatural beings, intuition and the invisible causes of illness helped him discover hydrogen and nitrogen. Paracelsus believed that "Elementals are unlike pure spirits for they are mortal, but they are not like man for they have no soul."

★ GNOMES ★

Gnome: *noun* - A legendary dwarfish creature, supposed to guard the Earth's treasures; diminutive spirits or small fey 'humanoids' in Renaissance magic and alchemy, first introduced by Paracelsus in the 16th century, known for their eccentric sense of humour, inquisitiveness, and engineering prowess; are typically said to be small, humanoid creatures who live underground.

Gnomes are a race of small, misshapen, dwarf-like creatures that dwell in the Earth and often protect secret treasures in vast caverns. Their actions are reflected in the presence of mineral deposits and other kinds of geological formations. Gnomes are the beings of craftsmanship. They are needed to build the plants, flowers and trees. It is their task to tint them, to make crystals and gems and to maintain the Earth so that we have a place to grow and evolve. As guardians of the treasures of the Earth, they are attuned to helping humans find the treasures within the Earth or part of it; this can be hidden riches, the energy of crystals and stones, or the finding of gold within one's life. Ultimately, they work with humans through nature. They give each stone its own individuality and essence. Indeed, they do this with every aspect of nature, and thus we can learn from each one, for every tree, rock and flower has something it can teach us.

According to Paracelsus, gnomes cannot stand the light of the Sun, and even one ray would turn them to stone. If you wish to retrieve any treasures that are buried underground or associated with the Earth, you must first appease the gnomes or they will cause you mischief.

The gnomes are the 'knowing ones', from the Greek *gnoma*, meaning 'knowledge'. The gnomes are the guardians of winter, the direction of the north, the physical world, and of fertility and abundance. The north is traditionally known as the gateway to inner wisdom. The Earth provides us with food and beauty in many forms. The gnomes are caretakers of everything that grows, from tiny flowers to towering trees. The King of Earth is Cernunnos or Ghob, its archangel Uriel, its magickal tool the pentacle or disc (which calls down the spirits into form), and its sacred ceremonial stone is the garnet in all its four colours. Perhaps Merlin sums up the gnome realm best: "From time to time, no doubt, these gnomes do make merry with the lives of human folk, having their ways in mischief and making jokes. And yet, for all their pranks and mischief, are these gnomes good and virtuous within their natures, and offer gifts of kindness when hard times come upon our lives."

INVOKING THE EARTH DEVAS

Gnomes are said to be the easiest of the devas to sense since their energy is almost tangible. Earth spirits can be very helpful since they embody practicality and common sense, and have an innate knowledge base around money, the material, and how to grow things. They relate to food, nourishment, health, treasures, fertility, protection, wealth, and all Earth magic.

Gnomes can also assist with the security of your home and are excellent guardians, so it is no accident that many gardens around the world are filled with representations of these powerful beings, as they are said to protect the home they are attached to. Gnomes can also be called upon to bring financial stability to your household, attracting the funds needed to pay a bill or to meet an urgent expense.

If you have a laborious task ahead, have job or financial worries, need to ground your ideals, or are in need of developing a special hands-on skill, ask the earth devas for their help. The easiest way to contact them is to spend some time outdoors around the Earth element and natural features, particularly rocks and thick-trunked trees. You may find it helpful to hold a crystal or stone of resonance when asking the Earth elementals for assistance.

THE NORTH DIRECTION'S CORRESPONDENCES

If you wish to work more with your particular element and direction, the following may help propel your wishes and magical journey:

Time of Day ★ Midnight
Polarity ★ Female, positive
Exhortation ★ To keep silent
Musical Instruments ★ Drums, percussion
Colours ★ Black, deep green
Season ★ Winter
Magical Instrument ★ Pentacle, stone
Altar Symbol ★ Platter
Communion Symbol ★ Bread, salt
Archangel ★ Uriel
Human Sense ★ Touch
Art Forms ★ Sculpture, embroidery
Animals ★ All domestic
Mythical Beast ★ Unicorn
Magical Arts ★ Talismans
Guide Forms ★ Earth, underworld goddess

Meditation ★ Fertile landscapes
Images & Themes ★ Caves, rocks, organic produce, Moon, stars, night, growth and life

HOW YOU CAN GET IN TOUCH WITH YOUR EARTH ENERGY

"The mountain's position is strong only when it rises out of the Earth broad and great, not proud and steep"
I Ching, hexagram 23, ken/k'un

★ Use Earth energy when making wishes around the following: Financial security and stability, material possessions, practical areas of your life, solidity, endurance and stamina, fertility and fertile opportunities, abundance, work and career, home and garden, children, manifesting anything on the physical plane

★ In magical practices, Earth can be represented by soil, salt, crystals and minerals. Earth spells are most powerful when performed outside. A forest, cave or mountain make naturally sacred spaces in which you can attune to the Earth's energy, infusing your work with the forces of nature. Use tools made with materials grown in the Earth, such as clay or stone, salt, herbs, sand, rocks and crystals - and try using a pentagram disc as a base to strengthen the links with your element

★ The best days on which to employ Earth magic are on a Saturday, ruled by the Earthy planet Saturn, or a Friday, ruled by the Norse Earth Goddess Frigg. If possible, choose dawn or dusk when the magical half-light is neither day nor night, a truly mystical time

★ Hike in the mountains

★ Indulge in some hot-stone massage therapy

★ Go camping

★ Spend time outdoors, connecting yourself to the Earth itself - in the form of trees, rocks, mountains and fields

★ Smell a flower, appreciate its fragrance

★ Heal your emotional body with flower essences

★ Red, brown and black-coloured crystals will activate your connection with the element of Earth and will nurture you and enhance healing

★ Exercise regularly, focusing your full attention on your body and its movements

★ Undertake physical activities that enhance your mind/body integration, such as t'ai chi or yoga

★ Learn to love your body

★ Eat Earthy foods and heavy foods which will help ground you, including breads, and rooted fruits or vegetables that grow in soil

★ Aim for greater order and organisation in your life, with regard to time, resources and possessions

★ Cook. Consciously attune yourself to the meals and food you prepare

★ Climb trees

★ Hug trees

★ Lie down in a field of flowers

★ Meditate on the Pentacles suit in the Tarot (the Pentacles suit represents the Earth element)

★ Collect and carry stones, shells, gems and wood, and any other products of the Earth that you find meaningful

★ Study the Earth sciences, such as geology, crystallography or environmental studies

★ Plant, grow and tend your own garden. Flowers, cacti, fruits and root vegetables are ideal

★ Help others learn how to be more realistic, hands-on and practical; as an Earth sign, you are an excellent role model

★ Learn how to make pottery or sculpt using your hands

★ Wear and surround yourself with the colours green, brown and other Earthy tones

★ Cultivate a whole-body sensuality, by giving and receiving massages regularly. You're a natural!

★ Attune yourself to the Earth goddess Gaia

★ Formulate and maintain a regular schedule and routine to help stabilise your energies

★ Devote yourself to finding a home, space or plot of land to call your own, helping to provide you with a foundation and a sense of rootedness in the one place

★ Invest your money in something secure and long-term

★ Surround yourself with friends who are also bodily-oriented and practical; they will help to reinforce and strengthen these facets of yourself

★ When working with the Earth element in magical practice, stand at the North quarter of your magical space, as the North is its domain, and invite its living essence into your 'circle'

★ Earth spirits are also known as fairies, gnomes, tree devas or elves. They provide grounding and attend to emotional healing, so Earth signs would be wise to adopt one (or all) as their very own spirit guide.

YOUR MODE ★ MUTABLE

Each sign belongs to one of the three quadruplicities, Cardinal, Fixed and Mutable. If we closely examine the Earth's yearly cycle, we can form a very accurate picture of the nature of these quadruplicities, for they correspond directly with the manifestation of the seasons. Each season has three months: the first month brings the new phase of the cycle, the second month brings a concentration of the season's energy to its fullest expression, and the third month represents the transition from the current season to the next one. The astrological quadruplicities represent the three basic qualities in all life: creation (Cardinal), perseveration (Fixed) and destruction (Mutable). Every thing that is born, from a period of time to a human being, experiences a life and then dies. In this context, death can be taken to mean that the form of the energy changes; but the energy itself can never be annihilated, for form is mortal, whereas essence is immortal.

The Mutable mode covers the signs Gemini, Virgo, Sagittarius and Pisces, and is the most flexible group of the three modes (the others being Cardinal and Fixed), able to shift and change to facilitate action. You instinctively know how to go with the flow and you adapt most easily to new situations and have diverse interests, but can lack perseverance and are prone to restlessness. Operating with flexibility and mobility, you are adaptable to change and have a circulating quality. Cooperative and friendly, you can fit in almost anywhere, put up with anything and turn any situation to your advantage. You can steer projects through periods of transition and can also bring them to a conclusion, but are conspicuously absent when hard work, long hours or persistent effort is necessary (with the exception of Virgo). Although gentle, generally easy going and likeable, you can be childish, sulky and ruthless if threatened. And although you have a natural benevolent streak and love to help animals and people, you can also be paradoxically selfish. The natural versatility of the Mutable quadruplicity can develop into a willingness to change and compromise, which gives an enormous sense of resourcefulness to these signs. Being so versatile, you are constantly seeking ways you can make improvements to yourself and your life; Mutable signs can always be relied upon to think of new and ingenious ways of dealing with changing circumstances. However, without the proper focus, centralising force, direction or persistence, your energy can become easily scattered, flighty, wavering and disoriented - and thus ultimately ineffective. You often lack a fixity and determination of purpose, which are needed to concretise goals. Your essential energy is one of movement, flow, fluidity, adaptability, adjustability, harmony, and versatility. Your feelings can switch and shift easily and you can be moody, indecisive, inconsistent and unpredictable. And although resourceful and ingenious, you can often project nervousness and worry. You may act as the intermediate between the Cardinal and Fixed signs. Mutable also indicates the ending of seasons, which are times of change and transition, merging into new territories and changing conditions.

Being of the Earth element, Virgo is the least changeable of the Mutable quality; however, you can easily end something that was firmly established if it doesn't suit. You are critical and analytical of all changes that do occur, and will never do anything without weighing it up carefully first.

YOUR RULING PLANET ★ MERCURY

The Great Communicator, Learner
& Eternal Student

Planetary Meditation
I am my Earth (my body),
and my Sky (my transcendence)
I am my Sun (my spirit),
and my Moon (my soul)
I am my Venus (my pleasure),
and my Jupiter (my faith)
I am my Mars (my courage),
and my Saturn (my lessons)
I am my Mercury (my thoughts),
and my Uranus (my truth)
I am my Neptune (my dreams),
and my Pluto (my transformation)

"Visualise the guardian of Mercury in swirls of coloured smoke surrounded by herbs and potions, crystals and gleaming phials of jewel-coloured healing liquids, writing in huge books in strange writing. He is ageless, in some lights an earnest young scientist, in others one of the ancient alchemists who have spent a lifetime in study.
Cassandra Eason, *A Complete Guide to Night Magic*, Piatkus, 2002

Each planet has its own distinctive and original meaning which, according to its position in the zodiac, combines with the qualities that are inherent in each of the twelve astrological signs. If a planet is your sign's ruler, however, it exerts a significant influence upon your life, regardless of its birth chart or zodiacal position.

Errant ★ Associated with the Mind, Communication, Intellect, Learning, Transport, Information Transmission ★ 88 Day Cycle

★ KEY WORDS ★

Information, Communication, Movement, Mobility, Intellect, Change, Adaptability, Rational Thinking, Learning, Analysis, Dissemination, Synchronicity, Perception, Inventiveness, Correspondence, Short Trips, Transportation, Eloquence, Knowledge, Assimilation, Cunning, Coordination, Logic, Expression, Interpretation, Thought, Deduction, Adaptation

★ KEY CONCEPTS ★
★ Mental Processes ★
★ Active Intelligence ★
★ Communication & Expression ★
★ The Neighbourhood Experience ★
★ Mind, Logic & Reason ★
★ Short Trips & Travel ★
★ The Movement of Goods & Ideas ★
★ Thieves, Theft, Trickery & Cunning ★
★ Early Education ★
★ Transmitter of the Spiritual to the Material ★
★ Negotiations ★
★ Sales & Marketing ★
★ Youthful Vitality ★

Day ★ Wednesday

Number ★ 5

Basic Energy & Magic ★ Speed, Communication

Colours ★ Yellow, Silver, Blue, Metallics, Mixed Hues, Checks, Plaids

Gods/Goddesses/Angel ★ Hermes, Mercury, Raphael

Metals ★ Quicksilver, Zinc

Gems/Minerals ★ Citrine, Agate, Opal, Beryl, Tiger's Eye, Topaz

Trees/Shrubs ★ Hazel, Forsythia, Filbert, Myrtle, Mulberry

Flowers/Herbs ★ Bittersweet, Fern, Lavender

Wood ★ Beech

Fabric ★ Linen

Animal ★ Monkey, Magpie, Hare

Element ★ Air

Zodiacal Influences ★ Rules Gemini; Exalted in Virgo; Detriment Sagittarius; Fall Pisces
Zodiacal Signs ★ Gemini, Virgo

Mercury was discovered around 5,000 years ago, and was one of the five known ancient planets.

This versatile and variable planet has a duality which shows in the signs it rules. It governs Gemini, the sign of immediate relationships (positive expression), and Virgo, the sign of analysis and discrimination (negative expression). The extrovert Gemini and introvert Virgo are two sides of the same essential function - the way we communicate and move, and the way we discriminate and think. Practical, analytical, methodical, determined and deliberate is the way Earthy Virgo will express its Mercurial nature. In Virgo, Mercury denotes the reality principle. It expresses thoughtfully and with consideration for the facts, is stable-minded, not easily swayed by emotion or passion, and has an essentially practical, sensible and focused thinking style.

Connected to writing, speech, journalism and information-gathering, Mercury represents the power of communication, interpretation and self-expression, intelligence, reason, the ability to perceive relationships and connections, and to gather facts, mobility, adaptability to environment, siblings, young people, writers, travellers, speakers, students, teachers, editors and transport workers. It tells us about our intellects and the way in which we express our ideas, and also how we relate to and deal with our siblings, neighbours, neighbourhood (the area in which we live, our place in it and how we interact within it), and immediate environment. Overall, its action is to quicken, enliven and add mobility.

The Egyptians saw Mercury as Thoth, transporter of souls, the conductor of sleepers to dreamland and souls of the dead to Hades, while the Greeks and Romans saw him as Hermes and Mercury, the messenger of the gods. Always pictured with wings on his feet, to represent the speed of thought and the ceaseless activity of the mind, Mercury symbolises all things intellectual and linked with communication. In some mythology, he is a direct descendent of Hermes, the messenger of Zeus, and the god of travels. The deity of roads, protector of travellers, god of doorways, commerce and thievery, of good and bad luck, of treasure troves, of honest and dishonest gain, Mercury is widely known as a thief and a cunning trickster. Using the nimble wit for which Mercury was noted, he was an immortal go-getter, a lightning flash whose mental frequency was always switched to 'high', a god who got things done. This is how we interpret Mercury's role in astrology. If we think of doorways and roads, and forces which channel, direct and concentrate energy from one source to another, we can begin to form a picture of how Mercury works. Mercury gathers the energy from any information we attract, and compresses it into usable form; it can be likened to the wire through which the current flows. As such, it encourages listening and responding, learning and reflecting.

However, Mercury's charm, quick wit, speed, fluidity and cleverness requires positive direction, for he can just as easily turn into a prankster and cheat as into a brilliant scientific genius. Pure Mercurial intellect needs to be humanised, to connect with something worthwhile and significant, to discover lofty purpose, otherwise it can lose itself in the frivolity of its own emotionally detached efficiency (when operating through Gemini at least).

Mercury symbolises the eternal and willing student, highlighting all channels of language, interpretation, reflection, verbalisation, perception, study, teaching and writing. It indicates our urges and levels of interest in exploring and sharing ideas with others, and is also connected with networking.

Mercury relates to our education (particularly early education), our early learning experiences, the foundations of learning rather than abstract thinking, principles of interchange, relatedness, seeing links and connections, and how we use our knowledge and skill to function and articulate effectively. The planet in closest aspect to Mercury is the most important as Mercury is very much coloured by its contacts with other planets and by the sign it is in. Mercury is the bridge between our inner selves (Sun) and the people we wish to share with (Venus). People with a strong Mercury in their chart are quick thinkers and fast talkers, often intelligent and learned, can think and talk too much and have a lot of nervous energy with a sensitive nervous system, and are likely to be interested in writing and journalism, communications, social networking, and information-gathering.

Astronomically, Mercury is the swiftest moving of the independent planets and makes rapid changes of declination in the sky. At inferior conjunction (when Mercury lies between the Sun and the Earth), its magnetic field deviates the stream of electrified particles emitted by the Sun; these particles have an influence on the nervous systems of living organisms on Earth, hence astrological tradition linking Mercury's with the nervous system in medical astrology. Mercurial types, such as those with a strong Mercury placement, or those born under its rule, i.e. Geminians and Virgoans, are prone to restless energy and tend to be nervous, neurotic, flighty or frequently suffer from other types of nervous disorders and disturbances.

In medieval astrology works Mercury was a significator of youth and young people, and those with a strong Mercury, Gemini or Third House in their birth chart, often seem to be 'Peter Pans', possessing a glittering, lively charm and never quite growing up. This youthful quality may mark a highly creative, inquisitive person, or a completely undeveloped naïve individual - sometimes both. Such is the trickery of Mercury. Jungian analysts call this personality type the *puer aeternus*, the 'eternal boy', and indeed having all the innocence of children, these characters float effortlessly through life with no noticeable purpose or direction.

Mercury is the closest planet to the Sun and therefore completes its revolution most speedily, linking it with speed and haste. Ancient people rarely saw Mercury in their skies, and when they did it was for a brief period of time. Since it can never be more than 28 degrees from the Sun, it is only when it is farthest from the Sun that it can be seen for scant amounts of time just before or after sunset - and due to its close proximity to the Sun, it can never be seen in the night sky, being swallowed by the Earth alongside its Solar neighbour.

Being prominent in your chart as your ruling planet, Mercury gives Geminis a quick wit, ingenuity, adaptability, humour and a love of study and argument. If it is disharmoniously aspected, however, it can give you a changeable, cunning or exaggerating mind, a nervous and excitable temperament, and a tendency to be quarrelsome, superficial or indecisive.

As your ruling planet, Mercury gives you good mental ability, quickness, ingenuity and some secrecy or slyness. You are inquisitive but rather superficial and restless, and a good talker, often more head-based than heart-based. But what you lack in passion and emotion, you more than make up for in bubbly mercurial effervescence.

Like its namesake, those quicksilver globules that are ever-moving and never still, Mercury is a hard one to pin down. Three of its main keywords - communication, intelligence and knowledge - are equally difficult to define. The actual process of communication is a complex series of skills, emotions, experiences and other human capacities that defy simple or universally-accepted description. The mechanisms may be there for communication, but nothing can really happen until they are activated by some impulse, like an electrical current. This is where Mercury comes in. Intelligence is also tricky and indefinable, for through the senses Mercury may pick up and transmit signals to the mind which then trigger feelings and mental programs and 'files' lodged in the brain, but it is neither intelligence nor the mind itself per se, but the *current* that makes the mind work. Mercury is not knowledge either, but the means by which it is collected, codified, deciphered and dispersed. So although these three words are associated with Mercury, the planet's nature itself is really more nebulous than any of them, as it is the facilitator, the fuel that brings the mechanisms of the mind to life, the measurer of circumstances and the digester of meanings. In short, Mercury is a two-way street, linking the external environment with our minds and vice versa.

Mercury can also be likened to a chameleon, changing its colours to suit its surroundings and, being rather neutral itself, is very influenced by the sign and the house in which it is found in the birth chart.

Associated with quickness, astrologers have always examined the speed of Mercury to determine the speed or agility of a person's mind or thought patterns. The slow-moving, stationary or retrograde * Mercury describes a slower intellect, people who take longer to come up with answers and solutions, working things out slowly and carefully, while those with a faster-moving Mercury are quick to answer and possess minds which move at great speeds and are one mind-step ahead of everyone else.

The Greeks called this innermost planet 'the twinkler', and it is easy to see how appropriate this name is from the astrologer's point of view.

The glyph (or symbol) for Mercury is a complex symbol, open to various interpretations. It appears as the cross of matter sitting below the circle of spirit, surmounted by the crescent of soul. This stands for the triumph of mind over matter, as in an intellect that can channel energies from above and below. In essence, this emblem stands for active intelligence.

The combination of the crescent, the circle and the cross, shows receptivity resulting from the exaltation of spirit over matter, which you are destined, if you haven't already, to master. This icon suggests manifested (crescent) spirit (circle) over matter (cross), and indeed, Mercury's function is to link the spirit to everyday matters to facilitate this process.

Another well-known symbol for this planet is the caduceus of Mercury, which depicts two serpents coiled around a magic wand or herald's staff whose heads are facing each other. On top of the wand or staff is often a pair of wings and a circle, again symbolising spirit. This symbol attests to Mercury being a giver of the healing arts, and it is still used today as the emblem of modern chemists and the medical profession. The caduceus is a complex symbol, but in simple terms it represents the power of wisdom which can bring happiness and good fortune. It protects messengers, who traditionally carried it, as well as its associations with health and healing.

In medieval times, Mercury was also known as Mercurius, the god of the alchemists. Mercurius is 'the alchemical androgyne', lending the astrological Mercury an androgynous quality, that is neither male or female. As Mercury has neither a feminine or masculine energy to it, it is neutral and objective, and works in accordance with its aspects to other planets, its brothers and sisters, effectively plugging itself into their forces and being driven by the resulting power. (According to a Greek myth, the union of Hermes and Aphrodite produced the being known as hermaphrodite, who was both male and female). The mind itself, which Mercury is said to represent, is beyond masculine and feminine polarities, although it could be asserted that the rational or analytical aspect of the mind may possess a masculine flavour, for the hemispheres of the brain have a distinctly male (right) and female (left) quality. But the entire spectrum of the mind that Mercury encompasses, is a different concept altogether, for it seems to transcend these separations. This can be illustrated by the fact that in some Tarot decks, the Magician card is depicted as Thoth or Hermes. He stands before the four elemental symbols which represent the four functions of the human psyche - thinking, feeling, intuition and sensation. Mercury, the true alchemist of times past, possesses the ability to unite these elements into a single whole. But the power to separate and regroup positive and negative impulses in such a way as to bring you what you want and send away what you don't want is not restricted to magicians. It is available to us all and we are constantly making use of it, either consciously or unconsciously.

The Sun and Mercury's relationship describes the intellect's link with a sense of direction, purpose and will. If these factors marry up harmoniously, the individual's expression will come forth accordingly. It is believed, however, that when Mercury forms too close a conjunction to the Sun, it can metaphorically 'combust', and burn out. The two can also produce too intense an energy, so it is arguably more desirable for them to occupy different signs, or at least be as far away from each other as possible so that the energies of both signs can more easily complement each other by virtue of their distance and consequent objectivity. However, having said this, a close conjunction can just as easily signify a powerful focus of that sign's qualities. Further, one's intellect may be somewhat detached from one's central purpose if Mercury is at its maximum distance from the Sun, but in the case of a close conjunction it can symbolise that the mind and will are united. Mercury, as the smallest and nearest planet to the Sun, and a symbol of the rational mind, is intimately linked with our sense of spiritual direction (the Sun).

There seems to be a strong link between Mercury and Uranus. Uranus, according to esoteric astrologers, is the 'higher octave' of Mercury, and is the archetype of rebelliousness, the inventor, the bohemian, and any relationship between it and Mercury will reveal a person's attitudes towards traditional thought. The well-aspected Mercury-Uranus type is stimulated and spurred on by progressive technology, especially that which advances the speed and style of communication, and seeks to forge new pathways of thought, after shattering any boundaries to mental growth. When teaming up with Uranus, Mercury's powers are intensified, for Mercury likes also to improve things, to add to Universal knowledge through inventions. A planet of progress through experimentation, Mercury is never satisfied by established, ingrained thought and rather is ever seeking new avenues for his agile mind to explore.

A symbol of the rational mind, Mercury is intimately linked with our sense of spiritual direction (the Sun), in that our mind must serve our sense of purpose. In its evolved manifestation, it relates to how we transform our spiritual energies into matter. Mercury affects the transmission of information from one point to another, thereby aiding or interfering with the thought process, communications, technology and travel. Other functions influenced by Mercury include modes of travel as well as commerce, including sales, bartering, negotiating, contracts, importing and exporting. Physically, Mercury governs the hands and fingers, meaning that those with a prominent Mercury in their birth chart will have advanced fine motor skills and probably use hand gestures a lot when talking. Others may have good dexterity, beautiful handwriting or exhibit strong mechanical abilities.

Unlike its high-minded Solar system companion, the planet Jupiter **, which represents one's faith and beliefs systems, Mercury has no in-built bias, nor is it concerned with principles or ethics. Mercury is completely amoral and deals solely in rationale and concepts. It can be likened to the postal officer who delivers your letters; he or she is not responsible for the writing of the letters, nor the contents or the reactions they engender; Mercury, like the postal officer, simply operates as a neutral medium for the interchange of information.

Mercury governs our intelligence, our intellectual approach, learning styles, how we perceive things, and our subjective understanding of ourselves. Having established a sensitive contact with the world, we then try to understand it and make our own interpretations of what we see. We then use our intelligence to express this perception - intelligence being a tool for expression and communication. Our intellect is also a very key feature in our relationships with others.

Mercury is associated with manuscripts, registers, puns, conferences, speaking, buying, employees, busybodies, stammering, reports, questions, short journeys, atlases, stenographers, diaries, maps, scholars, education, speech, ideas, spokesperson, post offices, reason, pens, servants, contacts, statistics, topics, psychiatry, research, skill, dictation, investigation, schools, journalists, publishers, criticism, pencils, school pupils, libraries, dictionaries, mentality, deliveries, scripts, merchants, selling, apprentices, decisions, signs, messages, proverbs, speed, details, language, envelopes, desks, mind, information, boys, quotations, trains, mouth, trade, porters, reading, interviews, invoices, relatives, stationery, labels, secretaries, telephones, writers, testimony, words, textbooks, wit, whispering, walking, vouchers, cablegrams, signatures, letters, names, conversation, announcers, patterns, narrators, neighbours, instruction, nervous, calculations, cabs, publishers, traffic, pickpockets, statements, inquiries, knowledge, news, newspapers, signals, brainy, notes, short travels, records, stamps, translation, hands, dexterity, novels, correspondence, shorthand, intellect, thought, vehicles, typists, vocabulary, interpreters, lectures, diaries, coupons, literature, couriers, drafts, posters, editors, petitions, visitors, logic, prose, mail, encyclopaedias, observations, errands, essays, explanations, facts, billboards, cars, handwriting, autographs, tutors, fiction, files, fingers, tellers, books, commentators, gossip, the press, buses, grammar, graphology, inspectors, telegrams, catalogues, transport, keys, voice, bicycles, learning, linguists, bills, chatter, printing, luggage, biographies, twins, lungs, tongue, magazines, theories, clerks, manicures, advertisements, stories, certificates, arms, young people, auditors, charts, advice, agents, ambassadors, pamphlets, streets, broadcasting, clever, business matters, periodicals, columnists, talking, communication, orators, papers, witnesses, study, comprehension, pairs, writing, concentration, typewriters, respiration, tales, restless, rhymes, roads, rumours, satire, teachers and youth. I'm sure you get the idea!

This Mercurial energy and influence, throughout your whole life, gives Virgos the gifts of logical thinking, rational thought, an above average intelligence, cleverness, attentiveness, sharp perceptions, an inquisitive intellect (which manifests in Virgos as breaking down through shrewd discernment, discrimination and analysis). Too much of this Mercurial energy can make one restless, critical, superficial, lacking in imagination, argumentative, inconsistent, non-committal, insubstantial, cynical, immature, overly mind-based, neurotic, nervous, tense, flighty, unreliable, and unable to see the forest for the trees. But the Virgoan's key phrase is "I Analyse," and as your thoughts are always directed to this end, this is a perfect banner for your refreshingly discerning nature and powers of breaking down the big picture into bite-sized, manageable pieces. And this can be your biggest downfall or your greatest strength. How will *you* use your phenomenally powerful Mercurial influence?

* Retrograde means that these planets appeared to be travelling backwards at the time of birth. Despite the fact that this is only an apparent phenomenon, a planet in retrograde motion tends to internalise its effect and direct its energies inward. Its energy is internalised and sometimes suppressed, rather than expressed externally. Retrograde planets indicate energies that function in an indirect, ineffective, compulsive or other unconscious manner. Even though all the planets but the Moon and Sun will go retrograde for a period of time, it is Mercury's retro gradation (three times a year for approximately three weeks at a time) that has earned the reputation as a time when everything gets a little chaotic, especially around communication, travel plans and correspondence. While Mercury is not responsible for the breakdown of its associated correspondences, such as computers, phones, air travel, fax machines, commerce and information services, there is a widespread notion that these breakdowns most often happen when Mercury is retrograde.

** The relationship between the mind and will is imaged mythically by the relationship between Mercury and Jupiter. Jupiter serves to focus one's consciousness. It could be said that Mercury is the servant of Jupiter, i.e. the intellect must be directed towards a higher purpose.

A VERY BRIEF MYTHOLOGY OF HERMES

In mythology, Hermes was the son of Zeus and was renowned as a prankster. The legend tells us that he was born at dawn and by noon he had slipped away from his mother to explore the world. He found a discarded tortoise shell, stretched three strings of plaited grass over it and invented the lyre, and whenever his mother tried to scold him he would charm her by playing sweet music on this beautiful instrument. From then on, Hermes would be involved in much mischief, but always seemed to charm his way out of anything with his cunning, wit, eloquence and persuasiveness. His legacy arguably lives on in the sign of Gemini, and to a lesser degree, Virgo.

YOUR HOUSE IN THE HOROSCOPE ★ THE SIXTH HOUSE

The Sixth House indicates your work, duties, obligations, service, duties, responsibilities and the daily minutiae of your life. It is connected with your health, diet, how you feel about helping others and your attitudes towards routine.

A house is one of the twelve sections dividing the terrestrial globe, viewed from a precise time and geographical place, into sectors from the poles to the horizon. The horoscope, or birth chart, is divided into these twelve sections called houses. Each house governs a different area or 'department' of life, such as relationships, career, leisure and even karma. The reason for this division of the Earth into houses can be understood when we consider that the Sun's rays affect us differently in the morning, at noon and at night, and also in summer and winter, and if we study the cause, we will readily observe that it is the angle at which the ray strikes us or the Earth which produces that difference in effect. Similarly, with the stellar rays, astrologers have observed that a child born at or near midday, when the Sun's rays strike the birthplace from the Tenth House, has an improved chance of public or career advancement in life than one born after sunset. By similar observations and tabulations, it has been found that the other planetary rays affect the various departments of life when their ray is projected through the other houses, and therefore each house is said to 'rule' or govern certain departments of the human life experience.

The Sixth House, ruled by Virgo, is the house of daily work or employment, service, duty, day-to-day routines, and health. It also concerns small animals and pets.

It covers everyday work, daily chores, the usual work environment, employment and labour skills, competence, training, the use of time, routine tasks, basic organisational skills, efficiency, co-workers, employees, staff, hired help, the workforces, the working classes, servants, our place of work, and the conditions under which any work is done. As the House of Work, it is also concerned with colleagues, obligations, duty, responsibilities, and which type of daily work routine and environment most suits us. While the Tenth house relates to one's career, the Sixth House is primarily concerned with the everyday aspects of one's work. The Sixth House specifies the type of work we do, the workplace, and working conditions, and our job as opposed to our career, as well as our level of service, servitude and the employment of servants.

Strongly associated with health, it also encompasses tendencies towards self-improvement, conditions of the body, our health status, and overall it shows our general health, sickness, hygiene and dietetics. It is a truly holistic house, being linked with the integration of the mind, body, soul and spirit, and how this integration or dis-integration is expressed: a state of overall sound health reflects an inner harmony, while dis-ease indicates an inner discord of some kind. The Sixth House is connected with our daily life and rituals, hygiene habits and aspects of hygiene, tendencies to certain illnesses, diet, nutrition, exercise, healing capacities, nutrition, diet, and lifestyles fostering healthy and efficient body functioning. It describes our overall self-discipline, especially with regards to our everyday wellbeing and routines, as this house governs a wide range of matters which come under the basic categories of work and health.

The Sixth House is responsible for our own inner discipline, gives down-to-Earth advice and never shirks its duties. It is where we recognise what needs to be done and where we learn to improve ourselves, through patience, hard work, common sense and practicality. The service and duty carried out in this house comes from the heart or from a true calling, without thought of reward or recognition. This is a dedicated and devoted energy, which also indicates the type of assistance we give others in need. It reveals activities carried out to benefit someone else - whether these are acts of pure altruism or the result of duties tied to your work or your family. As this sphere signifies where your obligations lie, it also contains a degree of self-sacrifice; how selfless or selfish you are in daily life will depend largely on planetary and sign placements in this house.

The first level of the Sixth House concerns physical wellbeing, service, daily routine and rituals. The second level regards introspection, and one's awareness of the need for personal growth and improvement. At the third and highest level, it deals with the acceptance of self through accepting our imperfections, our altruism, charity and helpfulness towards others, and the ability to deal with our self through analytical, honest judgement. Service to ourselves and to others, stress management, analysis, personal discernment and fussiness or sloppiness, coherence, focus, discrimination, tasks, structured time, physical wellbeing, how we feel 'centred' and well, our housekeeping style, attitudes towards health, what we need to accomplish in our work to feel fulfilled, meditation and yoga as a means to grounding, centring and focusing (not in the transcendental sense), and regimentation, are all Sixth House concerns.

YOUR OPPOSITE SIGN ★ PISCES
WHAT YOU CAN LEARN FROM THE FISH

If we look at the zodiac, we can see that it can be broadly divided into two hemispheres, this division being based on the natural division of the year by the two equinoxes. Astrologers often refer to the first six signs, the hemisphere in which the day predominates (the days being longer in the spring and summer months), as the Personal Sphere of Experience, and the second six signs, the hemisphere in which nights are longer, as the Social Sphere of Experience. These two halves of the zodiac perfectly balance and complement each other, and each individual 'personal' zodiac sign has something to teach its directly opposite 'social' zodiac sign. To generalise, the signs of the personal sphere tend to experience life through a type of self-projection and self-interest which is often socially uncomplicated, unsophisticated or naïve. Their objective is to learn greater social awareness and thereby integrate themselves with the larger, more Universal human collective. On the other hand, the signs of the social sphere are prone to experience life through the use of their more developed social consciousness. In essence, the personal signs (Aries, Taurus, Gemini, Cancer, Leo, Virgo) usually provide stimulation and new energy to their environment, while the social, more Universal signs (Libra, Scorpio, Sagittarius, Capricorn, Aquarius, Pisces) provide experience, opportunities for wider expression, and give a more broad-minded approach and perspective to their surroundings.

Each sign in a pair seeks and is attracted to the qualities of its complementary opposing sign. Virgo seeks the complete selflessness of Pisces, while Pisces desires to be able to discriminate in its self-assertions. Virgo dwells within the realm of the distribution of *personal* services, while Pisces resides within the realm of the distribution of *social* services.

Although the word 'opposite' conjures up feelings of separateness and differences, the astrological polarities should not be seen as two signs in conflict with each other - their positive expression is to create a natural balance and equilibrium. Each sign has something to learn from its opposite, but also has a contribution to make towards the other sign's more evolved expression. The Sixth (Virgo) and Twelfth (Pisces) House polarity is concerned with daily 'seen' life versus spiritual 'unseen' life.

The work and service represented by the Sixth House is taken into deeper, wider and more complex areas by the affairs of the Twelfth House. The Sixth House shows work for its own sake -practical and useful - whereas the Twelfth House concentrates more on the concept of service for the collective or Universal good, allowing the individual ego to retire to a more subordinate role.

Negative and Mutable, this is the polarity of service and sacrifice. Virgo represents meticulous, hard-working efficiency and Pisces demonstrates compassionate, generous self-sacrifice. Both have much to offer the world, but also much to teach the opposite sign. Virgo can reduce everything to statistical analysis, dissecting the whole and using each part wisely so as to achieve maximum effectiveness. The expression of Mercury needs the wider, more generous application of Jupiter or the sensitivity of Neptune. Pisces shows that hard work and service are enriched by humanitarian application and fuelled by spiritual inspiration. But if the Piscean does not seek to learn from the Virgo, then ideals become merely pipe dreams and sense of purpose is diluted by indiscriminate compassion and sacrifice.

The discriminating, self-disciplined, dutiful and refined individual, adept at craftsmanship and motivated by a quest for purity, perfection and self-improvement (Virgo) seeks the sympathy and feeling for the unity of life which will allow her to offer her services through love rather than through duty (Pisces). The compassionate, imaginative and understanding individual, sensitive to the needs of others and gifted with a flow of creative ideas (Pisces) seeks to develop the skill, discipline and discrimination which will allow her to offer service and help others in a practical and truly helpful way (Virgo).

Virgo relates to spiritual oneness achieved through service and involvement with others, but it also relates to worry and anxiety when things aren't perfect or don't go as planned. On your quest for compassion and faith, you sometimes trip up due to your tendency to insist on rigidly building structure and order in your own personal world. You can also demand too much cleanliness and sterility of yourself and others and become judgemental of those who don't live up to your standards. Pisces, lacking the discrimination you possess, is far less judgemental and sterile, and has much to teach the Virgin about loosening up. Pisces intuitively knows that your fussy attitudes are blocking your understanding of your oneness with the Universe, and can teach you how to develop greater spiritual awareness around this. The Fish, being deeply instinctive and relying on emotions and feelings, can also impart lessons on trusting your intuitive faculties. Virgo, being so perfectionistic, critical, judgemental and harsh, needs to adjust expectations to a more realistic level by relying on feelings rather than past conditioning and societal expectations about how things 'should be'.

If you are a typical Virgo, you are constantly plagued by a guilt complex. Oddly enough, this stems from a kind of unidentified inner pride which leads you to be overly demanding of yourself and others. Deep down, you actually have little trust or faith in yourself or other people, and you doubt everything. You lack self-confidence to the point of mistaking helpfulness for over-servility, which enslaves you and traps you in vicious cycles or ruts out of which you cannot climb. You are eternally dissatisfied as a result, but Pisces can help, for she can show you the well from which you can draw a faith so strong that it could change your life. But first you must call upon your intuitive faculties and follow them without judgement, questions or restrictions. Your doubts will soon dissolve, faster than the Fish can swish her tail and swim off to help some other being in distress.

Conformity is another Virgoan trait which, when taken to extremes, can keep you in a rut or a cycle of senseless obedience. Learn from the Fish how to swim away from things which you are only doing out of your overwhelming and often incapacitating sense of duty and responsibility. Or better still, shun convention and rules from time to time, by burying your head in the sand or taking off on a one-way cruise and intentionally getting lost at sea. Shirk your obligations occasionally; you will feel much lighter for it. This the Fish knows, for she is forever floating along with the flow in a weightless daydream.

In our materialistic modern societies, there seems little room for love that is given expecting nothing in return; in essence, ruled by pragmatism and profitability, there is scant regard for the values that Pisces embodies. We may catch a glimpse of their qualities through movies, television or fantasy books, that make us dream, imagine and fantasise, but there is little practical education around cultivating such principles in real life. Although we need to learn the qualities of the Virgo's sphere, that is those of limitation, order, logic, analysis, discernment, application and reason, we also need to incorporate their polar and complementary opposite qualities: those of transcendence, dreaming, trust in the unseen, quests for the unusual, spirituality and an all-embracing empathy with others.

Pisces can teach you to see the broader, more Universal picture. While Virgo tends to dissect everything into tiny little pieces for the purposes of analysis, Pisces will merge all the broken pieces together to re-form the whole. This is, after all, the way it should be according to Pisces - for she believes that nothing is separate and everything is connected. In the process, she abandons all those characteristically Virgoan traits - pedantry, nit-picking, scepticism - and blends them together with such effortless ease that it is difficult to tell they existed in the first place. In summary, Virgo compartmentalises their experiences; Pisces lumps them all together under the one umbrella of the collective human experience. You need to move from the tangible into the unknown delights of the intangible, from facts to faith, from sense-based perceptions to soul-based perceptions, from mortal to immortal, from finite to infinite, from the world of form to the creative life force. Indeed, in her eternal glory, the Fish will swim beside you every wave of the way. Abandon fear and worry, for the Fish has been doing this for millennia - and she knows that there is no resistance if you just go with the natural flow of where the water will take you. And she instinctively trusts that there is no such thing as losing your ground - especially not if you're floating.

WHAT THE FISH CAN ULTIMATELY TEACH THE VIRGIN

Release ★ Negativity, over-analysis, rigid structures, harshness, perfectionism, worry, self-criticism, judgement of others, coldness, aloofness, tension, doubts, resentment, meanness (lack of generosity), uptight-ness, control, regimentation, only believing in tangible realities or that which can be proven

Embrace ★ Intuition, spirituality, imagination, going with the flow, emotions and feelings, affection, compassion, sensitivity, meditative practices, inspiration, faith, trust, innocence, Divine connection, believing in the intangible

Pisces is intuitive, imaginative, highly sensitive, perceives the whole, is synthesising, undiscriminating, accepting, disorganised, chaotic, confused, careless, flowing, mysterious, surrendering, avoiding, otherworldly, escapist, impractical, spiritual, transcendent, idealistic, self-pitying, ethereal, compassionate, devoted, responsive, tender, self-sacrificing, easily victimised, selfless and elusive.

You essentially need to develop more Piscean traits and characteristics in order to fully evolve into your highest potential. Some Piscean traits to help you develop your soul's highest potential are compassion, idealism, sensitivity, romanticism, appreciation of arts and poetry, gentleness, kindness and genuine sympathy and empathy with others.

Through the above characteristics, the Piscean can teach the Virgoan how to achieve enlightenment and unity with your mystical side and with the Divine; to take things less seriously; to *feel* rather than think; to go with the flow of life; to let the heart/intuition lead rather than always living in the mind; to develop spiritual wholeness; to spend less time analysing and more time daydreaming; and the calming therapeutic benefits of meditation.

Your ultimate karmic goal, and one which Pisces has already accomplished, is to reach enlightenment and to be at one with the Divine. Virgo needs to get more in touch with her spiritual side, and Pisces can act as your prime guide.

MAGIC, DRAWING, ATTRACTION, SPELLS, RITUALS, WISHING & POWER

A Note on the Universe

Within each of us resides the merging of the Sun and the Moon, the dance of the constellations, the vibrations of the planets, and the vast microcosm and macrocosm of the entire *Universe*. Uni means 'one' and Verse means 'song'; therefore, the word Universe literally means 'One Song'. If you learn to tune yourself in, you can even hear it!

What is Magic?

Magic is a kind of special energy that is beyond description, and like most kinds of energy it has its own rules and ways of being manipulated. It remains an elusive term, and no definition has ever really found Universal acceptance. Attempts to separate it from superstition, religion and other-worldly phenomena on the one hand, and 'science' on the other, are ridden with difficulties. However slippery the term 'magic' might be, there is a general agreement that most of us wish for more of its presence in our lives and often fall short of achieving this wish.

Those performing spells, 'asking the Universe', wishing, praying, or undertaking rituals, are using this very special energy to draw things to them. Learning to manipulate energy in these ways is never hard (and shouldn't be), but it can be complex and does require knowledge, practice, creativity, patience and above all, imagination. Most of us use simple magic every day, whether by saying little prayers, making wishes, visualising, and exchanging - sending out and receiving - good, positive or hopeful vibes. When you understand that all the forces and magic you need are *within* you, and you learn to *believe* in that power, you are then able to make all manner of changes to your life and, most importantly, yourself.

Magic is an invisible force which connects and permeates everything. Every thought you have and every action you take, will affect the strength of this force, and can be influenced and directed towards a specific purpose by using certain means. The most important of these are your intentions, facing in the direction of your desired outcome, your will and your *belief* that it works. The more you want something to happen, and the clearer you can visualise the desired outcome, the stronger your will and feelings towards it will be, ensuring an avalanche of amazing people, events and circumstances will flow into your experiences, gathering speed, momentum and power as it nears your goal or dream.

The Universe (or whichever higher power you believe in) works for us and through us. Ideas are given to us but they must be carried out *through* us, in the form of asking or acting or performing a ritual or casting a specific spell. The Universe's abundance is your abundance, and it flows through your mind into manifestation. The Universe or Divine Being in which you believe, gives you the necessary ideas and clothes them with all that is needed to bring them into form when we ask *believing*.

Based on ancient human beliefs, systems and superstitions, declaring what you want and acting out your deepest desires can actually help to make things happen. Magical ideas include the notion that thought affects matter and that the trained imagination can alter the physical world, that all aspects of the Universe are interdependent and that we can discover connections and correspondences between everyday occurrences and cosmic, or Divine, energies. A miracle or a wish coming true can suggest something is going on that extends beyond the laws of nature, that something unseen has occurred; but just because we cannot see it or touch it, it doesn't mean it's not there. Magic exists, especially if you truly believe it does, but science is so far incapable of capturing its essence or the rationale behind it. Personally, I prefer to leave that task to the higher powers of the Universe.

To help your dreams come true and to use your inborn power to its full effect, you can employ boosters based on the special energies and qualities of your Sun sign. These 'boosters' are chosen to be in alignment with the purpose of a particular goal, and contain energies of their own which will enhance the strength of your spell, prayer, ritual or 'asking'. Specific magical energies can be invoked by carrying out a spell or ceremony using specific herbs or colours, or on a particular day of the week, according to either your Sun sign (to heighten the power of the asking), and/or that is in sympathy with that for which you are asking (I have included days of the week for other Sun signs and spell types).

Some materials and boosters you can use to increase the power, magic or energy in any area of your life include: candles, wish lists (written on an appropriate piece of paper written with a specially-chosen writing tool), symbols, affirmations, chants, incense, herbs and flowers, locations, colours, days of the week, elements, crystals and gemstones, animal symbols, charms, talismans, amulets, gods and goddesses, essential oils, planetary hours and your Solar totem animals. All are covered, some more briefly than others, for your very special Sun sign to radiate the energy to powerfully draw your wildest dreams towards you!

Overall, it pays to remember that the Universe (or whatever higher power/s or force/s you happen to believe in) creates *through* you that to which you give your attention. What you contemplate becomes the law of your being, and through your pure unwavering belief, is eventually brought through to manifestation on the material plane. What you think about is entirely up to you. But just be mindful that whatever you think about the most becomes your dominant thought, then your main point of attraction, and is ultimately magnified until it becomes your reality or your experience. So choose your thoughts with care. And to quote Ralph Waldo Emerson, "Be careful what you set your heart upon, for it will surely be yours." I carry a copy of this beautiful prophecy in my purse as its words resonate so strongly with me. In other words, be mindful about what you're wishing for, for you will most probably get it, whether it's good or bad - magic, after all, doesn't discriminate. Just make your dominant thoughts good ones, and you will attract everything you set your heart and intentions upon. Good luck!

ASTROLOGY & MAGIC

"Everyone practices magic, whether they realise it or not, for magic is the art of attracting particular influences, events and situations within human life. Magic is a natural phenomenon because the Universe is reflexive, responding to human thoughts, aspirations and desires …"
David Fideler, *Jesus Christ, Sun of God*

Astrology is the most sublime of the occult * sciences, while at the same time it is one of the most practical for everyday application, for it divines the human soul itself. The cosmos, particularly the patterns that formed across it at the exact moment we were born, indicates the road along which our mental and spiritual endowments are likely to impel us, therefore enabling us to prepare in advance for life's battles, pitfalls, milestones, celebrations and of course to make the utmost of opportunities. Such is the magic of the human mind, that it can 'see' into the future and relive the past without having to be physically present in either, and when combined with astrological *knowing*, particularly the knowing that springs from understanding some of the dynamics of our natal chart, however basic, our inner - and outer - magic can be lifted to phenomenal heights.

In ancient times, not only was astrology the ardent study of the most learned and powerful minds, but among the masses of ordinary people its authority and guidance was accepted and followed without question. How this powerful knowledge was used was - and still is - up to the individual, but all who used it applied it to their perceived advantage.

As primitive humans observed the skies, no doubt they gradually realised that certain stars upon which their fate depended accompanied the seasons, or certain times of the year. They may also have reasoned that if governed their fate, they also governed their bodies, and it is therefore conceivable that the skies were associated with Divine influence. Certain celestial influences were believed to emanate from the thirty-six decans of the signs, and the mysterious but apparent effect that they exercised upon humans were thought to be due to a subtle ether shed by the heavenly stars and spheres on the Earth, that affected not only people, but also other animals, plants and minerals. For the ancient mind, linking magic with astrology may have also provided a much needed sense of predictability and patterns.

Early astrologers named and made associations with the imaginary divisions of the twelve signs and the twelve houses, and people born under a certain sign were said to inherit to an extent, its properties and nature. They also believed that the influence of the planets and stars corresponded with the medicinal properties of certain plants and minerals. They therefore asserted that the influence of a star or planetary position would affect the type of medicine or healing they would offer a subject to attain the most beneficial outcome. Throughout the writings of early philosophers and theorists, there is constant reference to this unmistakable mystic connection between the seven known planets and Earthly affairs and ailments. The seven metals were connected with the seven planets, to which the seven colours and the seven transformations were added. So the alchemist came to share the astrological doctrine that each planet ruled some mineral: The Sun ruled gold, the Moon silver, Mars iron, Venus copper, Saturn lead, Jupiter tin, and Mercury quicksilver. Consequently, in alchemical symbolism the same sign came to represent the metal and its corresponding planet.

In subsequent years, astrology became closely related to alchemical knowledge and development, and the alchemist came to be regarded as an authority not only on the transmutation of metals, but also on astrology and magic. This goes some of the way to explaining how magic and divination, which had always been inseparably bound up with astrology, came to be associated with alchemy. In all the occult sciences, the supreme power was believed to be in the stars above, and from their mysterious emanations all the metals, crystals, minerals, plants and herbs derived their special properties over time. Further, as alchemy became ever more spiritual and concerned with more abstract and philosophical concepts, eventually it was considered that the transmutation of lead into gold was simply a metaphor for the transformation of base matter, in this case the human soul, into a much purer and higher state of wisdom and being.

The Sun and Moon were believed to have greater influence over the human body than all the other heavenly bodies, and to exert their influence in various ways whenever they entered a certain sign of the zodiac. And although the Moon was traditionally regarded as the most important factor of a horoscope, the Sun has come into its own in later centuries, with the result that almost everyone knows their Sun sign but only those who have delved deeper are aware of the sign their natal Moon falls in. For this reason, I have chosen to focus this book series on the twelve Sun signs, as this is what the majority of people are most familiar with.

The following pages contain methods, energies, materials and objects which may be used to increase the magic and power of your Sun sign's influence upon you. Precious stones, flowers, colours and so on, are regarded as having a potent effect upon good fortune by attuning your mind to receive harmonious vibrations from the astral forces that surround you.

Finally, a basic working knowledge of basic astronomy and astrology is an asset when working with luck, abundance, wealth and personal power. You can attract more of these things when you align yourself with the workings of the wider Universe, the movement of the Sun, stars, Moon and planets and become aware of the correlations between the outer cycles of the skies and the inner cycles within yourself. Also, for those who are knowledgeable about Moon phases, equinoxes and solstices, a world of lucky possibilities can also magically open up to you. You don't need to know about astrology's deepest complexities to understand how everything interrelates; just learning the basics will give you an edge - and hopefully the following lucky tips will provide you with at least a small glimpse into the insights gleaned from your Sun sign, which I am certain will endow upon you the potential for amazing results to manifest in your life - and maybe even a step up one further rung towards the heavens!

* The word 'occult' comes from the Latin *occultus*, which literally means 'knowledge of the hidden'.

USING COLOURS, CRYSTALS, DEITIES, PLANTS, FOODS & MATERIAL SUBSTANCES FOR INCREASING POWER & MAGNETISING MAGIC

Alchemist, reformer and mystic Henry Cornelius Agrippa, born in 1486, in his principal work, *On Occult Philosophy*, expressed his belief in the doctrines of astrology and in the theory that the spirit of the world exists in the body of the world, just as the human spirit exists in the body of man. He contended that this spirit also abounds in the celestial bodies and descends in the rays of stars, so that the things influenced by their rays become conformable to them. By this spirit every occult property is conveyed into metals, stones, herbs and animals, through the Sun, Moon and planets, and even through the stars beyond and higher than the planets. A firm believer in the efficacy of charms, he stated that they may "be worn on the body bound to any part of it or hung around the neck, changing sickness into health or health into sickness." I believe the same effect could be applied to wishing and the thinking of positive thoughts, to mean, "Changing thoughts and dreams into manifest reality." He also recommended that these charms be worn in the form of finger rings (that have been created using the materials in agreement and harmony with your Sun Sign's magical energy).

Material substances are connected with abstract purposes by a complex but highly usable and accessible system of correspondences. Use these time-honoured connections in your own spells and wishes to magnetise your desires to you. The following pages will give you some materials, energies, forces and ideas you can summon the power of in order to enhance your magic and luck.

PLANETS

The Planetary influence of the day is important when 'asking' for something. If you are wishing for luck, for example, try working with your Sun sign's inherent energies combined with the perfect day of the week for it. So a Virgoan might try using her natural intellect and articulate expression, to ask for greater luck on a Thursday, which is Jupiter's Day and Jupiter is renowned for being a lucky planet, or better still, ask for luck on a Wednesday, which is Mercury's Day, planetary ruler of Virgo, at the time of day when Jupiter's influence is at its most powerful (information about planetary hours for each day of the week can be found on the Internet or in books on the subject, and can be complex and detailed. It is an art to memorise the correct times, days and energies for the correct spells. If you are determined enough to achieve your dream or goal however, you will be determined enough to put in the research to do it properly!) Here is a simplified rundown of the days of the week and their meanings:

DAYS OF THE WEEK & THEIR POWERS

MONDAY ★ Moon
Cancer

The Divine feminine, changes, intuition, emotions, secrets, dealing with women, purity, goodness, perfection, unity, psychic ability, magic, spirituality, invoking a goddess's or angel's guidance, anything that fluctuates, contracts, increases or decreases.

TUESDAY ★ Mars
Aries & Scorpio

Enthusiasm, competition, passion, energy, courage, protection, victory, anything requiring assertiveness, standing up for yourself, or a 'fighting spirit', determination, vitality, sexuality, self-confidence, men's power, men's mysteries, drive, ambition, achievement, triumph, masculinity.

WEDNESDAY ★ Mercury
Gemini & Virgo

Education, travel, exams, study, communication, making connections, thinking, dealing with siblings, writing and speaking, knowledge, learning, adaptability, charm, youth, absorbing information.

THURSDAY ★ Jupiter
Sagittarius & Pisces

Increase and expansion of anything (remember to be careful what you wish for), luck, growth, influence, worldly power, accomplishment, fulfilment, gambling, philosophy, higher education, abundance, optimism.

FRIDAY ★ Venus
Taurus & Libra

Love, luxury, the arts, indulgence, beauty, marriage, money, prosperity, fertility, women's power, women's mysteries, grace, charm, appeal, hope, pleasure, decorating, self-worth, self-esteem, personal values, business partnerships, romance, creativity, sharing, bonding.

SATURDAY ★ Saturn
Capricorn & Aquarius

Long-term goals, career, institutions, establishments, security, investments, karma, reversal, structure, protection, solitude, privacy, determination, ending, blocking, renewing, transforming, anything to do with the public.

SUNDAY ★ Sun
Leo

All-purpose, success, wishes, generosity, happiness, optimism, spirit/essence, recognition, health, vitality, material wealth, invoking a god's aid or guidance, personal empowerment, spirituality, the Divine masculine.

YOUR NATAL MOON PHASE

Although this book is aimed at enhancing your life through the energy of your Sun sign, a bit of Lunar help can give your wishing a boost! As well as using the planetary days and hours system to add a bit of zest to your wish fulfilment, try combining your Sun sign's power periods with your natal Moon phase (your natal Moon phase can be calculated using a number of sources on the internet, or through an astrologer), or even studying which constellation the Moon is situated in at certain times, to increase the power of your spells and asking rituals. For example, you might like to 'ask' for a promotion at work during a New/Waxing Moon period, particularly if the Moon happens to fall under an auspicious sign for career advancement, such as Capricorn. Your natal Moon phase can also be used to similar effect, by researching when your Moon phase will coincide with a certain Lunar constellation position.

In most astrological interpretations the Sun is regarded as the most important, central feature of a natal chart. But to many the Moon is equally, if not more, important than the Sun sign. Many ancient cultures considered the Moon sign to be more significant. The Moon passes through the 12 signs about every 2.5 days, usually covering the whole zodiac in around 27.3 days. The Moon symbolises our inner world, the world of feeling, emotions, habitual responses, instincts, intuition, security and the subconscious. It describes our nurturing style and needs, our emotional response to life, our attitudes and likely reactions to others, our instinctive and habitual responses, the receptive feminine side of ourselves, our experience of our mother or mother figure, and our childhood experience. It represents the soul. In relationships it symbolises how we like to be nurtured and cared for, and the potential depth of our involvement on personal intimate levels.

For many centuries, people across the world have recognised that the Moon influences the affairs of all living things on planet Earth. The waxing Moon appears to have a drawing, increasing and enhancing effect, whereas the waning Moon has a decreasing, receding and withdrawing effect. All things that come into being are stamped with the qualities of the prevailing Moon stage. It seems that people born during certain Lunar phases tend to share specific attributes with other people born during this same phase. In turn, their attributes will be subtly different from those of individuals born during any of the other stages in the Moon cycle. Knowing exactly which phase of the Moon you were born under gives you all kinds of extraordinarily valuable insights into your character, emotions, behaviour and motivations in life. It can make you aware of your deepest underlying drives, the fundamental purpose that you are drawn towards in life and the contribution you can make to others and society during the course of your lifetime. This knowledge may enable you to intuit and make the most of your own personal cyclical pattern that you go through each month, and allow you to know when the most auspicious periods of time are for you and your affairs, nurture yourself and channel your energies in the most positive directions.

Because this Lunar pattern repeats itself every month, you will find that you can even pace yourself on a long-term basis. This will enable you to effectively target your efforts and goals on periods of time that you know will be potentially fortunate for you. You may in fact find that your birth phase corresponds with the days of the month when you have abundant energy, feel inspired and can generate new ideas with ease. During this period, you should work towards the fruition of your efforts, bring your dreams into light and reach for the stars!

The Lunar Phases Are:

★ New Moon
★ First/Waxing Crescent
★ First Quarter
★ Waxing Gibbous Moon
★ Full Moon
★ Waning Gibbous / Disseminating Moon
★ Last Quarter
★ Waning Crescent / Balsamic Moon
★ Back to the New Moon

SPELLS, MAGIC & WISHING WITH MOON PHASES

Though the Moon has eight astronomical phases, it is the three phases corresponding to maiden, mother and crone that are the most significant in spells, ritual, wish magic and psychic work. By tuning into the physical Moon we can understand and harness these distinct energy phases in our daily lives and magical worlds. The four primary Lunar phases are the New Moon, First Quarter, Full Moon and the Last Quarter. Depending on what sort of spell you wish to perform, your spell should take place during one of these cycles or time periods. Each phase of the Moon is good for some types of magic, but not so much for others.

NEW MOON, WAXING & FIRST QUARTER

In astronomical terms, the New Moon occurs when the Moon rises and sets at the same time as the Sun. Both bodies are found in the same position compared with the Earth. Therefore, a Solar eclipse can only ever occur at the New Moon, when the two luminaries are found, for a short time, in a perfect line relative to the Earth, with the Moon positioned between the Sun and the Earth. The New Moon's sunlit face is hidden from the Earth.

In astrological terms, the New Moon occurs at a time when the Sun and the Moon are found in the same degree of the zodiac and therefore occupy the same zodiac sign, forming a conjunction, or a 'fusing' of energies.

In astronomical terms, the First Quarter occurs seven days after the New Moon. Seen from the Earth, this phase makes the Moon like a crescent, forming the shape of a capital D.

In astrological terms, it occurs when the Sun and the Moon form a ninety-degree angle, or the square aspect, inside the zodiac, the Moon always preceding the Sun.

As the New Moon marks the beginning of a new cycle, it symbolises fresh starts. This is an exceptional time to work magic and make wishes for new beginnings, and for the conception and initiation of new projects. Use this Moon phase for improving health, the gradual increase of prosperity, attracting good luck, fertility magic, finding new love, friendship or romance, job hunting, making plans for the future and increasing your general spiritual or psychic awareness.

Overall, the Waxing Crescent and First Quarter Moon phases are appropriate for spells, rituals and workings that involve growth, healing and increase. This is a period of time lasting approximately two weeks, to draw things toward you and increase things, such as love, prosperity and new opportunities. During this period is the time to bless new projects, anything that requires energy to grow, such as gardens, business ventures, new homes, or educational pursuits. Personal growth and healing are accented, as is 'attraction magic' - drawing something to you such as love, abundance, health, success or a new path - and if done well, you can expect results by the next Full Moon. Magical workings for gain, increase or bringing things to you should be initiated when the Moon is waxing (or New, going from Dark to Full). A time for divination of all kinds, spells of spiritual intention, and for any creative project you wish to see birthed, with magical and fruitful results.

While making a wish within the first forty-eight hours after the New Moon is a powerful way of helping it come to fruition, the most potent time for making wishes is actually within the first eight hours of the exact time of its position. Write down your wish list within this first eight hours on a piece of appropriately coloured paper with a special writing tool, and be sure to capture the essence of your wish by wording it in a way that charges your emotions and simply feels 'right'. Make a maximum of ten wishes (less is perfectly fine too), as making too many wishes might disperse their energy too much to be effective. After writing down your list and releasing your wishes to the Universe in whichever form you feel happy with, keep your list and check on it in a few days', weeks' or months' time to assess whether anything has shifted in the direction of your listed dreams, desires or goals. I'll bet it has - or at the very least, something even better has arrived in its place!

Although the first forty-eight hours after the New Moon is the most potent time to make a special wish, you can begin Waxing Moon magic when you can see the crescent in the sky and continue until the day before the Full Moon. The closer to the Full Moon, the more intense the energies. In fact, a personally devised ritual using any special Lunar-associated materials over three days up to and including the Full Moon is excellent for something you require urgently or within a short timeframe.

In some cultures, people turn over silver coins or jewellery three times when the crescent Moon appears in the sky and make a wish. As the Moon grows, it is believed that prosperity and good fortune will grow too.

While the New Moon is not known as a time for 'banishing' or releasing things we no longer want in our lives, I feel that if we are to ask and wish for things, we need to make room to receive them. Making room means that the Universe can slot it right into our lives where we have cleared our paths for it. Clutter, unwanted things, unhappy relationships, possessions that no longer serve us, are all things we can banish. So, to help what you are asking for come into your life quicker, the New Moon is a particularly opportune time to throw a few things out so you can make way for the new and clear up some space for that which you are wishing for. What are you waiting for? Start creating a space for your wishes today!

FULL MOON

In astronomical terms, the Full Moon occurs 14 days after the New Moon, on the day when the Moon sets at the same time the Sun rises, or conversely. The two luminaries are effectively facing each other, with the Earth in between, the Sun shining its light onto the reflective Moon, giving it the fully lit up appearance of a giant, bright, perfectly round sphere. Indeed, its entire face is bathed in sunlight. A Lunar eclipse can only occur at the Full Moon, when the Sun, Moon and Earth are all in line, and the Earth hides the lit side of the Moon to us.

In astrological terms, a Full Moon occurs at the time when the Sun and Moon are 180 degrees apart inside the zodiac, and therefore positioned in opposite signs, forming an opposition aspect.

The highest energy occurs at the Full Moon, making this is a powerful time for all manner of magical workings. Use the Full Moon phase for any immediate need, a sudden boost of power or courage, psychic protection, a change of career or location, travel, healing acute health conditions, the consummation of love or a commitment, justice, ambition and promotion of all kinds. This phase lasts approximately 3 days - 24 hours before the exact Full Moon, the day of, and 24 hours after it, according to many sources - giving us 3 full days to perform our spells. However, we are not strictly limited to a three-day period; the power of this phase can actually be accessed for seven days - three days prior to, the night of, and the three days after the Full Moon. The Full Moon period is when the Moon is at her most powerful, being the most luminous and radiant part of the cycle. Known as the 'high tide' of psychic power, the Full Moon represents culmination, climax, fulfilment and abundance. The Full Moon governs all kinds of magic, including manifestation, banishing, and is particularly good for calling forth protection and heightening your intuitive abilities. The Full Moon contains magic that calls forth personal power, fertility, spiritual development, and psychic awareness. Cleansing of ritual tools, crystals, wish lists, Tarot decks, and the like can be done during this phase. Magic worked during the Full Moon often takes one complete cycle to come to fruition. Try also reaffirming your desires during the New Moon to give them an added nudge in the right direction.

LAST QUARTER OR WANING MOON

In astronomical terms, the Last Quarter, or Waning Moon, occurs twenty-one days after the New Moon. The time difference between the rising and setting of the two luminaries is reduced to what it was at the First Quarter. Viewed from the Earth, the Moon resembles a crescent whose lit up area is decreasing in size, forming the shape of a capital C.

In astrological terms, the Waning Moon occurs when the Sun and Moon are positioned at ninety degree angles of each other in the zodiac, forming the square aspect again. However, during this phase, the Sun is instead *ahead* of the Moon.

The Waning Moon represents the Lunar cycle from Full to Dark. Any spells and magic performed during this period is based purely around banishing and releasing. It could involve releasing things which no longer serve you (such as behaviours, material things, relationships and attitudes), banishing negative energies, and removing obstacles which are standing in the way of achieving your goals or dreams. The Waning Moon is the best time for cleansing, gently releasing, eliminating, expelling and completion. It is of great assistance when you are wanting to let go of something, or someone, gradually. The Dark of the Moon, the period when the Moon is no longer visible to the naked eye, until the New Moon, is the most useful time for divination of all kinds.

★ What is your natal Moon phase type?
Can you think of ways you can combine it with the power of your Sun sign to effect change and bring about wonderful happenings? ★

HARNESSING YOUR PERSONAL MOON MAGIC ★ MOON IN VIRGO

When the Moon is in your sign of Virgo, it is a great time for working magic around: Structure, diligence, research, exam success, the finer details of a project or goal, thrift, study success, restraint, duties and obligations, sincerity, analysis of anything, self-discipline and order. Suggested operations could be around rituals and spells to help you make a difficult choice by breaking it down and weighing it up (making a decision with the head and not the heart), precision, finding solutions, and anything related to health and healing. It is also an opportune time to cleanse, detox, give something up (Moon in Virgo exudes a fantastic energy of self-discipline and dedicated focus on overcoming addictions for example), or simply focus on better nutrition. Spells to help strengthen your resolve in anything, increase your brainpower, or undertake a more effective study ritual to ensure academic success are best performed during a Virgo Moon. Down-to-Earth, simple wisdom is accentuated during this Moon, so purify and cleanse your thoughts or space at this time also - clearing out clutter of mind or environment would be most effective if undertaken while the Moon is in Virgo. With the Moon in your sign, you can also seek to create order out of a chaotic or unwanted situation, cultivate self-analysis to aid your self-improvement efforts, or uncover an elusive medical or mental condition that seems to be baffling doctors. This is great intellectual and self-discipline magic!

THE MOON ★ WHAT IT REPRESENTS IN THE HUMAN PSYCHE & NATAL CHART

The Moon in the sky shines with the reflected light of the Sun. Although not a planet, the Moon is our nearest celestial neighbour and exerts a great influence upon us. The gravitational pull of the Moon affects our body fluids, which contribute to about 90 per cent of our biological make-up. It moves at approximately half a degree per hour and takes an average of 27.3 days to pass through all twelve zodiac signs, staying in each for around 2.5 days.

In astrology the Moon corresponds with the way in which we reflect and respond to what is going on around us. It has to do with our feelings, emotions and instincts and, in the same way the Moon influences the tides on planet Earth, it symbolises the ebb and flow of our emotional nature, our moods, fluctuations and changeability. The Moon is the archetype of the Mother, which is within us all, and represents the primary feminine principle in the natal chart. It is through the Moon that we express our parental instincts - caring, nurturing, protecting, sensitivity. The Moon has links with the past and the subconscious and it is from this almost primitive source that our natural instinctual forces flow.

The Moon is essentially a feminine principle and associates with the inner personality, receptivity, passivity and inward-oriented feelings. It can act as an inner guide to the deeper self, the unconscious self, figures half-shrouded in mystery, linking the hidden personal world of the subconscious to the clearer world of personal awareness.

The Moon is the innermost core of our being, private feelings, habitual reactions and subconscious habits. It is the caring, nurturing sustainer of life, the 'mother' of the zodiac. It tells us about how we seek security, our urge to nurture, our nurturing style, our responses and feelings and moods. The innermost core of our being, private feelings, subconscious habits. It is concerned with habits, mothering, habitual/instinctive responses and personality. It is our karma, our soul, our past.

The Moon represents our mother or mother figure, our feminine side, maternal instinct, our nurturing style and needs, our unconscious self, our emotional reactions, the subconscious, our feelings, instincts, intuition, receptivity, habits, what we need to feel secure, fluctuations, cycles, moods, and our childhood. Its position in the birth chart is very significant, because as well as revealing feminine qualities and the potential gentleness and tenderness of a being, the Moon also reveals important information about the experiences and expression of the five senses.

The Moon is essentially receptive and passive; it reflects the life experience rather than initiating it. Fluctuating and cyclical, the Moon is the planet (although technically a satellite) of the childhood experience, and instinctual reactions. It represents the mother (a child's experience and expectations of their mother), maternal instincts and the feminine principle, indicating how strongly these manifest in an individual, male or female.

As it represents what our childhood experience is likely to be, and childhood is essentially a time where our consciousness has not yet fully developed, our Moon sign traits seem to be more apparent in our younger years. We will usually show our Moon sign traits more so than our Sun sign traits during this developing period of infancy and early childhood, until we have the presence of mind to more consciously develop our ego and true core self (the Sun).

The symbol for the Moon ☽ is a representation of its crescent in its waxing phase from new to full, but it can also be seen as two half circles - these form a bowl shape, a receptacle, a feminine container that 'receives' and 'holds' anything put into it. The half circle, unlike the full circle of the Sun, is finite and incomplete, almost as if striving for wholeness.

The Moon represents our *soul*.

YOUR MOON SIGN

The Sun / Moon Polarity
Conscious & Unconscious, Night & Day, Yin & Yang

"Man does, woman is."
Edward Edinger

Your Moon Sign, representing your soul, and your Sun sign, representing your spirit, work together to form the foundation of your basic personality, expression and nature. If you know what your Moon sign is, look it up below and read how it works with your Virgoan Sun to blend your mind, soul and spirit.

♈ **With the Moon in ARIES, Sun in Virgo,** you are likely to be ★ Devoted, dutiful, persistent, self-contained, emotionally cool, impatient with others' shortcomings, pragmatic, self-motivated, adaptable, fussy, resourceful, meticulous, professional, mentally quick, sensual, analytical, choosy, pragmatic, a workaholic, bossy, detached, critical of others, competitive, aloof, precise, skilful, picky, overly cerebral with emotions, demanding, self-controlled, caustically witty, dedicated to work, critical, a good delegator, self-sufficient, verbose, diligent, forthright, a perfectionist, impatient, irritable, steady, rational yet feisty, and in possession of an indefatigable resilience and an unwavering belief in yourself and your abilities.

Sun/Moon Harmony Rating ★ *6 out of 10*

♉ **With the Moon in TAURUS, Sun in Virgo,** you are likely to be ★ Stable, modest, dependable, cool, calm and collected, deliberate, sensual, greedy, consistent, level-headed, pragmatically intellectual, dedicated, critical, stubborn, dutiful, supportive, self-sacrificing, domestic, routine, unimaginative, staid, materialistic, nature-loving, certainty-seeking, fruitful, loving, self-restrained, Earthy, a craftsperson, diligent, financially savvy, organised, reserved, black-and-white in your thinking, kind, affectionate, in possession of a shrewd business sense, infinitely patient, slow and steady-paced, persevering, enduring, loyal, emotionally placid, nervous yet grounded, flighty yet rooted, devoted, dry-humoured, logical, stoic, faithful, peaceful, capable, resourceful, peace-loving but strong-willed, reliable, realistic, sensible, persistent, and dedicated to working hard for an income and thereby gaining security.

Sun/Moon Harmony Rating ★ *8 out of 10* **

♊ **With the Moon in GEMINI, Sun in Virgo,** you are likely to be ★ Changeable, hot and cold, skilful, critical, dissatisfied, fitful, adaptable, intellectually bright, discerning, debonair, cerebral, emotionally versatile, shallow, a jack-of-all-trades, effective, unsympathetic, efficient, perceptive, discriminating, analytical, narrow-minded, observant, applied, prone to worry and over-thinking, clever, rational, inquisitive, an eternal learner, clear-thinking, precise, practically intelligent, pragmatic, objective, able to apply your mind, in possession of mental ingenuity, refined in taste, persuasive, unemotional, mobile, logical, anxious, nervous, self-critical, torn between solitude and social activity, communicative, able to work alone and with others, concise, articulate, alert, unsentimental, and a good reasoner.

Sun/Moon Harmony Rating ★ *6.5 out of 10*

♋ **With the Moon in CANCER, Sun in Virgo,** you are likely to be ★ Gentle, sensitive, caring, nourishing to others, tenacious, retiring, emotionally articulate but moody, kind-hearted, dutiful, sentimental, sympathetic, fertile, self-repressed, conscientious, defensive, nervous, tense, principled but flexible, doting, self-reflective, shy, a complainer and whinger, self-critical and self-pitying, easily depleted, easily stuck, reticent, private, logical yet imaginative, poetic, considerate, concerned for the welfare of others, devoted to family, helpful, companionable, protective, giving, withdrawn, a good counsellor, easily hurt, sensual, enduringly loyal, dependable, supportive, reliable, and able to analyse and process your emotions.

Sun/Moon Harmony Rating ★ *8 out of 10*

♌ **With the Moon in LEO, Sun in Virgo,** you are likely to be ★ Proud, individualistic, hard-working, artistically refined, aesthetic, honourable, discreet but radiant, emotionally articulate, expressive, verbose, hospitable, dutiful, calm on the surface with a great strength within, self-controlled, gently artistic, quietly generous, warm-hearted, capable, trustworthy, sensually romantic, affectionate, snobbish, gently passionate, conflicted between vanity and modesty, controlling, devoted, patient, comfort-seeking, helpful, encouraging, supportive, skilful, an elitist, noble-minded, and masterful.

Sun/Moon Harmony Rating ★ *7.5 out of 10*

♍ **With the Moon in VIRGO, Sun in Virgo,** you are likely to be ★ Judgemental, nervous, hard-working, a thinker *and* a doer, cool, calm and collected, aloof, critical, studious, a perfectionist, discriminating, methodical, studious, devoted, dedicated, practical, modest, reserved, helpful, focused on health, analytical, discriminating, thoughtful, productive, consistent, supportive, kind, unassuming, caring, rigid, conventional, down-to-Earth, attentive, industrious, constructive, resourceful, efficient, objective, rational, cool-headed, logical, neglectful or unaware of your deeper potential, dutiful, self-critical, scathing, willing to help and do what needs to be done, pragmatic, skilful, reliable, persevering, stable, altruistic, humble, modestly wise, lucid, responsible, poised, and in possession of a good deal of common sense.

Sun/Moon Harmony Rating ★ *7.5 out of 10*

♎ **With the Moon in LIBRA, Sun in Virgo,** you are likely to be ★ Harmonious, peace-loving, introverted, aesthetically aware, orderly, aesthetic, pleasant, courteous, polite, elegant, ethereal, sentimental, attractive, artistic, sensual, able to work with principles easily, quietly sociable, refined, graceful, well-balanced, moderate, easy going, loving of simplicity, charming, a hider of feelings, distanced from your true emotional power, gracious, hospitable, detached, pleasure-seeking, romantic, modest, endearing, delightful, gently persuasive, artistically sensitive, charitable, helpful, cooperative, reasonable, tolerant, a practical idealist, and conflicted between self-reliance and needing others.

Sun/Moon Harmony Rating ★ *8 out of 10*

♏ **With the Moon in SCORPIO, Sun in Virgo,** you are likely to be ★ Intense, discriminating, meticulous, substantial, an extreme worker, deeply anxious, single-minded, robust, highly resilient, subjectively responsive, acutely intelligent, tight, pious, scrutinising, passionately dedicated, persistent, committed, repressed emotionally, self-sufficient, charged, astute, concentrated, tightly controlled, serious, unable to relax, resourceful, alternating between being extreme and being modest, highly critical and judgemental, strong-willed, ruthless, sensually passionate, obsessive compulsive, unyielding, sustaining, controlling, shrewd, persevering, thorough, hard-working, penetrative, analytical, secretive, probing, intensely loyal, emotionally stoic, tense, strategic, perceptive, self-reliant, exacting, manipulative, and in possession of a difficult, cool temperament.

Sun/Moon Harmony Rating ★ *6 out of 10*

♐ **With the Moon in SAGITTARIUS, Sun in Virgo,** you are likely to be ★ Giving, gregarious, helpful, dutiful, rational but idealistic, versatile, intellectually enthusiastic, restless but controlled, interested in philosophy, spirituality and religion, articulate, philosophical yet logical, broad-minded, moralistic, grounded yet seeking, perceptive, adventurous yet conventional, quick-witted, urbane, a dedicated student and thinker, embracing of novel ideas, honest, reasonable, frank, studious, intelligent, mentally dextrous, prone to preach and boss, a good guide or mentor, distant from your feelings, emotionally nervous, mentally agile, gently optimistic, ardently sensual, gently exuberant, a lover of learning, aspiring, objective, ambitious, broad-minded yet rigid, adaptable, and guided by reason and logic rather than emotion.

Sun/Moon Harmony Rating ★ *7 out of 10*

♑ **With the Moon in CAPRICORN, Sun in Virgo,** you are likely to be ★ Dedicated, staunch, disciplined, conscientious, devoted, refined, shrewd, rational, dependable, cynical, down-to-Earth, steadfast, pragmatic, modest, a workaholic, controlled, emotionally repressed, cool, aloof, dictatorial, resourceful, committed, driven to succeed, conventional, ambitious, reserved, pessimistic, withdrawn, polished, methodical, frugal, quietly dignified, realistic, logical, industrious, self-restrained, helpful, organised, productive, efficient, reliable, organised, serious, critical, a perfectionist, tight-fisted, timid, sensible, introverted, understanding of practical applications and wisdom, economical, practical, honourable, uptight, socially rigid, self-contained, and willing to work long and hard to achieve your goals.

Sun/Moon Harmony Rating ★ *7 out of 10* **

♒ **With the Moon in AQUARIUS, Sun in Virgo,** you are likely to be ★ Tolerant, objective, contrary, nervous, detached, cool, aloof, discontent, living an unusual lifestyle in some way, paradoxical, attracted to health fads, socially timid, a progressive thinker, dispassionately critical, acutely aware of the human condition, kind, pragmatically helpful, contradictory, quirky, an intellectual, untouched by passions, rational, thoughtful, cool-headed, observant, applied but scattered, a naïve eccentric, philanthropic, dedicated to worthy ideals and causes, well-meaning, open to the unusual, unemotional, helpful, sensible yet rebellious, changeable, dissatisfied, unique, a humanitarian, uncertain, respectful, sceptical, shrewd, conflicted between solitude and social stimulation, realistic, committed to principles, embracing of abstract concepts, analytical, scientific, independent, and devoted to social causes.

Sun/Moon Harmony Rating ★ *7.5 out of 10*

♓ **With the Moon in PISCES, Sun in Virgo,** you are likely to be ★ Loving, sympathetic, sensual, caring, able to mix realism with mysticism, insightful, idealistic yet grounded, compassionate, wholesome, a natural counsellor, inspiring, refined, discreetly generous, self-critical, good-natured, gentle, kind, impressionable, affable, inconsistent, pessimistic, unstable, unsure, prone to depression, self-doubting, sentimental, modest, downplaying of own abilities, supportive, a pragmatic poet, able to bring dreams into reality, needy, introverted, withdrawn, despondent, easily discouraged, self-sacrificing, diffident, torn between being impractical and practical, procrastinating, evasive, melancholic, self-pitying, an escapist, sensitive, cleverly intuitive, perceptive, and in possession of an innate love of beauty, art and peace.

Sun/Moon Harmony Rating ★ *7.5 out of 10*

** If your Moon is in Taurus or Capricorn, your Sun and Moon will form what is known in astrology as a trine aspect. This aspect is the easiest, most flowing and harmonious astrological aspect, ensuring that your Sun and Moon, or spirit and soul, are well integrated. With both luminaries in Earth signs, this gives them the best possible degree of complementary energy - a blending of the elements suggests a balanced expression of personality. One drawback of the trine aspect lies in the fact that its easy flow can be *too* harmonious; if our path is too smooth and difficulties don't arise to challenge us from time to time, we can often become lazy and complacent, stunting our growth and spiritual evolution. As Earth signs, you share the art of practical application, devotion, rational thinking, logic, a love of beauty and peace, determination, pragmatism, sensibility, conservatism, realism, sensuality, fruitfulness and a gentle, caring approach to all your relationships and endeavors, but may be staid, rigid, unimaginative, materialistic, slow, lazy, narrow-minded and lacking in enthusiasm and zest.

YOUR BODY & HEALTH

"A physician without a knowledge of astrology has no right to call himself a physician."
Hippocrates (born c. 460 BC)

Hippocrates, the fifth century BC Greek physician and 'father of medicine' and supposed author of the Hippocratic Oath, maintained that no one should be allowed to practise medicine who had not first studied astrology. Another Greek physician, Claudius Galen, brought together a huge range of knowledge and ideas in the second century AD which dominated medical practice until the 17th century. Among his teachings was a diagnostic technique which assumed that illnesses and their treatments were affected by and governed by the phases of the Moon. For centuries, astrology was a compulsory component of medical training (and still is in some natural medicine degrees), albeit only one aspect of diagnosis and treatment.

Medical or health astrology concerns particular ways of determining and interpreting an individual's horoscope with particular reference to health issues - diagnosis of current dis-eases, identification of areas of bodily weaknesses, and the prescription of natural cures and remedies. In ancient times, and still even today, the movement of the stars and planets was believed to affect bodily functions, and to cause ailments, or cure them.

During the Middle Ages, many drawings of the 'zodiac man' were made, which showed which signs of the zodiac were related to each part of the body, providing information as to the best times of the year to undertake cures for ailments affecting the corresponding body parts.

Health astrology persists today in many forms and among astrologers themselves, from whom clients seek counsel on health-related issues, and while it certainly cannot be used diagnose a condition or dis-ease, one's Sun sign, along with other factors of the natal chart, can definitely indicate potential problem areas of weakness or possible troubles. This branch of astrology has been found to be surprisingly accurate in most cases. While mostly accurate, none of the following information should ever be used as a substitute for professional medical advice should you be personally concerned about any of the conditions or afflictions listed for your Sun sign.

VIRGOAN HEALTH

Virgo is associated with the Intestines, Digestive System, Lymphatic System, Duodenum, Gall Bladder, Pancreas, Spleen, Nervous System, Abdomen, Colon, Hands, the Enzyme Production of the Liver, and Fingernails and Toenails. As Virgo governs the abdomen, intestines and bowels, it makes Virgoans susceptible to a wide range of digestive complaints. Ulcers are a threat to you, as your delicate nervous system, coupled with your sensitivity to many foods through your precarious digestive functioning, may result in such flare-ups.

Virgo represents the energy of discrimination and assimilation. Its nature is cold, dry and adaptable. You fare best in a cool, crisp climate with natural surroundings, and fresh, unpolluted air. Principal rulerships include the absorption and assimilation of nutrients, the abdomen and Solar Plexus, and the autonomic nervous system through its control of the digestive system, and affinity with hygiene, sanitation and diet.

As a general rule, your health is good, though you are prone to worry and fuss incessantly over things, and to resort to all kinds of different remedies. A morbid craving for drink or drugs may also be experienced. Typical Virgos are usually health-conscious and healthy, but if worried, unhappy or upset, you are prone to succumb to the Virgoan tendency toward hypochondria; you are quite prominent among the hypochondriacs of the world, inclined to take far too many pills, potions, tonics and vitamin shots to supplement a highly selective and specialised diet. You are very fussy about checking that any preparation you use is the real thing; all ingredients must be pure and products true to their label. In fact, yours is the most pedantic when it comes to label-checking, analysing and even verifying.

Generally, quite strong in constitution, you are one to have frequent medical check-ups, if for nothing else but your peace of mind. You certainly don't allow any symptom to go on too long without reporting it. Because of this, an illness seldom develops to the stage where it is difficult or impossible to treat.

Nervous system conditions may also be in evidence, so you would benefit considerably from relaxation techniques such as conscious breathing, yoga and meditation, to calm your overactive mind and soothe your frayed spirit. Additionally, as a result of stress and woes, you are often vulnerable to migraines, stomach aches, depression, headaches and even various psychosomatic complaints. You tend towards being a workaholic and can consequently neglect other areas of life, for example working through your lunch break or failing to get adequate fresh air or exercise due to your duties and responsibilities in the workplace, or long work hours.

As a child of nature, it is essential that you spend as much time as possible in fresh air and natural surroundings. Virgos are naturally drawn to health, nutrition, and lifestyle and alternative medicines, and are more suited to the vegetarian way of life than most. Medically-administered drugs don't suit many Virgoans, and you should always watch carefully for any allergy. Holistic and homeopathic remedies seem to agree with your mental and physical constitution and are often favoured, with excellent results. To you, balance and moderation are always the best answer to any health issues, and you are a sound advocate and example of the benefits of these virtues.

Lymphatic system complaints are often associated with Virgo, as are digestive conditions such as appendicitis, indigestion, constipation, colic, constipation, malabsorption, bloating, malnutrition, hernias and diarrhoea.

The typical Virgoan will usually live to a ripe old age, and yet, for most of your life you are inclined to worry about your health and to take all kinds of protective measures against illness. Undoubtedly you have good reason for this health-consciousness, which can sometimes border on obsessive/compulsive, because your sign represents the meeting point of the nervous system and digestive processes. If it's not your nerves affecting your digestion, it's the other way around, ensuring you are always ultra-aware of your diet and your emotions. Many Virgos are food faddists, even bordering on radical, with many of you adopting a lifestyle that involves veganism, organic foods or fad diets. But it is still vitally important to you to only ingest those foods that agree with you.

Your ruling planet Mercury governs the Nervous System, Sensory Nerves, Nerve Fluid, Right Cerebral Hemisphere, Tongue, Bile, Buttocks, Hearing, Speech, Hands and Body Tubing. Mercury is believed to control the whole nervous system, and there is an emphasis on the mental processes, which are usually bright and quick in those under its influence, but also makes you vulnerable to nervousness and unspent restless energy. Mercury is also associated with respiration and the mental faculties, such as memory, and nervous or mental disorders may manifest if you do not take care to nurture your mind's health. Mercury rules the brain and mind; it is changeable in nature. These are all your possible weak spots. As a Mercurial child, you may be afflicted with headaches, speech impediments, all manner of respiratory ailments, poor dietary assimilation, intestinal gas, lung and breathing disorders, asthma, and hearing loss.

Keeping yourself in excellent health overall, with a special awareness of Virgos' vulnerable points, is key to achieving all you set out to do, and getting the most out of your life!

THE CELL SALTS ★ ASTROLOGICAL TONICS

Homeopathy and astrology have colluded to provide a wonderful list of astrological tonics, one particularly suited to each of the twelve signs. These are called 'homeopathic cell salts', 'tissue salts' or 'biochemic cell salts', and are available in most health food stores, are inexpensive and easy to take. They are considered to be gentle, effective and safe, even for children, people in fragile health states, and the elderly. Although the full picture, drawn from a full natal horoscope, gives a fuller, more accurate idea of an individual's unique constitution, even simply working with one's date of birth can be enough for the medical astrologer to suggest the use of a cell salt based upon the correlation with an individual's Sun sign. As well as the cell salts having a significant effect upon physical ailments, they can also profoundly influence the subtle energy bodies, including the mental, emotional, etheric and spiritual. Although the most common use of these salts is based upon each salt's correspondence with a Sun sign, use of the cell salt related to one's Moon sign can assist with addressing deeper underlying emotional issues, such as anxiety, depression, panic and fear. Use of the cell salt relating to your Moon sign will therefore help to restore your sense of safety, balance, security and emotional resilience. In the first seven years of life, when the Moon is the most influential sphere in our lives, Lunar cell salts are the most appropriate choice as a remedy or tonic.

For specific health problems, take both the salt of your Sun or Moon sign, *and* the salt that pertains to the specific condition. The same principle applies to the Ascendant sign, as the First House represents one's physical health, and especially if the Sun or Moon is a rising planet, which means rulership of the whole chart. For the purposes of this book, however, the cell salt that correlates with your Sun sign only is outlined.

TISSUE SALT FOR VIRGO ★ KALI SULPH.

Kalium Sulphuricum, or Kali Sulph. (Potassium sulphate) is the cell salt for Virgo. Found in the epidermal and epithelial cells, it carries oxygen to the cells. Used with Kali Phos., it assists in the oxygenation of skin cells, and is the lubricant that keeps the body mechanisms functioning properly. Used for a wide variety of physical and mental ailments, such as skin eruptions, hot flashes, bronchial and sinus complaints, chills, heaviness, boxed in feelings, giddiness, inflammatory conditions, toothaches, headaches, palpitations, dandruff, nail dis-eases, psoriasis, weariness, anxiety, fear, sadness, and limb pains, especially those that occur in closed-in, warm rooms or the warm air of summer. Virgo diets need to tend to the processes of elimination through the skin and the liver, and this cell salt helps to cleanse the body. Kali Sulph. improves the body's condition and ability to take up nutrition efficiently, which can particularly benefit Virgo considering it rules the intestines, spleen and lower alimentary system. This tissue salt also enhances the body's ability to produce and distribute oil throughout the system; a deficiency can therefore lead to dry skin or hair, and conditions which involve rashes or scaling of the skin. It is mostly used for skin ailments and is indicated in the late stages of all inflammations.

EARTH SIGN VIRGO & THE MELANCHOLIC HUMOUR

Greek physician Hippocrates (460 - 370 BC) theorised that certain human behaviours were caused by body fluids, called 'humours'. Later, Galen of Pergamon (AD 131 - 200), a Greek physician, developed the first typology of temperaments to encompass many facets of the human psyche and physiology. These also related to the classical elements of Fire, Earth, Air and Water - as choleric, melancholic, sanguine and phlegmatic respectively. According to the Greeks who developed the temperament theory (the word stems from the Latin word *temperamentum*, meaning mixture), temperament is the 'mixture' of qualities that combine to form elements in physics and humours in medicine. The Greeks sought equilibrium in the four qualities of hot, cold, wet (moist), and dry, the elements of Earth, Air, Fire and Water, and the four humours of choler or yellow bile, melancholer or black bile, blood and phlegm. If balance was achieved, the person was said to be well- or even-tempered, and the importance of determining the temperament allowed for imbalances to be treated.

In ancient times, each of the four types of humours corresponded to a different personality type, which were associated with a domination of various biological functions. It was suggested that the temperaments came to clearest manifestation in childhood, between around the ages of six and fourteen of age, after which they become subordinate, but still influential, factors in our personality. It is important to note that your temperament is not your personality. However, your personality can incorporate parts of the temperament in its expression. Personality is shaped by both external and internal factors, whereas the temperament is innate, an inborn, inherent part of each individual.

The Earth element corresponds with the humour melancholic, which is characterised by long response time delay, and response sustained at length, if not seemingly permanently. Driven by the fear of rejection and the unknown, you tend to be rigid, moody, anxious, sober, pessimistic, unsociable, responsible and quiet.

The melancholic temperament is analogous with the Earth, which is the main element in autumn (or Fall), the season with which Earth signs have many points in common. The nervous system and physical and mental powers reign supreme in melancholic types, although they may often behave in nervous, worried or unstable ways, too. The Mercurial (Virgo) melancholic is distinguishable from the Saturnine (Capricorn) melancholic through the former's obviously more eccentric and less withdrawn mannerisms.

A melancholic disposition represents anxiety, peace and inflexibility. Its taste is sweet and astringent, its nature alkaline, its indication black bile. The melancholic humour is associated with the physical and *solid* body ^, and with cold and dry conditions.

^ A couple of thousand years ago, the Mesopotamians, Chinese and Egyptians, and more recently the Arabs, practised a medicine called 'of three bodies'. According to the doctors of the ancient world (who often practised as astrologers as well), a human being had three bodies: the physical body, the ethereal (or vital) body and the astral body, imparting a holistic approach to health. In modern medicine, usually only the physical body is focused upon fully. According to tradition, this physical body comprises three principles or states corresponding to three primordial elements: *solid* (Earth), *liquid* (Water) and *gas* (Air). This is the material body, the physical outer cover of muscles, nerves and organs held together by the skeleton. The Fire element corresponds with the *astral* body, which sits outside the physical body in one's auric field.

MONEY ATTRIBUTES

Colour for Increased Earning Power ★ Yellow

The following plants can be used by all zodiac signs to assist in attracting money ★ Ginger, Allspice, Clover, Orange, Marjoram, Cinnamon, Sassafras, Woodruff, Bergamot, Tonka Beans, Heliotrope, Alfalfa, Coltsfoot, Thyme, Mace, Irish Moss, Clove, Almond, Corn, Honeysuckle, Sesame, Nutmeg, Vetiver, Poppy, Jasmine, Dill and Elder Flower. To attract luck and success, try using any of the above, combined with any of the following: Alfalfa Seeds, Basil, Mustard Seeds, Vervain Leaves, Poppy Seeds, Rosemary, Lemon, Anise and Holly.

Striving for financial gain and abundance with a healthy inner moral compass is, in my view, one of the most noble goals we can set for ourselves. When we have more money, we are better placed to help ourselves and of course others; after all, as Abraham Maslow's Hierarchy of Needs model (1943) attests, once our primary and base survival needs have been satisfied, we can then advance higher towards loftier achievements, such as self-confidence, creativity and self-actualisation. Prosperity allows us to turn our attention to these more transcendental matters - to reach for lives not just of material comfort and luxuries, but of meaning, generosity, balance, harmony, fulfilment and joy. Our Sun sign can offer clues as to how we go about acquiring, earning, saving, maintaining, and allowing the overall flow of giving and receiving money. What's *your* money style?

Virgos are hardworking and meticulous in their acquisition of money and you are cautious and even have a tendency to be financially mean. You analyse all monetary decisions before taking a calculated risk and are naturally financially literate and intelligent. Virgo is thrifty, budgets carefully, and rarely spends money on frivolous purchases, preferring to shop around, compare prices and seek out bargains. By living modestly and spending below their income, Virgo always seems to have money in the bank and knows where any money goes. Financial planning and analysis ensures investments that grow slowly but steadily in value are always chosen.

Virgos are good at balancing money and you take great care to save. Sensible to a fault, you like to save your pennies for a rainy day and always have some left over to give - but only if the recipient is deserving, otherwise you can be rather stingy with your money. Bills are paid on time.

You tend to spend your funds on things of quality, preferring to wait until you have the finances needed to make your purchase - debt makes you squirm. In fact, you view being indebted as a weakness and aim to avoid it at all costs.

Anything you find worthwhile enough to save money for is usually of the highest possible standard and you never indulge in impulsive or meaningless spending sprees. It is a rare Virgo who makes a purchase they regret later. Nor do you waste money, for it is a precious and useful resource that can buy a comfortable lifestyle if you use it for noble and sensible purposes only. Retail therapy is not your style, unless of course it is 'investing' in a state-of-the-art juice extractor or the like, that you have carefully researched. In fact, you view such purchases as a kind of health insurance.

Sincere, dependable and honest, you are not one to flash your money or status symbols around for others to see, but the true, modest Virgo has usually accumulated quite a mass of wealth and prosperity under her cool, controlled façade as the years roll on.

COLOURS

Chromatomancy, or divination by colour, is a form of energy therapy that has been used for thousands of years by many different cultures. It works on the principle that we make both instinctive and rational choices or preferences based on circumstances which are already present in ourselves; colour also has an effect on the energy in an environment, and we in turn respond consciously or subconsciously to our surroundings. If we look at the causes, and try to understand the reasons, as to why we are so receptive to one particular colour over another, we will see that there is a subtle link between certain hues and our emotional and instinctive individual reactions. The colour which we give to things results from a combination of three elements:

1. The light or the vibration of a body;

2. The context in which it is found and the interaction between its own light and that of its environment;

3. The sensitivity of the eye's retina which sees the body in question. Because of this, a colour can vary, depending on the individual's perceptions, namely, his sensitivity, his mood, and his view of reality. For a long time, people have understood that their vision of reality depends a lot on their moods, feelings and emotions.

Chromatotherapy, or colour healing, stems from this body of evidence, and its main application is the use of colours for healing purposes. Colours are generally associated with characteristics, feelings, stones, metals, plants and flowers, planets and even the zodiac signs. In varying cultures, they play a significant role in ceremonies and regalia.

We vibrate to the frequency of colour, shown through its continual movement and change in our aura ^. One of the most beautiful examples of colour is the rainbow. This architect of colour is caused by the refraction and internal reflection of light in raindrops. Colour can be perceived as either a pigment, or as illumination. The colour spectrum can be divided into eight main colours: red, orange, yellow, green, turquoise, blue, violet and magenta. Each colour has a wavelength and frequency that carry different therapeutic qualities which have indirect effects upon our health and bodily systems, and because of this, coupled with the fact that we as living energy centres emanate colour, colour can be a great medium in healing, calming, energising, increasing and attracting.

Aristotle, in the fourth century BCE, considered blue and yellow to be the true primary colours and related them to life's polarities: Sun and Moon, male and female, stimulation and sedation, in and out, expansion and contraction. He also associated colours with the four elements of Fire, Earth, Air and Water. Hippocrates, the father of medicine, used colour extensively in medicinal healing and recognised that the therapeutic effects of a white violet differed from those of a purple one. In the fifteenth century, Paracelsus placed particular importance on the role of colour in healing.

Each Sun sign and planetary body has a specific colour or colours which when used in combination with wishing rituals, can enhance their power immensely. Coloured candles can be used to good effect, as the fire energy of the flame/s increases the power of any wish, and flames are also a useful aid to meditating on, focusing upon or clarifying what you want. Coloured candles help to focus the energy for whatever purpose the colour is in sympathy with (e.g. green for money, pink for romance, orange for joy, etc.)

With all this in mind, wearing or using your Sun sign or ruling planet's magical colour/s on a regular basis will undoubtedly bring great benefits.

^ The aura is defined as an energy field, which interpenetrates with, and radiates beyond, the physical body. Clairvoyantly seen, the aura is full of light, colour and shade. The trained healer or seer sees or senses indications within the aura as to the spiritual, physical and emotional state of the individual. Much of the auric colour and energy emanates from the chakras.

YOUR LUCKY COLOURS

For Virgo ★ Mixed Hues, Grey, Navy, Pale Gold, Pale Blue, Brown, Beige, Green, Blue-Greens, Black, Yellow, anything spotted or speckled

For Mercury ★ Yellow, Jade Green

Ruled by Mercury, the planet of the communication and the intellect, yellow is your primary colour, followed closely by more conservative, smart and Earthy colours such as green and dark brown.

Each of the eight colours of the rainbow spectrum also has a complementary colour to which it is matched. Red is complementary to turquoise, orange to blue, yellow to violet, and green to magenta. If these colour pairs enhance each other's most spellbinding qualities and energies, perhaps you could try wearing your Sun sign's lucky colour with its matching complementary colour in order to produce extra magical results! Your lucky Virgoan colours are green, which complements magenta, and yellow, which complements violet. Now you know your colours, you can dress for success!

FEATURE COLOURS ★ GREEN &YELLOW

★ GREEN ★

Planetary Associations ★ Saturn, Venus

Complementary Colour ★ Magenta

Healing Qualities ★ Balancing, Harmonising, Calming, Comforting, Relaxing, Soothing, Wellbeing, Freshness, Generosity

Keywords ★ Prosperity, Growth, Money, Springtime, the Emerald City, Abundance, Fertility, Good Luck, Harmony

Green is a colour of balance and harmony; from a psychological perspective, it is a great balancer of the feelings and the emotions, creating an equilibrium between the head and the heart. The most restful colour on the eye, it is the middle colour of the rainbow - a bridge between the colours of physicality and spirituality. Green is the colour of Venus and of the element of Earth. It shares the Heart chakra, Anahata, with pink and when the hues of this energy centre are in balance you feel an abundance of love and happiness. Its healing powers come from its alignment with the natural forces and rhythms of the Earth. It is the colour of nature, which can reconnect us to planet Earth, and we instinctively lean towards this colour when in need of peace or harmony. Green is also connected with spring, and the abundance of baby animals and seeds sprouting at this time, make it a youthful and playful colour.

Being the colour of balance and sympathy, it has the power to bring the negative and positive energies of a person into balance. Likewise, it has the strength to integrate the right and left hemispheres of the brain, the right hemisphere being intuitive and the left being intellectual. It is also the colour of Spring, of growth, of rebirth and renewal. Green, being such a pervasive colour in the natural world, is regarded as a symbol of peace and ecology. It can be used in healing to promote fertility and beauty. In Feng Shui and other spiritual disciplines, it is said to attract money through its vibrational energy. As mentioned earlier, Green is the colour of the Heart chakra and bridges the gap between the physical and the spiritual worlds. Opening the Heart chakra allows one to love more, feel compassion and empathise with others. Meditating with a green crystal held over the Heart chakra can help to balance emotions. However, green can also evoke feelings of jealousy and envy when out of balance, hence the terms 'green with envy' and the 'green-eyed monster'. Darker shades of green can also symbolise wealth, avarice and greed. Despite some less desirable connections, this colour works to make your mood more like it: caring, contented, accepting, loving, nurturing and joyful. Green can also balance the three aspects of a person's being, namely the body, mind and spirit, creating a sense of wholeness and integration. Green is the midpoint colour of the rainbow spectrum, being neither at the hot nor the cold end. It occupies more space in the spectrum visible to the human eye than most colours. Positioned right in the middle of the rainbow spectrum, it gets along well with other colours and can be used alongside them to complement their effects and enhance and brighten duller hues such as grey or brown, rather than overpowering them.

Coupled with blue, green is a great stress-reliever and natural tranquilliser. It is not always regarded as a gentle colour; for some, it can signify illness, such as when one's skin turns green if sick, and for others, it has connections with ghoulish monsters, aliens, zombies, vampires and dragons. Also strongly associated with the fairy world, it is linked with elves, sprites, dryads and leprechauns - who can all be very helpful to humankind, but can also be 'impish', mischievous, spiteful and malicious. But despite some negative associations, overall, there is no better colour if you are looking for new ideas or a fresh start, as green is the colour that symbolises and supports growth and natural change. Green is a wonderful all-round soother, balancer and harmoniser, and a beneficial tonic for the mind, body, spirit and heart.

★ YELLOW ★

Planetary Association ★ Mercury

Complementary Colour ★ Violet

Healing Qualities ★ Self-confidence, Optimism, Happiness, Life Force, Brightness, Energy, Cheerfulness, Long-term Memory, Nervous System

Keywords ★ Sunniness, the Sun, Vitality, Energy, Healing, Intellect, Confidence, Eloquence, Travel, Movement, Enthusiasm, Creative Imagination, Communication, Upbeat, Open-mindedness, Philosophy, Attraction, Charm, Persuasion

Yellow is a colour of the Sun and can also represent Air or Earth. It is a bright and happy colour, uplifting and energising your emotions and inspiring the mind and spirit. Yellow brings hope and cheer and is a high-visibility colour that can signal danger, being used in hazard signs, albeit to a lesser extent than red. It is used for mental stimulation, improving the memory, communication, travel and even wealth. Yellow is an optimistic, warm, dynamic colour that encourages positivity and inner power. It strengthens the nervous system and soothes stress-related tension. Yellow is the dominant colour of the Solar Plexus centre in our body's chakra system and is related to the mind and intellect, power and control. When in balance, it endows you with a positive outlook - free, self-confident and happy. Bridging the gap between the emotions and the intellect, it promotes dynamism and increased creativity.

Yellow represents the nervous system which it is said to stimulate, tone and strengthen. A yellow environment is a powerful space in which to work or grow, so is an ideal choice when one wishes to increase positive vibes, versatility, energy, self-expression and creativity. Yellow, representing the power of thought and stimulating mental activity, makes it a good colour to have in a study or work environment. It dispels fear and melancholy, being emotionally healing and lively. Being the colour of detachment, it can also help us to detach from unhelpful thoughts, feelings and habits. Yellow has many 'happy' associations, such as daffodils, sunflowers, the robes of Buddhists and Hindus *, and prosperity, in both a material and spiritual sense. In both colour and crystal therapies, yellow, with its summery disposition and associations, can help alleviate the symptoms of seasonal affective disorder (SAD). Overall, yellow rays carry positive magnetic currents which are inspiring and stimulating, and these currents strengthen the nerves, impart vitality and stimulate the higher mind.

* Yellow is associated with enlightenment, which is why Buddhists and Hindus wear yellow robes.

Green and yellow and their respective complementary rainbow spectrum colours magenta and violet, are Virgo's special LUCKY colours! These can be worn or otherwise used together to dazzling and mesmerising effect.

VIRGO'S CHAKRA CORRESPONDENCE ★ THROAT

The word 'chakra' comes from the Sanskrit and means 'wheel', disc' or 'circle'. Chakras are vitally important to your physical health, emotional wellbeing and spiritual growth, and are regarded as a complete integrated system that works holistically. The chakras are funnel-shaped spinning energy vortexes of multi-coloured light. These swirling vortexes of energy absorb and distribute life-force, the subtle energy known as *prana*. The seven master chakras - Root, Sacral, Solar Plexus, Heart, Throat, Third Eye and Crown - lie in the centre line of the body, with the first five embedded within the spinal column. Each chakra vibrates at a different vibrational frequency and on a different note, and responds to specific life issues or 'thought forms'.

The lower body chakras deal with physical issues. As we move up the body, the chakras correspond to increasingly spiritual concerns. As a consequence, each chakra's energy vibrates at a different rate, depending on whether they govern earthbound or ethereal issues. The lower chakras have slower and denser vibrations, while the higher chakras spin at faster speeds with higher vibrations.

Because the chakras have no physical manifestation and cannot be located using any scientific instrument, they have tended to be viewed with scepticism by many Western medical professionals, a distinction they share with energy points in acupuncture and the notion of meridians. Instead, they are believed to have been sensed intuitively by many people over many centuries, and indeed people in yoga positions and in deep meditation have reported experiencing the sensation of a surge of energy rising from the base of the spine and emerging through the top of the head. Some people have even said they have seen points of blue light when their *kundalini* energy has risen from the lowest chakra to the highest, as well as experiencing a profound sense of happiness and ecstasy.

In summary, the Universal Life Force enters the body through the Crown chakra at the top of the head. As it works its way through the body, it flows through the other centres. As it spreads to the Base chakra, it is said to arouse the kundalini energy, which yogis believe sleeps in a coiled serpentine form.

The chakra associated with Virgo is the fifth, or Throat chakra, which governs self-expression, beliefs, speech and communication, and actions involving verbal exchanges.

THROAT CHAKRA

Location ★ Throat Region
Colour ★ Blue
Concerned with ★ Communication, Speech & Self-Expression

Gland ★ Thyroid
Essential Oils ★ Cajeput, Blue Chamomile, Elemi, Cypress, Myrrh, Eucalyptus, Palmarosa, Ravensara, Black Pepper, Rosemary, Yarrow, Sage
Animals ★ Bull, Elephant, Lion
Shape ★ Downward Triangle
Element ★ Spirit/Ether
Planet ★ Mercury
Zodiac Signs ★ Gemini, Virgo
Flower ★ 16-petalled Lotus
Energy State ★ Vibration
Mantra ★ HAM

Positive Expression ★ Spiritual, self-expressive, willing to work with the Divine, articulate, cooperative, effective communication

Negative Expression (Blockage) ★ Indecisive or wilful, idealistic versus realistic, arrogant, deceptive to self or others, judgemental, problems with self-expression (expression of own truths), inability to communicate ideas or uncontrolled, low-value or inconsistent communication, problems with creativity, manipulative

The Throat chakra is located at the base of the throat. Its Sanskrit name is *vishuddha*, and its symbol is a sixteen-petal blue lotus flower whose centre contains a downward-pointing triangle within which is a circle representing the full Moon. Balance in this chakra is expressed as easy communication with ourselves and others on all levels. It corresponds to the thyroid and parathyroid glands and the pharyngeal nerve plexus. Crystals that can be used to cleanse and balance this chakra are mostly blue stones, including: Blue Lace Agate, Amazonite, Blue Fluorite, Chrysocolla, Blue Chalcedony, Angelite, Aquamarine, Azeztulite, Azurite, Blue Calcite, Larimar, Lapis Lazuli, Aqua Aura Quartz, Malachite, Blue Sapphire, Turquoise and Blue Tourmaline. Amber also helps cleanse and balance this area.

LUCKY CAREER TIPS & PATHS THAT WILL MAKE YOUR BANK BALANCE & SPIRITUAL SELF SOAR

The branch of astrology known as 'vocational astrology' encompasses the areas of one's calling, career path, or ideal profession. Careers, jobs, professions and occupations can all mean different things to different people, but to simplify the definition, I refer to a vocation as one's true calling, one's authentic path, and a dynamic way of life which pays an income in some form and leads to a deep fulfilment of personal and spiritual needs. An ideal vocation will provide self-fulfilment, ego satisfaction, and feed one's inner drive to achieve what they ultimately wish to achieve, whether that be to gain recognition, wealth or approval, to travel, to learn and fulfil an inner need for knowledge, an urge to serve others in some way, or an urge to improve personal, societal or Universal conditions.

In order to gain ultimate fulfilment and self-esteem, we all need a purpose in life. Many people gain this through their work, providing the job or career they choose suits their temperament, talents and aspirations. If our professional life is unsatisfactory or disharmonious in any way, frustration, unhappiness and even despair can result. Although your whole horoscope would need to be drawn up and interpreted in order to gain more substantial, deeper insights into your ideal career and purpose, you can begin by being guided by your Sun sign, which can give you many pointers to a suitable, and therefore successful, career path. You just never know, something in the following might jump out at you and make your soul dance immediately - and hopefully all the way to the bank!

With your Sun in Virgo, your analytical and managerial skills are unsurpassed. Yet you are usually modest and introverted, so would rather avoid the limelight and are happy to let others shine. Information, financial, medical, healing and service industries all appeal to the Virgoan spirit and suit your multitude of skills. You are multitalented and smart, and your ideal vocation utilises your mental and manual dexterity, your problem-solving abilities, and your healing 'touch', as well as providing a healthy, clean, safe and peaceful environment.

Most Virgos are practical and methodical, with a natural ability to deal with routine work and fine details. Your concise and usually accurate judgement is more likely to be influenced by facts and logic than by fantasy or idealism, as your planetary ruler Mercury keeps you rooted in reason and rational thought. Down-to-Earth, you will normally tend towards vocations where the ultimate goals and tasks are realistic, measurable and achievable.

In many ways Virgo is a follower rather than a leader, and your unassuming, humble nature often keeps you in 'safe', secure occupations where you happily carry out any duties assigned to you. As attention to detail is one of the hallmarks of your sign, this skill can be put to excellent use in the following fields: Accountancy, Research, Engraving, Statistics, Microscopic Analysis, Critic, Clerical and

Secretarial Work, Libraries, Computer Programming, Watch-Making, Editing, Design and Drawing, Mathematics, Electronics, Languages, Switchboards, Cataloguing, Disseminating Data, Mapping, Proof-Reading, Pathology, Microsurgery - and many other activities which entail fine detail, counting, calculating or small components.

Virgo is specifically related to health, cleanliness and hygiene, and most Virgins are particularly fussy and careful about what they eat. You like to know how it has been prepared or cooked, and you also read labels, examining what chemicals, 'numbers', or artificial colours, flavours or preservatives have been added to foodstuffs. Because of this, and your emphasis on and interest in nutrition and a healthy lifestyle, the following careers may hold appeal for you: Working in a Health Food Store, Health Resort Worker, Retreat Operator, Health Inspector, Health Researcher, or Health Supplement Manufacturer. A career as a Nurse, Chemist, Doctor, Social Worker, Osteopath, Naturopath, Chiropractor, Dietician, Nutritionist, Hygienist, Psychologist, Herbalist, Physician, Nurse, or any other type of medical, healing or health worker could be very rewarding too.

With their Earthy nature, urge to serve others, eye for detail and discriminating natures, many Virgos can also be found in the areas of Horticulture, Personal Assistants, Teaching, Food Supplies, Nature Photography and Public Health, Safety and Hygiene.

Overall, you make a valuable asset in any vocation, as you are dutiful, orderly, efficient, helpful, and everything you undertake has a distinct purpose. Any career where you can combine your need for routine and high standards with you urge to serve and help others, is ideal. You are at your best when working in the background, giving stability and practical assistance to all around you.

LUCKY PLACES WHERE YOUR ENERGY IS HEIGHTENED

As the Earth element and melancholic humour correspond with cold and dry conditions, arid but cool places suit your constitution, disposition and temperament. The following nations and cities are also places whose vibrations are closely allied with the sign of Virgo: Brazil, Kurdistan, The Eastern Mediterranean, Mali, Croatia, Mexico, West Indies, Iraq, Switzerland, Greece (Crete), France (Paris, Lyon), Turkey, Germany (Heidelburg) and North America (Boston). Silesia, Niger, New Caledonia, Armenia, Belarus, St Marino, North Korea, Saudi Arabia, Egypt, Honduras, Costa Rica, Honduras, Estonia, Guatemala, Ethiopia, Trinidad and Tobago, Malta, Gozo, Qatar, Papua New Guinea, Salvador and Uruguay are also in tune with the Virgoan energy, as are libraries, research facilities and health farms and retreats. Visiting the scenic countryside, anywhere where you can learn something new, places of intellectual greatness, advancement or history such as famous universities, book stores, laboratories, research institutions and museums, taking self-guided touring through places that are peaceful and away from the hustle and bustle, health retreats of all kinds, yoga and meditation getaways, and indulging your senses in fresh air, healthful food or a cleansing regime to restore or refresh your body and spirit, could very well be your ticket to Virgoan heaven!

GEMS & CRYSTALS

"People love stones, and apparently stones love people. Like the angels they may be, they seem endlessly willing to serve the wellbeing of humans and to help us achieve our desires ...Unlike people of the ancient past, we now have access to virtually the entire mineral kingdom. We have the opportunity to work like modern alchemists, combining and arranging the stones and their currents, looking for combinations and patterns that can help us enhance our inner and outer lives."

Robert Simmons, *Stones of the New Consciousness*

Each crystal and mineral of the Earth embodies different qualities, patterns or potential expressions of the Divine language, the silent whispers of the Universe. If we can accept the fact that the human body is a sophisticated, multi-faceted antenna system comprised of a crystalline matrix that is constantly transmitting and receiving all manner of energies, it could then be assumed that energy and body workers who use quartz, shells and stones, which are also crystalline materials, have the power to promote resonant interactions with the liquid 'crystal' structures found in human tissues. It could even be said that we are all made of essentially the same substances and structures, and that crystals and gemstones vibrate at varying energetic levels which can connect with our own in order to 'buzz' and dance together to make a harmonious Uni-verse both within and without.

All crystals work through vibrational balancing and by channelling energy. The magic of crystals is in their colour, which is determined by the rate at which their atoms vibrate; these vibrations can be matched to the energy given by your own body's aura. And just as light can be focused and refracted through gemstones, so too can all kinds of psychic energy, from healing energies to Divine communications.

Gemstones can help us attune to higher vibrations and bring them into our own experience and being. This theory of crystal resonance suggests that the characteristic energy patterns emanated by any stone can be transferred into the 'liquid crystal medium' of our bodies through resonance. Our bodies, being composed of these tuneable liquids, can mimic and mirror any consistent vibrational pattern with which we come into contact; we can therefore resonate with the healthful qualities of various crystals and minerals.

Crystals and precious stones have been valued throughout world cultures over many centuries for their healing virtues and capacities to imbue courage, strength, invulnerability, clairvoyance, love and numerous other qualities. Wearing gemstones is one of the simplest and most effective self-healing practices you can undertake, and wearing or carrying those stones whose vibrations correspond with the qualities you wish to embody brings their energetic currents into engagement with your body.

Over time the phenomenon of energetic integration, may be felt tangibly and your own vibrational field may internalise the stone's currents and adjust to them and effectively 'store' them, making them, eventually, a part of your own vibrational make-up. And we seem to know from the resonances we feel within our bodies when in contact with these gemstones, that crystals emanate tangible, if oft immeasurable, currents.

Crystals act as transmitters and amplifiers of your will or intentions - as long as your will or intentions are in sympathy with the crystal's energy. The mineral kingdom refers to stones, minerals and crystals and the associations and vibrations they carry. When working with stones, we are working with several different layers of spiritual energies, and although they can be regarded as inanimate 'psychic batteries', they are actually moving, vibrating masses of energy which transmit potential and power into our lives. Some crystals and stones even have receptive powers, which means they can absorb energy and retain it within until cleansed or re-programmed.

Although it is untrue that the only stones you can usefully wear are the ones astrologically matched with your Sun sign or ruling planet, those which align with your Sun sign or ruling planet are your most fortuitous and therefore strongest 'attractors' and 'amplifiers'.

Twelve oracular gemstones were described in the Bible, as the author of *Exodus* (28-15 and 17-21) knew them. Yahweh spoke to Moses about the breastplate he would have to wear to train for priesthood, and described it to him in these words: "And thou shalt make the breastplate of judgement with cunning work; ... And thou shalt set in it settings of stones, even four rows of stones; the first row shall be a sardius, a topaz, and a carbuncle. And the second row shall be an emerald, a sapphire and a diamond. And the third row an opal, an agate and an amethyst. And the fourth row a beryl, and an onyx, and a jasper; they shall be set in hold in their inclosings. And the stones shall be with the children ... (all) twelve (of them)." Given that the compilers of the Bible lived during a time when astrological belief was prevalent in Babylon, it seems valid to assert that these previously named gemstones would have some astrological basis. Further, since these ancient people supposedly made correlations between each of the twelve precious stones, and one of the twelve zodiac signs, there are seven crystalline systems set down in crystallography (or the science of the laws which influence the formation, structure and geometric, physical and chemical properties of crystallised matter) as analogous with the seven traditional ruling planets of the zodiac.

However, nobody is under the rule of one planet alone. We are all in essence a complex mixture of every planet, many elements and varying aspects, depending on their positions, placements and prominence in our birth chart. Everything that goes on in the skies above us affects what is going on here on Earth, and also *within* us. Your lucky stones are to assist you to tune into your Sun sign's energy and planetary influences, but you are by no means limited to the ones listed for your sign alone. Above all, let your stones, whichever ones you choose, work for you and allow them to transport your very own unique and magical energy into the wider Universe.

> "Beautiful and strong is the material of stones, but more beautiful and much more powerful is the mystery that emanates from them."
>
> **Chinese Poet & Alchemist, Li Po, 8th Century A.D.**

★ CLEAR QUARTZ ★

The Master Healer ★ *For All Zodiac Signs*

A common, well-known and popular gem, clear quartz (sometimes known as rock crystal) is an all-purpose 'jack-of-all-trades' stone. It amplifies the magic of any work you do or wishes you make. It is connected with all the chakras and increases the power of all other crystals. Clear quartz is a deep soul cleanser, which unblocks and regulates energy and emotions on all levels. It is balancing and harmonising. In various cultures, quartz crystal is reputed to be the most powerful crystal, the 'grandfather crystal', and the 'chief of the Stone People'. Clear quartz is also considered to be the only gemstone that is modifiable to suit your needs *, as other crystals automatically contain and retain their own specific resonance or natural signature. In essence, clear quartz is the most easily programmable and the most overall healing and readily accessible crystals of the mineral kingdom, holding a unique importance in the Universe of gems. And because of its all-encompassing nature and wide-ranging healing abilities, it has zodiacal affinities with all the signs.

* To program your clear quartz crystal, simply hold it on your Third Eye chakra (between and just above the

physical eyes) and concentrate on the purpose for which you wish to use it. Be positive and receptive while you allow your crystal to fill with this energy. If you wish, you could also state the intention of the programming out loud, for example, 'I program this crystal for love / healing / meditation / abundance / protection or (insert your own word here)'. You could also run your clear quartz crystal under running water, allow it to dry naturally, then hold the stone with both hands, bring it up to your mouth and blow into it sharply three times in order to impregnate it with your own breath. Then, hold it firmly in one hand and silently invite and welcome it into your life as a friend, helper and guide.

VIRGOAN & MERCURIAL LUCKY CRYSTALS, STONES & GEMS

Virgo birth stones ★ Sapphire, Carnelian, Peridot, Sardonyx

August birth stones ★ Peridot, Sardonyx, Moonstone, Carnelian

September birth stones ★ Peridot, Sapphire, Lapis Lazuli

Sapphire, Carnelian, Peridot, Sardonyx (your four primary birthstones), Moonstone, Lapis Lazuli (August and September birthstones), and Emerald (Mercury) are your luckiest stones, and one or more of these gems should be worn about your person to ensure good luck and increase your magnetism. Banded Agate, Jade, Diamond, Jasper, Rutilated Quartz, Amazonite, Citrine, Opal, Magnetite, Blue

Topaz, Amber, Smithsonite, Moss Agate, Rubellite, Purple Obsidian, Sodalite, Sugilite, Dioptase, Chrysocolla, Amethyst, True Jasper, Snowflake Obsidian, Cat's Eye, Hawk's Eye, Grey Onyx, Grey Amber, Alexandrite and Garnet also align with Virgo's energy.

CRYSTALS & THE PLANETS

All the Vedic texts agree in relating gems to planets. This verse from the *Jatax Parijat* links each gem to a planet:

'The ruby is the gem of the Lord of the Day (the Sun),
The shining pearl is the gem of the cold Moon,
Red coral is the gem of Mars,
The emerald is the gem of noble Mercury,
Yellow sapphire is the gem of Jupiter, instructor of gods,
Diamond is the gem of Venus, instructor of demons,
Blue sapphire is the gem of Saturn.'

Each planet influences its gem, and their curative power varies according to the position of its planet in the zodiac. Ayurvedic medicine has always paid attention to these details in their healing practices, often advising people to wear their corresponding zodiacal stone as a ring or a talisman.

CRYSTALS & THE ELEMENTS

Crystals are inextricably linked to the four elements, from their original creation to their potency and use in magical rituals and healing. Formed by the combination, in varying conditions, of different physical elements, such as metals, non-metals and gases, some stones require the enormous heat generated by volcanoes or deep thermal currents to bond their molecular makeup, while others may require pressure or water sources. The effects of the four elements of Fire, Earth, Air and Water is evident in these formation processes. The heat generated by Fire, pressure from the Earth, and the chemical reactions involved in absorbing elements from the Air and Water, all demonstrate the four elements in action to produce the correct conditions and ingredients necessary for the creation of crystals, lending them each their unique qualities.

CRYSTALS & THE EARTH ELEMENT

The most obvious elemental force for crystals is the Earth, in which they are found. Crystals are formed over millions of years, which naturally links them with qualities of perseverance, endurance and patience. These gemstones provide the stability of the Earth and the ability to remain, or become, grounded.

Some Earthy crystals are ★ Jet, Onyx, Aventurine, Magnetite, Emerald, Crysocolla, Smokey Quartz, Malachite and Jadeite.

THE CRYSTALLINE SYSTEM OF YOUR RULING PLANET MERCURY

Associated with your ruling planet Mercury, are Tiger's Eye, Jasper, Agate, Coral, Beryl, Azurite, Sardonyx, Gypsum and Marcasite. This is the seventh crystalline system, which is analogous with Mercury, and is known as the monoclinical or clinorhombic system, that is having an oblique prism on a diamond-shaped base. The stone which perhaps represents this system best is Azurite, or copper hydro carbonate.

MERCURY'S GEMSTONE ASSOCIATIONS

★ **Emerald** ★ Emerald is a vivid grass-green precious stone belonging to the beryl family, whose name is derived from the Greek *beryllos*, meaning a green stone. Emerald is mainly blue-green in colour but can also be green-yellow and even yellow. Virtues ascribed to this stone are that of hope, purity, prosperity, love, dreams, kindness, healing, fertility and eternal youth; the ancients believed that it would bestow immortality and good fortune upon those who wore it. With its dazzling green brilliance, emerald has long been prized for its magical properties and as such has a long history of myth and folklore. Most important of all was emerald's reputation as a link with the Divine forces. It is said to enhance psychic abilities and clairvoyance. Emerald is a powerful stone, associated with natural elements such as the Moon, rain and water. It is also linked with alchemists and with Hermes, and its legendary healing powers are said to be closely linked to the occult. The ancients believed that the Greek god Hermes inscribed the laws of 'magic', the thirteen precepts, upon an emerald tablet, and indeed, emeralds were dedicated to Mercury, the winged messenger, by early astrologers.

Connected with the Heart chakra, emerald opens and activates this vital organ to heal all problems associated with the heart, whether they be physical or emotional. It is known as 'the stone of successful love' with which unconditional love can be pledged to a partner. Possessing a very loving vibration, emerald carried in the left pocket is said to attract this vibe to you. To increase the loving vibration of your interaction with others, i.e. what you send out, carry this stone in your right pocket. By promoting harmony and wholeness to every aspect of one's life, emerald dispels negativity and draws beauty, wisdom and healing to it. Emerald ensures emotional, physical and mental equilibrium and imparts strength of character to overcome setbacks and misfortunes. As a stone of regeneration and recovery, it can inspire a deep inner knowing, broaden vision, and enhance one's wisdom and integrity. Indeed, in ancient times, emerald was seen as a stone which could deliver knowledge of mysteries, bringing particular wisdom and inspiration, and served both as a remedy and a miracle stone. It encourages us to follow the laws of nature and, by imbuing us with a sense of beauty and openness, enhances our ability to appreciate the wonders of life.

Emeralds were a prime source of wealth in Ancient Greece and Egypt, and this legacy endures today. Emerald is believed to attract good fortune and encourages gratitude, helping you to recognise abundance in all forms rather than just monetary. Perfect, sellable emerald stones are rare; most are cloudy, unremarkable or otherwise flawed - but can still be effectively used for healing purposes. Life-affirming and inspirational, this brilliant green beryl instils a sense of vitality and energy and is an overall uplifting and healing tonic for the mind, body and spirit.

★ **Cinnabar Quartz** ★ Alchemy, magic, transformation, wealth, insight, manifestation and mental agility are all key words for this mixture of red cinnabar, white quartz and other trace minerals. Its element is Fire and it is connected with the Base, Sacral and Third Eye chakras. A very attractive stone, its colour is usually vermilion or scarlet red. It forms around volcanic vents and hot springs and may also occur in sedimentary rocks associated with recent volcanic activity. Cinnabar becomes cinnabar quartz when it forms in conjunction with quartz, and cinnabar quartz is the most beneficial form of cinnabar for metaphysical use. The quartz serves to increase the durability of the stone, as well as magnifying cinnabar's energetic properties. As a stone of the Magician archetype, cinnabar (or cinnabar quartz) can facilitate the alignment of personal will with Divine will, allowing one to 'tweak' the Divine currents so that one can influence creative material manifestation. Cinnabar is also aligned with the god Mercury, also known as Hermes or Thoth, and as such it can help increase mental agility, intellectual brilliance and clarity of thought, traits for which these gods were known. The usual colour of cinnabar, pure red, is resonant with the colour of one of the images of the Philosopher's Stone, the 'attainment' of which is the goal of alchemy. This is the Stone of the 'lovers of wisdom' (*philo* = love; *sopher* = wisdom, or Sophia), which helps the alchemists attain one of their loftiest aims aside from transmuting lead to gold - that of wisdom. For one's aspirations of spiritual growth and evolution, Cinnabar is a potent quickener, helping to speed up the process by which one's transformation occurs. Overall, it facilitates the process of alchemical change within the individual and brings about the experience and expression of one's newfound inner golden illuminated awareness.

* Cinnabar and Cinnabar Quartz contain Mercury, so caution should be exercised when handling this crystal.

VIRGO'S FEATURE CRYSTAL ★ SAPPHIRE (BLUE)

The hardest crystal after diamond, sapphire has long held a reputation for its amazing spiritual as well as physical properties. A variety of the mineral corundum, sapphire is a symbol of ultimate truth and imminent justice. Sapphire is found in a variety of colours, including blue, yellow, white, black, purple and green - but the blue variety is probably the best known. Known as the wisdom stone, each colour having its own particular wisdom, all hues bring prosperity and attract gifts of all kinds. Its name is derived from the Sanskrit word *Sani*, which means

Saturn. Sapphire has always been associated with love, fidelity, joy, prosperity, the heavens and the angels. In Vedic astrology, gemstones such as the blue and yellow sapphires are believed to work through physiochemical and electrochemical means. It was believed to encourage altruism and generosity, to stimulate the imagination and curiosity, and had the reputation of winning those who wore it numerous friendships. Especially prized by the ancient Greeks and appearing throughout their mythology, those who wished to put a question to the famous Delphic Oracle had to wear a sapphire.

There are many legends surrounding this luminous blue stone: The Ten Commandments were said to be written on tablets of sapphire, and King Solomon was believed to have used one to commune with God. An old Persian myth tells that the Earth sat on a giant sapphire which gave the sky its brilliant blue colour. In Buddhism, sapphire is known as the 'stone of the stones' because of its connection with the qualities of devotion, happiness, spiritual enlightenment and tranquillity. Due to its highly soothing and balancing effect, sapphire is beneficial for treating nervous conditions such as panic attacks, anxiety and stress. Labelled the 'Gem of the Heavens', sapphire was believed to bestow its wearer with strengthened vision, including prophetic visions of the future. It is a symbol of truth and constancy. Sapphires (especially star sapphires *) are good stones to work with to improve your psychic faculties or astral travel, stimulating the Third Eye chakra to enhance psychic experiences. Sapphire is also effective at stimulating the Crown Chakra, and is excellent for improving mental focus and clarity. Blue sapphire has a calming and balancing effect on emotions and may also be used to open up the Crown and Third Eye chakras to the angelic realms. Some sapphires are believed to be record-keepers and may aid you to access the knowledge of ancient civilisations when dreaming, 'journeying' or meditating. Use it to connect to your spirit guides and teachers and for interdimensional communication, as it connects mind, body and spirit. Overall, blue sapphire encourages you to reach for the stars, speak your truth, and stay on your rightful spiritual path.

VIRGOAN POWER CRYSTALS

Around six thousand years ago, in ancient Mesopotamia, the Sumerians started studying precious stones and minerals, as well as the stars, with a view of improving their lives in many ways by probing the secrets and mysteries of the Universe. Their esoteric interests and knowledge were such that they began to grasp the general connections between the Earth and the heavens, or the Solar system as they knew it, and the functions of stones and minerals as a link between the two. Their method of making these connections was by colour (for example the Sun was allocated all yellow stones), as well as other spiritual links. The gemstones listed for the portion of your zodiac sign are given their status as your 'power crystals' due to the links that can be made between your primary planetary ruler/s and your mutable planetary ruler (listed last), and each stone's particular colour, chemical and mineral compositions, healing properties, and the number they are given (based on the Mohs scale of hardness: for example, diamond scores a perfect 10 out of 10), all of which combine to align with your planetary rulers. Working mindfully with your planet's special crystals is one way you can increase the flow of power and magic into your life.

POWER CRYSTALS FOR FIRST HALF
VIRGOANS ★ (22 August - 5 September)

Influenced by Mercury and Saturn
Black Opal, Labradorite, Spessartine Garnet, Specular Hematite, Magnetite

BLACK OPAL ★ Opal is a delicate stone with a fine vibration, which enhances cosmic consciousness and induces psychic and mystical vision. The ancients believed the opal was the mineral bridge between heaven and Earth, for which reason they sometimes labelled it 'The Eye of the Universe'. Even more significantly it was, and still is, 'The Stone of Hope'. As it contains all the colours of the other stones, it can be used to amplify all other stones' energies. Unlike most other gemstones, opal is not crystalline in form, but rather is defined as a mineraloid. It is an amorphous silica variety of quartz, is comparatively soft, and owes its beauty to the wonderful play of colour from its surface. The mineral is formed from the shells or skeletons of very tiny plant and animal organisms. Until recently, the only black opals in the world came from a nine-square mile area in New South Wales, Australia, called Lightning Ridge. Now top grade stones have been discovered in Indonesia, where they cost less because their potential market value is less well understood. Both occurrences yield a semi-black opal as well, but the Indonesian 'Java Black', with its flashing, iridescent 'fire' - a range of colours covering the whole spectrum set against a brilliantly jet-black background - is a particularly appealing gem. Black opal resonates with the Sacral chakra and the reproductive organs, making it particularly useful for releasing sexual tension or repression that arise from an emotional cause. It is also a good stone to use for processing and integrating newly freed emotions. Like all black stones, black opal is useful for grounding, emotional security and alleviating negative feeling states by clearing energy blockages. Opals work well overall with the emotional, mental, spiritual and etheric bodies. Its focus is to clear and build. Black opal, like other opals, is also excellent for enhancing creativity and intuition, connection to the higher self, and providing a much-needed burst of energy, especially when you are lacking in self-confidence. Opal contains more water than any other mineral, up to 21 per cent, and is porous, so it should not be immersed in water or brought into contact with oils, as these may harm or destroy it.

LABRADORITE ★ In every sense, Labradorite is a Stone of Magic. It awakens within you, your magical abilities, psychic powers and mystical gifts. It is a crystal for shamans, healers, mystics, alchemists and diviners of all kinds, and opens up the doorways and paths leading to enlightenment and Divine connection with the Universe. It deepens meditation, connects to intuition, and aligns with the higher sources. A member of the feldspar family, Labradorite is an opaque deep grey, grey-blue or more ethereal pale grey * stone, possessing a brilliant blue and green sheen displaying rainbow colours. Due to the presence within this mineral of countless minute iron plates, Labradorite shows shimmering shades of peacock-blue, green, gold and greenish-yellow, giving it a whole-spectrum colour appearance if viewed from the appropriate angles. Like a dragonfly's wings and resonating with true Mercurial swiftness and flutters, the colours appear, then vanish, this optical effect being achieved for the most part by the interference of light in Labradorite's physical structure. It was named in 1770 when discovered in Labrador by missionaries, even though its history goes back for centuries. In Ancient Scandinavia, Labradorite was used as an oracle by the indigenous peoples, and it can still be beneficially used for this purpose in this age. American philosopher Ralph Waldo Emerson said of Labradorite: "A man is a bit like a Labrador spar, which has no lustre as you turn it in your hand until you come to a particular angle; then it shows deep and beautiful colours." Indeed, this special quality - labelled 'labradorescence' after the stone itself - makes it one of the most striking crystals around. Aside from its blue lustre, glimmers of green, yellow and red may also be seen in some specimens, making Labradorite an appealing rainbow-hued stone. When a specimen shows more green labradorescence, it is known as lynx sapphire. White pieces are often sold under the trade name of rainbow moonstone, despite not actually being moonstone, while transparent specimens are often referred to as black moonstone. Although most aligned with the Third Eye and Crown chakras, Labradorite can be used anywhere on the body with equally beneficial effect. Labradorite has a protective power against jealousy, combating negative influences and empowering the self.

Labradorite can help astral projection by strengthening your aura, acting as a battery to give you the energy and confidence to master the process. It also has many other uses as a magical aide and may help in dream recall, by acting as the 'rainbow bridge' between the conscious and the unconscious mind. It allows for access to prophetic dreams and altered states of reality. A highly spiritual stone, it is believed to have the power to attract a mentor by raising your vibrational frequency so that you attract helpful guides and beings on both the spiritual and material levels. It can also rise above anything that could sabotage your progress, gently pushing you forward toward your goals, increasing your stamina and encouraging you all the way. It transmutes anything negative that reaches it, providing a 'screen' for your personal energies, only allowing through that which it discerns is for your higher good. It deflects unwanted energies, but also prevents energy leakages from the aura. The gentle grace of Labradorite carries ancient spiritual wisdom at its heart and as such it can answer your questions about your spiritual purpose; it can also connect you with esoteric knowledge, Universal forces, initiation into the 'mysteries', and allow access to the 'Akashic Records' **. It is an excellent meditation stone, accelerates telepathic abilities and assists communication with your higher self. Stimulating intuition and psychic gifts, Labradorite bestows the art of 'perfect timing' and energises the imagination and wisdom. It is a beneficial crystal to use during times of change or transition, imparting strength and perseverance, and facilitating self-transformation. Labradorite will connect you to the corresponding element/s of your surroundings - wearing it to the ocean or a forest, for example, will enhance your connection to Water or Earth energies respectively. Overall, Labradorite is a magical and enchanting stone, a dispeller of darkness and a bringer of light.

* The pale grey, translucent variety of Labradorite gives better results than the darker, opaque types. In the pale grey, light plays more effectively on the stacked crystals within.

** The 'Akashic Record' is a cosmic record that exists beyond time and space, containing information on all that has occurred and all that will occur.

MAGNETITE ★ A metallic iron ore stone that is also known as 'lodestone', the most common use of magnetite as a charm is to attract things to you. As magnetite is magnetic, it is believed to attract love, loyalty and commitment. The Chinese call it 't' su shi', meaning 'the loving stone' *. This crystal is renowned for its magnetic attraction to iron and also for pointing to the north and south poles when hung from a thread. This stone has a powerful positive-negative polarity and is extremely useful in magnetic therapy, working with the body's own biomagnetic field and meridians, and with that of the planet in Earth healing. Magnetite acts as a grounding stone and connects the Base and Earth chakras to the nurturing energies of the ground beneath us, which sustains the life force and vitality in the physical body. Magnetite will attract and repel, energise and sedate, clear and build, and also aids telepathy, meditation and visualisation. It enhances a balanced perspective and trust in your own intuitive wisdom. Emotionally, it can be used to alleviate negative feeling forms such as grief, anger, fear, anxiety, and over-attachment, and usher in more positive mood states. Magnetite assists in the release of emotional trauma and gently but firmly pushes you towards change. It dissolves fear and reluctance around change while simultaneously protecting you and helping you to grow. It also helps to bring the intellect into harmony with the emotions in order to cultivate inner stability. Overall, magnetite is both grounding and energising, and aligns our subtle energy systems with the Earth's magnetic field, bringing security, strength and life-force renewal. Magnetite has a hardness of 5.5, aligning it with Mercury's number. **

* To attract more love into your life, obtain a piece of magnetite (or better still, a pair of lodestones) and consecrate it with the four elements.

** Magnetite is best placed next to the body rather than directly upon it, to avoid the body absorbing too much of its energies which may be toxic if overused. Likewise, when handling magnetite, hold it in a tissue or cloth.

POWER CRYSTALS FOR SECOND HALF VIRGOANS ★ (6 - 21 September)

Influenced by Mercury and Venus
Iolite, Carbuncle, Tiger's Eye, Vesuvian Lava, Meteorite, Obsidian

CARBUNCLE (GARNET) ★ Carbuncle is sometimes used as another name for garnet. Garnet is regarded as a symbol of sincerity, good faith, loyalty and honesty. This is a stone of vitality and dreams, and increases the flow of the body's natural energy systems. Relating to the mysteries of sex and regeneration, garnet is a stimulant and effective connector to our deepest memories. It is a useful stone to have during challenges and lawsuits, where courage or fortitude may be required. During such times of change or upheaval, it can provide a sense of grounding, calm and balance, making us feel safe and secure. It inspires service, cooperation, relaxation and 'going with the flow'. Garnet has an affinity for the Base and Sacral chakras, where it breaks down blockages and stimulates our untapped creative energy. It will also revitalise and balance energy in these chakras, bringing serenity or passion according to the need. Sometimes known as 'carbuncles' (when they are cut *en cabachon*, that is, flat at the bottom or with a convex rounded top instead of facets), garnets occur in many different shades, the most well-known being red. Garnet can help lift melancholy and will help you find your inner strength and full potential by releasing your fear of failure. It assists in boosting confidence, imparting courage, building strength of character, and enabling us to find our inner strength and resources. It can help with any sexual difficulties, both mentally and physically, and is a stone of love and commitment which brings warmth, devotion, constancy, faithfulness, understanding, sincerity, trust and honesty to a relationship. Innovative garnet encourages you to be more creative and stimulates the right brain, creating 'light-bulb' flashes of inspiration and thought. It is an energising and regenerative stone, especially for the two lowest bodily chakras, although it also works effectively on the Heart chakra. Garnet helps to dissolve unhelpful behavioural patterns and past hurts to allow you to become more self-empowered and move on. Further, if you are feeling impotent or stuck in plans that have not yet manifested, this stone assists in moving out of the stagnancy and into potent action. It is also useful in easing situations in which you feel trapped and there seems no way out, or where life has become chaotic or broken, offering hope in apparently hopeless circumstances. Garnet is a powerful attractor of abundance and it is traditionally believed that wearing a square-cut garnet encourages success in business dealings. Garnet draws prosperity into your experience and offers support during challenges. It is interesting to note that skyscrapers built on New York's Manhattan Island have deep foundations driven into the island's bedrock, which contains a vast amount of garnet. It can activate other crystals, amplifying their effect.

TIGER'S EYE ★ Resembling the gleaming eye of a tiger in the night, this stone has a golden streak of light which stretches full width across its polished surface, giving it an enchanting shifting lustre. A beautiful combination of yellow-brown and chocolate-brown, it presents pale, parallel silk-like ribbons of colour alongside deeper-hued velvety bands, transforming its colour order with each movement. A stone from ancient times, tiger's eye has been revered for millennia all over the world for its protective and healing powers. A popular semi-precious member of the quartz family, its shimmering gleam effect takes its name from the beautiful chatoyant (cat's eye) effect caused by refraction of light from fibres in the crystal. Depending on the colour of this stone, it can be named after other animals also - such as hawk's eye, cat's eye, falcon's eye, ox's eye or bull's eye. The commonly known yellow-brown shaded tiger's eye was considered Solar and was especially sacred to the Egyptian Sun god Ra. It's Solar associations also gave it a reputation for attracting wealth, abundance and luck. Added to a charm bag, the crystal becomes a good focus for attracting prosperity and good fortune. Tiger's eye has a particular affinity for the Solar Plexus chakra and its gold and brown colours bring together the energies of heaven and Earth, enabling us to lift our vibrations while at the same time feeling grounded, centred and stable. The ancient belief that tiger's eye enabled one to see through things, meant that it has long been used for psychic work. A piece of tiger's eye held to the Third Eye chakra before any divination practices such as reading the Tarot, runes or scrying, is said to aid visualisation and help you focus on sharper images. It is also thought to give clear form to dreams, desires and aspirations, and when used in combination with spells and magic, it can help you focus more clearly on what you really want, making manifestation easier. Tiger's eye is an excellent protective stone, and has a positive strengthening effect on the aura when worn or carried. As a protector, it dispels fear and anxiety, and has the ability to imbue us with willpower, purpose, courage and self-confidence. It also encourages mental clarity, allowing us to see a problem objectively, unclouded by emotions or judgement; it may therefore be used when our ideas are confused, helping us to see our goals clearly and to make the right decisions. Further, it differentiates between wishful thinking about what we *want* and what we truly *need*. It softens stubbornness, allowing us to see our true needs, free from our self-imposed, idealistic or rigid mental stances, and attitudes stemming from unrealistic desires for perfection. Tiger's eye balances mood swings, as well as our yin-yang energies, and releases tension. Overall, tiger's eye helps us to overcome obstacles and is a gem of pure bravery and an eliminator of doubt, empowering us to fulfil our life's work without the fear of failure holding us back. Tiger's eye is a mood enhancer which heals issues of self-worth, depression, pride, wilfulness, self-criticism, blocked creativity, and aids in recognising one's talents and abilities. It builds a firm foundation for spiritual expansion and above all, increases our personal power. But this is no heavy power, for truly enlightened souls are joyful, light and playful. Tiger's eye will teach you the right use of your empowerment and stop you from taking your life and your life's path so seriously.

METEORITE ★ Corresponding with Mercury's dense, Sun-baked surface, a meteorite has a hard crust made up of many chemicals which have become fused and clotted by heat and pressure. These are the remains of a large mass of primitive matter from the

Solar system generally believed to have originated in the asteroid belt between Mars and Jupiter. When flung out of orbit, the materials would have been automatically drawn by gravitation towards the Sun, and either by chance or by this pull-force, reached Earth's atmosphere, where it became white-hot and usually exploded. These fragments that arrived on our planet are known as meteorites. In general, these objects have done little harm. Indeed, most are so tiny that nobody ever finds them.

OBSIDIAN ★ Obsidian is a dark, glassy, non-crystalline rock of volcanic origin and is hence found in places of such activity, such as Hawaii, Japan and Iceland. It is also mined in Mexico, Guatemala, Ecuador and the USA, where it can be found in solid, glassy blocks known as 'apache tears'. Obsidian is usually black, but it comes in a variety of other colours, such as red, brown, blue, green, rainbow, red-black, silver, purple, mahogany, silver-sheen and gold-sheen. If it has lacy white flecks, it is called snowflake obsidian. Obsidian is named after its discoverer, Obsius. Not strictly speaking a mineral, obsidian is actually a natural glass once spewed from an erupting volcano. It is essentially molten lava that cooled so quickly it had no time for facets to form or to crystallise. This material, which is usually black, sometimes contains white and grey markings which have given rise to such descriptive names as 'snowflake', 'flowering' and 'apache tears'. This 'jewel of the volcano' has been used in magical ceremonies and ritual for thousands of years. Both the Aztecs and the Mayans used obsidians extensively - indeed, obsidian is easily broken into sharp-edged pieces or 'flakes', and in the absence of iron this was their main cutting tool. Spiritually, obsidian vitalises soul purpose and stimulates growth on all levels. It urges exploration of the unknown and opens up new horizons by eliminating energy blockages. It assists in helping you to know who you truly are, by compelling you to confront your shadow self and identify behavioural patterns that may be hindering you. Obsidian is a fierce, protective stone that helps to unlock the unconscious and make room for this shadow self to come forward and communicate. In fact, nothing can be hidden from obsidian. It has been described as the 'warrior of truth' that draws hidden imbalances to the surface to release them. Working extremely fast and with great power, it is truth-enhancing and merciless, exposing flaws, weaknesses and blockages. With its reflective qualities (many scrying balls * and magic mirrors are made from it), it challenges us to search deep within. In this way, it is best used under the guidance of a qualified crystal therapist as it may bring up negative emotions and unpleasant truths, but under skilful and careful supervision, its cathartic properties are invaluable, helping us to recognise disempowering conditions. It impels us to grow and provides support while we do so, forming a shield against negativity, strengthening us in times of need. Helpful for healers and highly sensitive people, obsidian blocks psychic attack and removes negative spiritual influences. As obsidian is so effective at soaking up negative energies, it is essential to clean the stone under running water after each time it has been used for this purpose.

Divinatory stones made from obsidian are an excellent aid in foreseeing possible outcomes of the future or a particular situation. It has a particular affinity for the Base chakra and is an excellent stone for grounding and anchoring us firmly to Mother Earth, making us feel stable and balanced. Obsidian is also beneficial when used to bring out your 'inner warrior'. If you are feeling particularly nervous about an event or a situation, holding a piece of obsidian can allow its strength to radiate through you.

* Crystal gazing - or scrying - using a sphere of clear quartz or obsidian is an ancient way of moving beyond the confines of the rational mind to gain information and insights that otherwise would not be available to one. Scrying makes intensive and extensive use of your intuition and perception of subtle-energy impressions. Recognising these subtle-energy impressions is also helped by using deep blue or indigo crystals during meditation experiences.

YOUR LUCKY NUMBERS

Your lucky numbers are ★ 8 for Virgo ^ & 5 for Mercury (also, see 'Lucky Magic Square of Mercury')

LUCKY MAGIC SQUARE OF MERCURY

In Western occult tradition, each planet has traditionally been associated with a series of numbers and particular arrangements of those numbers. One such method of numerological organisation is the magic square. Magic squares date back to ancient times, appearing in China about 3,000 years ago. The first Chinese square is seen in the scroll of the river Lo - the Lo-Shu, a scroll believed to have been created by Fuh-Hi, the mythical founder of Chinese civilisation. Certain squares came to be linked with the planets; these associations came from the Babylonians. Each *kamea*, or magic square, is linked with a particular planet, and each of the squares has a *seal*, which is the geometric pattern created by following the numbers in order of their value. This pattern touches upon all the numbers of the square and the seal is used to represent the entire square. An intelligence and a spirit are also associated with each kamea, derived from the key numbers contained within it, using a Hebrew form of numerology. This intelligence is viewed as an inspiring, guiding and informing entity.

The 'Magic Square of Mercury' is divided into 64 cells, or squares, eight across and eight down. The sum of the numbers in the vertical, horizontal and diagonal lines is a constant of 260. The total of these numbers is 2080. Therefore, the numbers 8, 64, 260 and 2080 are also assigned to Mercury.

YOUR NUMEROLOGY NUMBER & LUCKY SUN SIGN NUMBERS

"Everything that exists has a vibration. The vibration of sound, music, colour, matter, even our words, thoughts, and names show form. All vibration is measurable. To measure we need numbers. Numbers are the basis of all. Numbers are the key to all mysteries."

Shirley Blackwell Lawrence, *Behind Numerology*

Numerology is essentially the metaphysical * 'science' of numbers. The use of numbers in magic is its cornerstone of power. The ancient Greek philosopher and mathematician Pythagoras, born around 590 BC, embarked on a thirty-year spiritual quest studying with important religious and esoteric teachers and healers to find the mystery of 'The Hidden Light', and came to see mankind as living in three worlds: the natural, the human and the Divine. He asserted that all things can be expressed in numerical terms, because they are ultimately reducible to numbers. Pythagoras stated that "Numbers are the first things of all of Nature" and followed the theory that "Nothing can exist without numbers."

Many believe that numbers have an arcane, mystical relationship with words, and with inanimate and animate objects; the interpretations that arose from these relationships date back to a time when the dawning intelligence of primitive man first visualised the meaning of numbers and associated it with spiritual significance. Numerology is the science of the exploration of this relationship in order to discover hidden meanings, forecast the future or interpret the character of a person. In its more modern applications, a series of figures which correspond to an individual's name and date of birth are calculated, and practitioners believe one's prospects, fortune and character can be deciphered from the results ^.

So what is numerology and how does one use it? Everything in the Universe has a vibrational frequency, an energy, a force, all vibrating at various rates, and we as humans are no exception, the difference between one person and another is their rate of vibration. This force or energy is constantly in motion and changing, and we can even 'tune into' and feel our vibrations if we are still for long enough.

Along with letters, sounds, colours, crystals, and many other things, it is believed that numbers also have vibrations, and when we are able to familiarise ourselves with our own numerical frequencies, we can use this familiarity to add power and magic to our lives. The numbers of our birth date, the letters of our names, and the numbers of our Sun sign and ruling planets, all have a unique vibrational frequency, and herein lies the key to understanding our self and our journey through life. Numerology refers to the knowledge contained within the numbers of our birth date and our name, and this is our own personal magic which can greatly assist us through life.

* Metaphysics is the study of those sciences that extend beyond the physical or tangible

HOW TO FIND YOUR NUMEROLOGY NUMBER

^ Your Sun sign's number was added up according to the principle of corresponding a number with a letter, for example 1=A, 2=B, 3=C and so on in sequence and up to 9=I, then beginning again at number 1 for the next letter J and following this same sequence. Following this system, the sum of the letters in Virgo vibrates to the number 8.

Your personal numerology number is determined by adding up all the numbers in your birth date until they reach a two-digit figure. The two resulting numbers are then added together again to form a single digit, which is your personal numerology number. For example, someone born on 3 February 1983, would add the digits $3 + 2 + 1 + 9 + 8 + 3 = 26 =$ (reduced to two digits) 8. So that person's personal numerology birth number is 8.

Each primary number or birth number from 1 to 9 has a specific meaning and is governed by a planetary force. The principle of numerology reduces all numbers down to the following: 1 to 9, and 10, 11, 13 and 22 *. The last four numbers only apply to people specially concerned with the occult and spiritualism - and can be studied at greater length through other sources if so desired - and can in any case be reduced further to a single digit if preferred. Your birth number contains a unique power, and therein lie your strengths, shortcomings and opportunities. It is beyond the scope of this book to outline your individual numerology number possibilities, so for the purposes of astrological applications, I have only included your Sun sign and ruling planet's special numbers.

* The numbers 10 and 13, and the master numbers 11 and 22, can be further reduced to one digit if so desired; however, they can be interpreted as they are without further reduction. The choice is personal.

BASIC MEANINGS & KEYWORDS

1 ★ Sun. Masculine influence, beginnings, independence, inventiveness, originality, leadership, exploration, innovation, ambition

2 ★ Moon. Feminine influence, cooperation, partnership, tact, diplomacy, harmony, unity, emotions, imagination, adaptability

3 ★ Jupiter. Communication, expression, youthfulness, self-confidence, creativity, inspiration, optimism, curiosity

4 ★ Uranus. Order, form, security, stability, patience, restriction, work, values, practicality

5 ★ Mercury. Freedom, inconsistency, change, variety, travel, activity, learned

6 ★ Venus. Love, home, family, sense of duty, responsibility, marriage, justice, nurturing, balance, gentleness, peace, friendship

7 ★ Neptune. Analysis, wisdom, mystical, spiritual, solitude, precision, research, integrity, mystery, psychic perceptions

8 ★ Saturn. Money, power, success, organisation, hard work, business, health, purpose, control, authority, mastery

9 ★ Mars. Completion, endings, Universal, service, humanity, philanthropy, loyalty

10 ★ Fortunate, creative, vibrant, stable, optimistic, original, successful, determined, individualistic

11 ★ Master number. Prophecies, inspiration, moral courage, missionary, long-suffering, foolhardiness, enlightenment, invention

13 ★ Misunderstood, fearful, changeable, interested in the occult, fatalistic, flexible, sacred, beguiling

22 ★ Master number. Powerful, successful, idealistic, attracted to the occult, creative, wise, successful, masterful, spiritually understanding

★ THE NUMBER 5 - FOR MERCURY ★

Names ★ Quint, Quintuple, Pentad, Quinary, Quintet, and all names preceded with the prefix *pent*, from the Greek *pent* which means five: pentacle, pentagon, Pentecost, pentagram

Arithmomantic connections with the letters of the alphabet ★ E, N and W

Ruled by Mercury, this is a changeable number by nature. The number 5, symbolised by the five pointed star pentacle, is an intellectual vibration and is connected with freedom and movement, energy, travel and creativity. But the number 5 also represents unpredictability and instability, owing to the unstable and unbalanced nature of this number. This fickleness and uncertainty is associated with the number 5, as it carries no constant vibration and may change or shift. The quincunx, the number 5, or the Pentad, was regarded by the followers of Pythagoras, as well as other philosophers, as the symbol of health and prosperity, but on the whole it seems universally to have symbolised marriage, fecundity and propagation, this belief probably having its origin in the idea of 5 being the union of 3 and 2, or a male and female number (in Ancient Rome, its significance was emphasised by the burning of 5 tapers during the marriage ceremony). A fifth element indeed exists, and was described by Plutarch in the 1st century AD, in these words: "If we assume that the World in which we live is the only one there is … then it is itself made up of, as it were, five worlds which make Harmony of it: one is the Earth, another Water, the third Fire, the fourth Air, and the fifth Sky, with the last one being called Light by some and Ether by others and by yet others, Quintessence." It could be said that 5 is the number of transformation, representing the combination of the four elements plus spirit (or ether). The magical symbol of the five-pointed star is an Egyptian hieroglyph for the womb, as well as one form of the ancient Seal of Solomon.

Five is associated with magical gateways, and indicates that there may be challenges ahead, but these will help you develop your skills. Five - the number of the physical senses - symbolises the planet Mercury, and people born under this number are mercurial in temperament and characteristics. It is a quixotic number of quicksilver temperament and ideas, and signifies communication, an artistic streak and extreme creativity. Number 5s are the ideas people, who hate being tied down to anything resembling a routine or time schedule. Carrying the Mercurial vibe, this is the number of adventure and communication which embodies the concept of "variety is the spice of life." People under its influence will likely have many irons burning on as many different fires as possible at the same time. It can also indicate travel and movement so is perfect for all those with wanderlust and who welcome the world and new experiences with open arms. You are the great communicators of life and love to travel far afield, making excellent explorers and adventurers. It can be contrary and irresponsible, however it is often the number associated with fame and notoriety.

Commitment can be a big problem for 5s, because there is so much out there to investigate. You may also be chaotic, uncommitted, inconsistent, self-indulgent, unstable, careless, and attracted to immoral or unvirtuous activities. You are energetic, lively, impulsive, adventurous, daring, freedom-loving, versatile, curious, adaptable, sociable, flexible, sensual, quick-thinking, romantic, fun-loving, accommodating, witty, courageous and worldly, but may be highly strung and have trouble with your nerves. You are good at making money, especially by risk or speculation, and you bounce back easily from any setback. You make friends easily with people born under any other number, but close friends will probably be fellow number 5s. Wednesday is the luckiest day for the quicksilver number 5.

Alchemy ★ Five stands for dynamic focus, a combination of two and three. It can be sparkling, sexual or charismatic, or on the other hand, a decisive act of destruction. It can also represent the quintessential element which is a distillation of all four basic elements. A five-pointed star, the pentagram (five points joined by one line) or a pentagon (a five-sided figure) are its main representations.

LUCKY 'MAGIC HOURS' OR 'TIME UNITS'

One rule of magic, luck and power, as already outlined elsewhere in this book, can be found within the well-known phrase, "As above, so below." From the most ancient times, the planets were said to rule Earthly destinies and powers. Days of the week were named after the seven planets which were the only ones then known: Sun Day, Moon Day, Mars Day (French: Mardi), Mercury Day (French: Mercredi), Jove Day (French: Jeudi), Venus Day (French: Vendredi) and Saturn Day.

The planetary hours are based on an ancient astrological system, the Chaldean order of the planets. The Chaldean order indicates the relative orbital velocity of the planets, and from a heliocentric (helios = The Sun) perspective, this sequence also indicates the relative distance of the planets from the Sun (the Sun switching places with the Earth in this sequence), and the distance of the Moon from the Earth.

Before an action is taken in daily life, or a transaction undertaken, for instance, it is possible to choose the appropriate day and hour that will provide the greatest chances of success. By studying the planetary hours system, you will discover which actions are propitious to which of the seven planets or 'star-gods' and at what time it would be advisable to undertake them.

The planetary hours system uses this Chaldean order to divide time, and each planetary hour of the planetary day is ruled by a different planet. The order is repeated, starting with the slowest: Saturn - then, Jupiter, Mars, Sun, Venus, Mercury, Moon, then back to Saturn, Jupiter, Mars, etc., ad infinitum. The planet that rules the first hour of the day is also the ruler of that whole day and gives the day its name. So the first hour of Saturday is ruled by Saturn, the first hour of Sunday by the Sun, and so on. It is important, for the purposes of using specific planetary energies for our magic and wishes, to note that planetary hours are not considered the same length as our normal time-keeping slots of sixty minutes. Each day is split into time periods, day time and night time, beginning at around sunrise and sunset respectively. These two time periods are each divided into twelve equal-length hours, which are the planetary hours. So the planetary hours of the day and the planetary hours of the night will be of different lengths, except during the equinoxes when light and darkness are balanced.

In sequence, the Sun, Moon and the five visible planets each exerts its own special influence over a twenty-four-hour period. I like to call your planet's special day and hour the 'Magic Hour'.

Magic rituals to draw luck and love to you should be conducted at astrologically correct times and with the appropriate instruments, tools, cards, herbs, flowers, oils and plants which are linked with the ruling planet. For example, a love ritual, spell or potion demands a concoction of any or all of the above ruled by Venus. Do not underestimate rulerships, for they wield an unseen power that can help make our dreams, big and small, come true.

Further, as specific hours of each day are ruled by certain planets, if you are really serious about attracting some power, luck or magic into your life, it is imperative that you wish, pray or ask at the most opportune times for your Sun sign. There are two methods you can use for fine tuning your magical workings. The first method is to perform your spell, ritual or wishing on the day your Sun sign's ruling planet during the planetary hour that signifies the essence of what you are asking for (e.g. A Virgo who is looking for love might perform a love-seeking ritual on a Wednesday, during a Venus-ruled planetary hour). Alternatively, if you wish to summon the power of your Sun sign's own ruling planet, then that same Virgo might perform their love-seeking ritual on a Friday (ruled by Venus) during Mercury's planetary hour.

The nature of that which you are asking for, such as love, travel opportunities, money, career guidance, protection or friendship for example, should always be considered when choosing the day or hour during which your magic will be heightened.

The answer to the question why are there seven days in a week, is a very important one to know in unravelling the secret of your Magic Hours. Ancient people recognised the supreme importance of the seven heavenly spheres, which comprised those which could be seen by the naked eye: The Sun, Moon, Mercury, Venus, Mars, Jupiter and Saturn. They then named each of the seven days of the week after one of those spheres and assigned that planetary 'ruler' to one day of the week. As viewed from Earth, these seven spheres appear to move at varying speeds, and the ancients used this factor to arrange them in order of varying speed. If you intend to use your Magic Hours to attract wonderful things, you must memorise that sequence because it is what forms the basis of the whole system.

Whenever you intend to use your Magic Hours or, perhaps more accurately, Magic *Time Units*, it is important to find out the exact time of sunrise for the area in which you live, as sunrise marks the time when your planet's magic is at its most powerful on its specific day. So, at sunrise on Sunday, the Sun rules the hour following the sunrise, the Moon rules the first hour following sunrise on a Monday, and through the week the pattern is repeated, with each day's ruling planet beginning the cycle in that first hour after dawn. It is logical then, that the rest of the planets, in sequence, follow on with one planet per hour for that day thereafter for the rest of the 24-hour cycle, creating a Magic Hour or Time Unit for each planet throughout the day and night, depending on which planet rules that particular day and is therefore the first in line.

If you wish to explore the idea in more depth, it is worth noting first and foremost that each day contains twenty-four hours, but, depending on the season, day and night will be of varying lengths. In summer, daylight is longer than darkness, whereas the reverse applies in winter. During autumn and spring, day and night are usually about equal. Therefore, although a complete day always contains twenty-four hours, there are not always twelve hours between sunrise and sunset and another twelve hours between sundown and the following sunrise. So, depending on the season (and location), a time unit may be shorter than one hour, longer than one hour, or equal to one hour. So whenever you intend to use your Magic Time Units, it is important to find out the exact time of sunrise and sunset for the area in which you live. The next step is to divide the amount of day time (if day when you wish to work your 'magic', otherwise the same following theory applies to night time) into twelve equal sections by calculating the number of hours and minutes between sunrise and sunset and divide by twelve. An example is if the Sun rises at 6.27 a.m. and sets at 5.49 p.m., the amount of time contained in this day is eleven hours and twenty-two minutes. Convert this total into minutes (682) and then divide that figure by twelve (57). Therefore, each of the twelve daylight time units will be 57 minutes on that day.

Although this wonderful method of using astrology is very ancient, it may be completely new to you. You are in for a pleasant surprise though, because if you are willing to delve into a little research and put the system to the test, rich rewards are in store for you!

YOUR LUCKY DAY ★ WEDNESDAY

Planet ★ Mercury
Basic Energy ★ Speed
Basic Magic ★ Communication, Study, Information
Element ★ Air
Colours ★ Blue, Yellow or Silver
Energy Keywords ★ Expression, Activity, Communication, Siblings, Dexterity, Adaptability, Intelligence, Agility, Versatility, Analysis, Verbosity, Restlessness, Neighbours, Awareness, Articulation, Brilliance, Changeability, Efficiency, Discrimination, Precision, Reason

Wednesday is the day of Mercury, your planetary ruler. In commonly used calendars, Wednesday is the fourth day of the week, though in others it is the third. The English name is derived from Old English *Wodnesdaeg*, and Middle English *Wednesdei*, meaning 'Day of Woden' or a claque of the Latin *dies Mercurii*, or 'Day of Mercury'. The god Woden was interpreted in the Roman era as the Germanic Mercury. Ash Wednesday, the first day of Lent in the Western Christian tradition, is perhaps the most well-known day with which Mercury's day is associated.

In the folk rhyme 'Monday's Child', 'Wednesday's child is full of woe'. Wednesday is the time for Mercury's powers of communication, to link up with long-lost friends, to communicate with a passed over loved one, or write important correspondences. It is also an opportune day to ask for qualities such as versatility, agility, articulate expression, reason, wit, humour, adaptability, intellectuality, and overall efficiency - as all are themes of Mercury. Mercury or Hermes is the god of thieves, so if something has been stolen from you, now could be the time to ask for it back in some form or another.

MERCURY'S MAGIC TIME UNITS
(BASED ON THE PLANETARY HOURS)
FOR EACH DAY OF THE WEEK

SATURDAY ★ Sixth time unit after sunrise
SUNDAY ★ Third and Tenth time units after sunrise
MONDAY ★ Seventh time unit after sunrise
TUESDAY ★ Fourth and Eleventh units after sunrise
WEDNESDAY ★ First and Eighth time units after sunrise
THURSDAY ★ Fifth and Twelfth time units after sunrise
FRIDAY ★ Second and Ninth time units after sunrise **

Choose the Hour/s of Mercury for any transaction, initiative, exchange, activity or venture which involves communication, siblings, your neighbours or neighbourhood, education, writing, service, social gatherings, intellectual pursuits, pets, information-gathering and research, and short journeys.

** Please note that for the purposes of simplification, the information regarding 'Mercury's Magic Time Units' is a very diluted and simplified version of using magical times to your advantage. These hours cover only daylight hours, or the first twelve hours after sunrise, and do not take into account magical times after sunset or throughout the night. 'Hours' is also a deceptive term, as most 'time periods' used in this system are less than an hour, but for the purposes of simplifying the technique, I refer to them as Magic Hours (to keep with the tradition of the term 'planetary hours') rather than magic 'time units', which is what they really are. Should you wish to do further research on your ruling planet's most powerful time units, or require further information about the planet/s from which you are seeking 'energy' from in order to assist your wish-making, other sources may provide you with more comprehensive and detailed information.

A LITTLE NEW MOON / MAGICAL TIME UNIT WISH RITUAL

Step 1 ~ Choose the Magical Hour and/or day that matches your intentions. The first dawn hour of Sunday, ruled by the Sun, is a great time for all-purpose magic, success, joy, abundance, prosperity, bliss, personal power & all-round expansion.

Step 2 ~ Write out a little wish list with the appropriate coloured pen on the colour paper which corresponds to your desire.

Step 3 ~ Choose a small stone of your choosing that is connected to your wish (or a number of stones, that are perhaps linked with your planetary ruler's number, for example 5 for Mercury).

Step 4 ~ Find a nice patch of soil in your garden or any special place to you, dig into it, affirm your wish in your mind, place the crystal/s and piece of paper in the hole, then place a plant on top of the crystal/s and wish list.

Step 5 ~ Fill the soil back in over the roots of the plant and feed it with a little water out of a magical vessel (a small genie bottle would be ideal).

Step 6 ~ Thank the Earth, the Universe and the Sun (or whatever planet you are summoning the power from) for bringing forth your desires.

Step 7 ~ Repeat all day long: "Thank You, Thank You, Thank You!"

Step 8 ~ Watch your plant - and your wish - grow bigger and bigger as time goes on!

YOUR LUCKY CHARM/TALISMANS

The following are three 'materials' or talismanic symbols from which to make your lucky charms, and the planetary energy under which to do it, corresponding with your Sun sign:

VIRGO ★ Sapphire, Spider, Silver, Mercury

"When any star ascends fortunately, take a stone and
herb that are under that star, make a ring of
the metal that is congruous therewith, and in that fix
the stone with the herb under it."
Henry Cornelius Agrippa, *On Occult Philosophy*

Charms, talismans and amulets are among the oldest forms of magic. A charm or talisman is a symbol, often used to communicate a thought, prayer or wish to, or to make a connection with the Divine. It is usually in the form of an object, which has been imbued with mysterious and magical powers. A charm may be as simple as a stone, a flower or a feather, or it might be a parchment bearing writing; the meaning and significance that you attribute to the symbol is what is important. It can be created by yourself (to best effect) or by someone else, and works as a tool to activate our subconscious mind.

You can use general charms such as a cross, or a universally lucky symbol such as a horseshoe, but you will exude and therefore attract more potency and protection if you make and wear the appropriate charms with the matching gemstone, set in the right metal and created under the corresponding planetary influence. While most people wear silver or gold, cheaper tin or copper may be more appropriate and indeed beneficial for your Sun sign. An amulet (for protection) or a talisman or charm (for luck), must also be made, ordered, designed or purchased on the appropriate day of the week for its power to be most effective. Your day, as previously described, is Wednesday.

You can even go further and create or buy your amulet or charm at one of the hours and/or days when your planet is exerting its most powerful influence. It may sound complicated and requiring of forethought and effort, but if you are going to summon magic and are superstitious enough to truly *believe* that you can do this (and remember pure belief in something is the starting point of all manifestation), you should be scrupulous enough to do it properly. For your planet's day and time, please consult the information under the previous headings 'Your Lucky Day' and 'Mercury's Magic Time Units'.

GODS, GODDESSES, ANIMAL TOTEMS & OTHER 'GUIDES'

Gods, goddesses and guides can be summoned to help you live your life to its optimal best. Some are connected with your Sun sign, while others may be of your own personal choosing, ones you may feel particularly drawn towards. Those which align with your ruling planet and your Sun sign, give a good indication of those who will shine a guiding light along your desired path, but you can choose your own too, based upon exploration, observations, research, meditation or simple intuition - I believe choosing your own, based on your inner *knowing* or guidance system, is a very powerful magical tool. However, to get you started, following are some animal spirit guide ideas for your contemplation. Good luck!

YOUR LUCKY ANIMALS & BIRDS

Rooster, Cat, Magpie, Parrot, Squirrel, Mouse, Insects, Fox, Monkey, Beetles, Apes, Spiders, Hyena, Weasel, Bee, Brown Bear

"Somewhere beyond the walls of our awareness … the wilderness side, the hunter side, the seeking side of ourselves is waiting to return."
Laurens van der Post, *The Heart of the Hunter*

"(People) everywhere are being made acutely aware of the fact that something essentially to life and wellbeing is flickering very low in the human species and threatening to go out entirely. This 'something' has to do with such values as love, unselfishness, sincerity, loyalty to one's best friend, honesty, enthusiasm, humility, goodness, happiness … fun. Practically every animal has these assets in abundance and is eager to share them, given the opportunity and the encouragement."
Jay Allen Boone, *Kinship with All Life*

Some astrological systems, such as Shamanistic * or Native American Astrology, tell us that the Sun sign we were born under has a corresponding animal totem, which informs us about our characteristics and act as a kind of spiritual guide or mentor throughout our life's journey. These totems are described as Solar totems, because many of them share similarities with the Solar system and the sign the Sun was passing through at the time of our birth, and therefore relate to animals and animal behaviours which also correspond to environmental conditions and seasonal changes. These animals encompass many aspects of the Solar system, from seasonal relationships, to creature instincts, to reciprocal links with the planetary vibrations, and 'clans' within nature that you are inherently closely connected with through your date of birth.

Carl Jung, a master of dream analysis and interpretation, proposed that animals symbolise our natural instincts, operating through our dreams. He theorised that certain dream symbols, among them animals, represent core emotions and concepts, archetypes that will hold true for all of us the world over, regardless of so-called 'divisions' such as sex, customs, age or culture. In *Man and His Symbols*, Jung states that primitive societies believed that each person had a bush soul and a human soul. The bush soul incarnates as a tree or animal - a totem - and when the bush soul is harmed or injured, the human soul is considered injured as well.

Some of the most important and powerful spirit guides are those belonging to the animal kingdom. Both in ancient times and in some traditional modern tribal systems, people consult with animals for their wisdom and personal power. Even though most societies today have drifted away from this connection, it has never really left us, and different creatures continue to communicate with us on both the physical and spiritual planes in an attempt to speak to our souls and spirits.

As part of the teaching world, animals can bring us wisdom and survival skills, while others show us how to adapt, transcend or morph. Others still can remind us the importance of play and humour, and guide us around how to overcome life's challenges. Many are known for their loyalty and ability to love unconditionally and without judgement, while some have a grounded and healthy detachment, remaining true to themselves rather than pleasing others, an important lesson in itself. Whatever the qualities of the unique animal guides for your Sun sign, all have some enlightening soul-awakening traits that can teach us much about our own true inner selves. Ultimately, your animal spirit guides, and in particular your Solar totem animal, endow you with qualities that will enhance your life and help to activate your creativity, wisdom and intuition, helping to heal the broken or return the lost pieces of your soul and reconnect you to the natural world.

Your Solar totem animal (listed last on your lucky birds and animals list) is not the same as an animal spirit guide, which is based on metaphysical principles and is also based on your soul's mission in this embodiment - however, you can definitely make your birth Solar totem animal your spiritual guide if you wish, as you may find that its qualities, traits, symbolism and messages strongly reflect and define your own nature - or what you aspire to become, manifest or draw towards you. Your birth totem power animal comes from a place of trust and innocence, and represents the essence of your creative inner child. If you spend some time meditating on your Solar totem animal, asking what lessons it can teach, and reflect deeply on its character, life and habits, you may find it connects with you on a deep spiritual level and you can make the necessary changes to your life to draw in more magic and power.

Overall, if your life is stagnant or in need of healing or an energy boost, you can request your animal spirit or spirits to come and help you change your vibration, awaken your truth and arouse your inner forces. If you are aware of your animal spirit's presence in your life every day, you can use its particular energies to support, guide and teach you. And above all, pay attention to any signs and expressions of its lessons, and remember to thank your chosen animal guide for helping you.

* Shamanism is a traditional spiritual practice of the Native American culture. A shaman, one who practices this age-old art, is an intermediary between the human world and the world of the spirits. He inherits his magical powers at birth, but spends many years as an apprentice, so that he is usually much older in age before he is able to practice and call upon his skills. People ask for a shaman's help when there is a crisis on either a personal or wider spread scale, such as famine, drought, war or illness. The shaman makes contact with the spirits by going into a trance. First, he may perform a series of rituals, which usually include drumming, singing and chanting, and when these have brought on the right conditions, he leaves his body behind to travel to the other world. There he meets with the spirits of his ancestors, who inform him what must be done to relieve the suffering of his people. If the shaman is asked to cure someone of a dis-ease, then the spirits may accompany him to find the correct medicinal herbs or treatments for his patient.

YOUR FEATURE ANIMAL ★ BEAR

The Bear's Message ★ Embrace the power of your spirit
Brings the totem gift of ★ Fearlessness, leadership, inner power, protection, meditation
Shares the power energies of ★ Cave-dwelling (withdrawal), contemplation, protection, ferocity, strength
Brings forth and teaches the magic of ★ Dreamtime, vision quests, wildness, introspection

The Bear is a natural nurturer, protector and healer. It is usually docile, but shamans are able to summon its brute strength to help them. The Bear is a fierce ally who symbolises protection, who will actively defend you from all danger. The Bear is one of the most powerful spiritual guides and brings the gifts of intuition, self-knowledge and spiritual wisdom. It is strong and fearless, but also teaches us to be mindful of our limitations - sometimes we need to exercise caution, even in fierce and instinctive defence. Among the natives of Siberia, the northern islands of Japan, and parts of Alaska, the Bear is considered the luckiest of animals. Although hunters kill bears for food and fur, it is always carried out with prayers of apology, lest the killing bring bad luck. This powerful animal is believed to have supernatural powers, perhaps due to their ability to hibernate for long periods of time without food or water. Linked to the pole star, the Bear helps to guide us towards our highest principles. Calling us to honour our ancestors, the Bear teaches us to acknowledge where we have come from and where our true destiny lies.

When a steady and careful hand is needed, the pragmatic and methodical bear is the one to call upon. Practicality and level-headedness are coupled with a wonderful sense of business and duty, and the bear is also gifted with a big heart and a penchant for generosity. Although shy and modest, the Bear will shower generosity and affection upon her loved ones if in a loving environment. The Bear also has an enormous capacity for patience and temperance, but can tend towards scepticism, small-mindedness, laziness and reclusiveness. Due to their stable nature and sensible advice, Bears make ideal teachers, healers and mentors.

SPIRITUAL KEEPER ★ COYOTE

Your spiritual keeper guides your spiritual growth and brings illumination. Your spiritual keeper is determined by the season in which you were born. Regarded as the 'keepers' or 'caretakers' of the Universe, the four Directions or alignments were also referred to by the Native Americans as the Four Winds because their presence was *felt* rather than seen. The Direction to which your birth time belongs influences the nature of your inner senses. The South Direction's totem is the Coyote. The Coyote is a symbol of growth, fruition, emotions, productivity and fluidity. The Coyote is bold, impetuous, charming, youthful and creative, and as a spiritual keeper, can endow us with these qualities. In some native tribes, the Coyote is referred to as a trickster or joker. A clever, cunning and amazingly adaptable animal, its message is of wisdom and folly. Operating year-round, the Coyote doesn't try to trick us, but rather mirrors our own human capacity for stupidity and cleverness. Challenging the status quo, the Coyote sometimes becomes unstuck but is ever the triumphant survivor. To the Indian, this animal is a creator, teacher and keeper of magic, and even when the magic does not work, it serves a purpose; the Coyote knows there is always hidden wisdom.

Playful as well as skilful and agile, the Coyote teaches us not to take things too seriously, and that anything is possible if we understand that wisdom, balance, intellect and fun can all co-exist. Through this spiritual keeper, we can reawaken the child within, stimulate our intuition and open up the mind. Coyotes hunt in cooperative groups, in an organised fashion - while one chases, one will rest, then they switch - which can teach the value of teamwork. The howl of this animal is a social call, usually warning of danger or to bring attention to its loneliness, reminding us too of our own primal needs and connections. The Coyote's teachings can help you negotiate a difficult situation, and can highlight the traps we may be caught in, or ways we could be fooling ourselves. It is an especially powerful healer when it comes to relationships, because it is when we are in one that we often fool ourselves the most. Following the Coyote won't make you a fortune, but its lesson is to teach us that material wealth doesn't equate to true happiness anyway. Your animal keeper the Coyote is, above all, a potent symbol of the need for the balance between wisdom, trickery, skill, cleverness and cunning.

CLAN ★ TURTLE

Your clan animal comes from a place of inner knowing and intuition, helping you to discover the essence and magic of your true self. The Turtle is the totem of the Earth clan and in mythology, during a time when there was only water and nowhere for the people and animals to go, the Turtle made a great sacrifice by letting everyone come and live on her back. In the Far East a talisman carved in the form of a Turtle is believed to have power over all kinds of magic; the Chinese and Japanese also wear charms in the shape of Turtles to ensure a long life. In ancient times, the shape of a Turtle's shell suggested the dome of the sky and the creature became a symbol of heavenly virtue. The medicine of the Turtle is Mother Earth. The Turtle can be your guide to connect with our Earth Mother for healing and wisdom, and reminds us, in return, to tread gently and with respect. In fact, you have a responsibility to our Mother to protect her, and also to remind others to appreciate her bountiful beauty that provides so much for life itself.

People of this clan tend to be brave, stubborn, strong and loyal. Methodical and practical, you possess a great determination but also like to take things one step at a time - with steady, slow-paced grace. Although some Turtle clan people tend to be as hard as a rock, you have a need to personify roots, growth and stability, much like the Earth itself does.

You are revitalised most strongly by visiting natural places frequently and instinctively feel connected to rocks; in fact, you instinctively feel drawn to be around rock formations and need to have rocks in some form or another around you in your personal environment. Indeed, the rocks will speak to you, if you listen, but you must be careful not to become too much like them - that is, immovable, inflexible and too firmly rooted in the one place out of a need for comfort, safety or security. In essence, Turtle clan souls focus on the tasks at hand with the determination, persistence, diligence and perseverance of one who is aligned with a true Mission. To connect with your clan animal, visualise yourself walking at a slow and steady pace, with no worry for shelter as you carry your home on your back. You also have no concern for how fast you are travelling along the Path, for you know that you will arrive exactly where and when you are meant to. Nor do you fear attack from predators as you feel assured that the armour on your back will guard against attack. These lessons, once learned and incorporated into your life, are the blessings of being born of the Turtle.

YOUR CORRESPONDING CHINESE ASTROLOGY ANIMAL

The Chinese Zodiac, known as Sheng Xiao (literally meaning 'birth likeness'), is based on a twelve-year cycle, each year in that cycle related to a particular animal. These animals are: Rat, Ox, Tiger, Rabbit, Dragon, Snake, Horse, Sheep, Monkey,

Rooster, Dog and Pig. The selection and order of the animals that so influence people's lives, particularly in East Asian cultures, originated in the Han Dynasty (202 BC - 220 AD) and was based upon each animal's traits, characteristics, tendencies and living habits. Further, ancient people observed that there were twelve Full Moons in a year, and that, among other similarly related celestial observations, suggests its origins are also based on astronomical concepts.

The legend of the Chinese zodiac's story usually begins with the Jade Emperor, or Buddha (depending on who is telling the tale), summoning all the animals of the Universe for a race or a banquet. The twelve animals of the zodiac all appeared at the palace, and the order in which they arrived determined the order of the Chinese zodiac.

Each oriental animal corresponds with a Western astrology sign. For Virgo, it is the Rooster.

"I am on hand
To herald in the day,
And to announce its exit.
I thrive by clockwork and precision.
In my unending quest for perfection
All things will be restored to their rightful place.
I am the exacting taskmaster.
The ever-watchful administrator.
I seek perfect order in my world.
I represent unfailing dedication.
I am the Rooster."
Theodora Lau

Chinese name for the Rooster ★ JI
Ranking Order ★ Tenth
Hours ruled by the Rooster ★ 5 p.m. to 7 p.m.
Direction ★ Directly West
Season and principle month ★ Autumn - September
Corresponds to the Western sign ★ Virgo

★ ROOSTER ★ *Fixed Element Metal*

★ Keywords ★
Outspoken, energetic, protective, resilient, popular, stylish, bossy, competitive, clever, talkative, eccentric, always busy, opinionated, deep-thinking

The Rooster is the tenth sign of the Chinese horoscope. Although traditionally a yin sign, Roosters are associated with aggressive 'male' or 'yang' competitiveness, resilience and strength, and are typically vivacious, creative, generous and attractive. Your amusing outlook and sincere nature often make you the centre of attention. Outgoing, kind, independent and enthusiastic, you like to keep abreast of anything that is interesting or new, and are able to recover from any setbacks relatively quickly. Even if you are a more retiring type of Rooster, your inner extrovert will still express itself through your desire to appear chic and stylish. There tends to be an element of theatre in everything you do, and you dread tedious or mundane tasks; this is when you delegate it to others so that you can get back to organising your next adventure, trip, project or big plan. Energy radiates from you most of the time, and you will give almost anything a shot, especially things that are artistic or creative. Your creative endeavours and hobbies will rarely become a career, however, as you don't like to take chances with your financial security. Despite your usual choice of unconventional forms of dress or lifestyle, you are extremely conservative deep down. You like to be in charge and in control, and with your loved ones you like to be candid, humorous and helpful.

YOUR METALS

Virgoan power metals are Platinum, Copper and Quicksilver (Mercury)

Although the magic power of crystals is widely recognised and applied, the influence radiating from metals is often overlooked. Metal, too, emits a powerful energy and in fact, in Chinese philosophy, metal is considered so essential and powerful that it is classified as one of the elements, alongside Air, Fire, Earth and Water.

As already mentioned earlier in the book, throughout the writings of early philosophers and theorists, there are countless references to the unmistakable mystic connection between the seven known planets of the time, and Earthly affairs, ailments and objects. Seven metals were connected with the seven planets, to which seven colours and the seven 'transformations' were added. So the ancient alchemist came to share the astrological doctrine that each planet ruled a mineral: The Sun ruled gold, the Moon silver, Mars iron, Venus copper, Saturn lead, Jupiter tin, and Mercury quicksilver. Consequently, in alchemical symbolism the same sign came to represent the nominated metal and its corresponding planet.

PLATINUM

The word 'platinum' originates from the Spanish word *plata*, meaning 'silver', referring to the colour of the metal. Platinum was discovered in the early 1700s. It is so rare that two million pounds of ore may only contain about one pound of platinum metal. Its rarity makes it even more valuable than gold. Platinum nuggets are rarely larger than a pea - anything larger would qualify as a major find. The highest quality platinum comes from the Ural Mountains in Russia. It can be used for jewellery, but has less glamorous uses too: it is placed in anti-pollution devices in cars to trap dirt and toxic gases.

COPPER

Copper is a chemical element with symbol Cu (from Latin *cuprum*), and carries a special cultural significance in that it was the first metal to be used by humans, its use believed to be as early as 7000 BC. Indeed, there is evidence it has been in use for at least 10,000 years. In alchemy, the symbol for copper was also the symbol for the goddess and planet Venus. Aphrodite (Venus's Greek counterpart) and Venus represented copper in alchemy and mythology because of copper's lustrous beauty, its ancient use in producing mirrors, and its association with Cyprus, which had sacred links with the goddess.

Copper is prized by craftsmen for its elegance and lustre, and its ease of use in crafting things of great beauty. Pure copper is reddish-orange/gold in colour and is soft and malleable, and like aluminium, it is 100 % recyclable without any loss of quality. As one of only two coloured metals, its attractiveness makes it highly desirable for making ornaments and jewellery.

Copper's main modern-day applications are its use in electrical implements and electrical wires (having very high thermal and electrical conductivity, and being ductile enough to be drawn into wire or beaten into sheets without fracturing), roofing and plumbing, industrial machinery, scientific instruments, and of course coins. It is usually used as a pure metal, but when a greater hardness is required, it can be combined with other elements to make an alloy, such as brass or bronze. Copper's resistance to corrosion also makes it suitable for use in, or near the ocean. Brass, an alloy of zinc and copper, is used extensively in marine applications due to its non-corrosive nature.

Copper is even found in the human body in trace amounts and has various biological functions, mainly in the liver, muscle and bone.

Copper can also be made into jewellery, and it is believed that wearing a copper bracelet can relieve arthritis-related symptoms *^. It is also used in alternative medicine to various other ailments, as its absorption through the skin somehow creates a magnetic field, thereby affecting or treating nearby tissues ^.

Overall, copper serves many purposes and is arguably essential in keeping the world functioning, as it pervades in all facets of (comfortable) existence: it is found in your house, coin currency, computers, cars, and cruise ships.

* However, in various studies, no difference has been found between arthritis treated with a copper bracelet, magnetic bracelet or placebo bracelet

^ Please check with a medical professional before applying any remedy, treatment or concept outlined here

QUICKSILVER

Quicksilver, also known as mercury, is a chemical element with symbol Hg, is heavy and as its name suggests, is silvery in colour. A mysterious, much-maligned and paradoxical metal, although its surface reflects light like shiny polished steel, the fluidity of this substance does not allow it to maintain any shape. Mercury is nearly 14 times as heavy as water, its density meaning that heavier things can easily float on top of it. But like water, it evaporates, albeit much more slowly, and in the air it is much more noxious and dangerous than in its liquid state.

Mercury is an extremely rare element in the Earth's crust, and many former mines which produced a large proportion of the world supply, have now been completely mined out. Today China is the top producer of mercury, but because of the high toxicity of this element, the mining of cinnabar (the mineral from which it is mostly extracted) and the refining of it for mercury, are hazardous and can produce serious health effects through mercury poisoning.

Quicksilver is the only metallic element that is liquid at standard conditions for temperature and pressure. It is perhaps best - and menacingly - known as a toxin - and indeed, mercury poisoning can result from water-soluble forms of quicksilver, inhalation of its vapour, or eating seafood contaminated with it. Some countries have banned the use of mercury in all products and production methods, while many others agreed in the Minamata Convention on Mercury, to prevent emissions.

Because it is liquid like water and shiny like silver, mercury's name was derived from the word *hydrargyrum* (where the chemical symbol Hg comes from), a Latinised form of the Greek word *hydra-gyros*, meaning 'water-silver'. The element itself was named after the Roman god Mercury, known for his speed and mobility.

Found in Ancient Egyptian tombs that date from 1500 BC, in China and Tibet, mercury use was thought to prolong life, heal fractures and generally promote overall wellbeing and health (although it is now known that exposure to mercury vapour can lead to serious adverse health effects.)

Its use in alchemy was widespread. Alchemists thought of Mercury as the First Matter from which all metals were formed, believing that different metals could be produced by varying the quality and quantity of sulphur contained within the mercury, the purest of these being gold. Mercury was therefore summoned in attempts to transmute the base (impure) metals into gold, which was the ultimate goal of many alchemists. This quest left a lasting legacy: The Sanskrit word for alchemy is *Rasavatam*, which means 'the way of mercury'; and mercury is the only metal for which the alchemical planetary name became the common name.

Used in thermometers and other measuring equipment, float valves, vermilion paint pigment, fluorescent lamps, mercury switches and other devices, mercury is also used in industrial chemicals, for electrical and electronic applications, as an ingredient in dental amalgams, in some batteries, as a preservative in vaccines, and as a compound in some over-the-counter drugs, as well as some niche uses including skin tanner vapour lamps, 'neon lights' and some cosmetic mascaras.

Natural sources, such as volcanoes, account for approximately half of all atmospheric mercury emissions, but the human-generated half can be divided into estimated percentages, the highest of these emissions (around 65 per cent and around 11 per cent) said to come from coal-fired power plants and gold production respectively.

Despite its well-known dangers and sinister reputation as a toxic heavy metal, an increasing amount of quicksilver is being used as gaseous mercury in fluorescent lamps, and it is still used in some thermometers, especially those which are used to measure high temperatures. However most of its other uses and applications are being gradually phased out due to health and safety regulations, and are being replaced with less toxic but considerably more expensive alternatives.

* Mercury and most of its compounds are extremely toxic and must be handled with care, if at all. Mercury can be absorbed through the skin and mucous membranes and mercury vapours can be inhaled. The most toxic forms of mercury are its organic compounds, which can cause both acute and chronic poisoning. Pregnant women should avoid this metallic element at all costs, particularly by avoiding eating large species of fish and all varieties of shellfish, as ingested mercury is considered an

accumulative neurotoxin that can adversely affect the unborn foetus in numerous ways.

PLANTS, HERBS, SPICES, TREES, SHRUBS, FLOWERS, SCENTS & INCENSE

Plants have long been associated with magic, medicinal properties, superstition, nutrition and even astrology. In ancient times, some were endowed with magical properties based upon beliefs of the time, but also upon anecdotal evidence that some herbal concoctions, flowers or essences helped alleviate and even cure uncomfortable, painful or dis-eased physical or mental states. Whether these were based upon 'old wives' tales' or beliefs in supernatural forces matters little, for in modern times we can prove and indeed *have* proven through scientific research and controlled experiments, that plants have their place in our health and medicine cabinets. Some 'magical' plants have aphrodisiac or narcotic properties, while others have formidable toxic effects, but all are considered in some way to affect the human system on physical, spiritual and psychological levels. Plants such as cocoa, tobacco and coffee, which have accompanied humans over the course of millennia, are still, more than ever, an integral part of our daily lives. They still incite the same pleasures, the same fascinations, and the same dangers, and some still carry the same taboos. It is interesting to note that more than 80 per cent of chemical medicines in existence today, and found in pharmacists' dispensaries, are made from plants.

In modern astrology herbs are often associated with the zodiac signs and have evolved from an old system where a specific planet rules each herb. The planet that governs a herb is chosen according to its appearance, scent and where it grows; herbs are additionally categorised as hot or cold, and dry or moist. In this way you can see how the nature of the herb corresponds to the nature of the planet. If you are familiar with your ruling planets' basic associations, you will find it easy to match it to herbs. Although you can simply buy whatever herbs you wish to use for your magic, the optimum effect will be obtained if you can gather them at a favourable astrological time. Once you are armed with astrological knowledge, you can choose a time when the planet that rules your chosen herb is in a position of strength. Keep in mind that each planet rules a substantial amount of plants, so if one isn't easily obtained, it should be simply to find another one to use for the same purpose.

There sometimes seems to be a wide variance in the list of herbs associated with a specific astrological influence. This is because the different parts of the plant have different rulerships and uses. For example, whichever planet rules it, a plant that bears fruit is naturally related to Jupiter, its flowers relate to Venus, seed or bark to Mercury, leaves to the Moon, wood to Mars, and roots to Saturn. So, as well as the planet that traditionally rules the plant, it can be regarded as having a secondary ruler according to the part of the plant being used. Although you don't need to work with a highly complex system of deciding which herb will suit your purposes, you can make your magical workings more powerful by paying attention to some of these nuances.

Essentially, different scents, herbs, flowers and plants have their own specific vibrations. Their essences should be worn on your skin (you can make up your own combinations using essential oils or flower waters), burned in an oil burner, inhaled from a cloth, diffused in a bath or bowl of steam, or burned as incense sticks. Many plants, herbs and spices, however used, contain gentle yet effective energies which will affect not only your wishing ceremonies, but also your moods, associations and emotions, which can assist in carrying your wonderful Self in the direction of your dreams. Lifted up on incense smoke, for example, your wish is carried out to the wider Universe. Try making your own, out of any or all of your power plants, woods, flowers, shrubs, trees or herbs!

Thirty-three magical, mythical plants are: Cocoa, rosemary, tobacco, thyme, wheat, coffee, sugar cane, cinnamon, hemp, tea, pumpkin, foxglove, incense, amanita (a mushroom), tarragon, pepper, rice, belladonna, reed, ginseng, clove, ginger, sage, maize, mistletoe, lily, mandrake, St John's Wort, poppy, peyote, cinchona, verbena and the vine *. How many of your Virgoan 'lucky plants' (listed under the next sub-category, 'Your Lucky Plants, Herbs, Spices', etc.) can be found on this Magical 33 List?

YOUR LUCKY PLANTS, HERBS, SPICES, TREES, SHRUBS, FLOWERS, SCENTS, OILS & INCENSE

Hazel, Buttercup, Chicory, Foxglove, Elder, Liquorice, Primula, Balm, Skullcap, Forget-Me-Not, Fennel, Walnut Leaves, Summer Savoury, Poppy, Crosswort, Forsythia, Aster, Mimosa, Salad Burnet, Flax, Madonna, Lily, Cornflower, Horse Chestnut, Marshmallow, Alkanet, Yellow Archangel, Peppermint, Southernwood, Valerian, Morning Glory, Bittersweet, Narcissus, Mandrake, Fern, Caraway, Oak Leaves, Acorns, Cardamom, Basil, Dill, Parsley, Vervain, Cranesbill, Fenugreek, Marjoram, Cat's Ear, nut-bearing trees, and all small, brightly coloured and field flowers. *

For Mercury ★ Vervain, Lungwort, Sweet Marjoram, Aniseed, Olive. As Mercury relates to the Air element, the plants associated with it often contain divided leaves or stalks. Coriander, Fenugreek, Liquorice Roots are all related to this planet *

* Some plant products can be poisonous, toxic, hallucinogenic or even fatal if consumed. Always research first.

YOUR SPECIAL POWER FLOWERS

VIRGO IN GENERAL ★ Morning Glory

OTHER BIRTH FLOWERS ★ Buttercup, Pansy, Cornflower, Rosemary & Madonna Lily

AUGUST BORN ★ Poppy ★ Opium, used to relieve pain and induce sleep, was originally made from a variety of poppy commonly found around the Mediterranean, before its cultivation spread along the Silk Road through Asia and finally China, where it became the catalyst for the Opium Wars of the mid-1800s. The Greeks associated it with Hypnos, the god of sleep, and Morpheus, the god of dreams (morphine is made from opium and was named after Morpheus). In Greek mythology, Persephone was picking poppies when Hades abducted her. Since World War I, the poppy has been adopted as the flower of remembrance in the British Commonwealth, and millions of artificial poppy flowers are sold each year to be worn on Remembrance Day. Because it produces a large amount of seeds, the poppy is associated with fertility. The poppy's many blessings are a capacity for renewal, and an understanding that there's a time for every purpose: beauty, loss, loyalty and courage.

SEPEMBER BORN ★ Aster ★ Grace, modesty and a sweetness of disposition are bestowed on those given the stylish aster, which is considered emblematic of elegance, friendship and secret love.

YOUR FOODS

Your puritan soul likes pure food and you'll hector anyone and everyone to know the nutritional and fat content as well as the holistic properties of whatever you eat. Virgo is the wholefood vegetarian of the zodiac. Pulsing beneath the solid composure of the Virgin is a taste for the sensual - but it must also be pure, organic *and* biodynamic. Stable, devoted and methodical, recipes were made for the Virgo, because you seem to be the most likely to follow them - to the word. The notoriously fussy Virgo is often difficult to please when it comes to food. You enjoy most cuisines, as all types of foods appeal to you, particularly if they're nutritionally-dense, however you are not adventurous or imaginative and are often too timid to try new things. You would prefer to stick with the tried, tested and true, even if it's boring and bland. A predictable routine is best suited to you, as you don't like eating at strange hours or on the run. Fast food is the most off-putting concept you can conceive of, and you would rather pull your own teeth out than eat deep fried food, as you have done your research and found out the truth about what it does to your insides.

Virgo rules the digestive organs, so you are sensitive and likely to suffer food allergies and intolerances, even if they are just a symptom of your hypochondria. But you also lean towards obsessive-compulsive tendencies, so it is not uncommon for you to scrub an apple raw before you eat it; hygiene, purity and nutrition are that important to your peace of mind. You are essentially a sensible eater and consume mostly that which you deem to be nutritional, healthful, cleansing, or otherwise useful in some way. Overall, the more untouched, natural, healthy and nutritionally-rich the dish is, the more appealing you will find it! Health fads and 'superfoods' were made for the Virgoan palate. Being so frugal and economical, you will never reject leftovers, because you hate food wastage as well. You can, however be inconsistent at times: although you will gladly eat a humble cheese sandwich if offered, you are used to perfection and precision, and will demand that whatever you are served is presented on a starched white tablecloth, with well-polished cutlery (yes, even for a sandwich!), sparkling crystal and pristine plates. Spirulina powder, chia seeds, dried fruits, smoothies, sprouts, quinoa, dark berries, and coconut *everything* are ideal for your discerning dietary needs. Rushed, fast, deep-fried, poorly presented, messy, exotic, sloppy, extravagant, unhealthy, fancy and adventurous are definitely not on the menu for the Virgin.

VIRGO POWER FOODS

"Let food be your medicine; let medicine be your food."
Hippocrates

Health Foods, Blackberries, Almonds, Wheat, Endive, Corn, Millet, Rice, Barley, Rye, Oats, Swedes, Plantain, Turnips, Strawberries, Fennel, Subterranean Vegetables (Kohlrabi, Carrots, Celeriac, Potatoes),

Mushrooms, Peas, Okra, All Kinds of Beans, Nuts, Bird Meat, Gooseberries, Loganberries, Pomegranates, Cress, Beetroot, Figs, Mulberries, and all foods that grow under the Earth. Your power beverages are Sparkling Drinks (Mineral Waters, Champagne), Health Drinks, Protein Shakes, Smoothies, 'Superfood' Powders, Wheatgrass Shots and Organic Wine. *

* Caution: Always use essential oils, alcohol and/or herbs with caution and research each one prior to use, as not all are safe for use by certain people, or under certain conditions such as pregnancy, intoxication or illness. Some herbs and oils may be hallucinogenic, toxic in high doses, or produce other undesirable effects, and may be considered potentially harmful or hazardous if used or consumed before operating machinery, driving, or combined with alcohol or other drugs. Always consult a qualified practitioner or undertake thorough research from reliable sources before use or consumption of any of the listed essential oils, herbs or foods.

YOUR LUCKY WOODS ★ BEECH & HAZEL
(Great to make a magic wand out of!)

Native Americans referred to trees as 'Standing People' because they stand firm, obtaining strength from their connection with the Earth. They therefore teach us the importance of being grounded, while at the same time listening to, and reaching towards, our higher aspirations. In Norse mythology, Yggdrasil, the tree of life, is a cosmic map that represents all life. The tree has its roots in the Underworld, is linked to the Earth through its trunk and its branches reach into the air of the Otherworld of spirit. The dryad, or tree's spirit, needs to be respected and asked when 'taking' from a tree for the purposes of magic. The essence of tree magic lies in understanding the qualities of each type. These can be drawn on for such things as healing and spell-casting. For example, the rowan tree grows high up the sides of mountains, often in hard-to-reach places, so if you need to develop tenacity or access to difficult spiritual spaces, you can call on this tree; the oak tree is durable and strong, so if you are needing fortification or firmness, you can gain power from this tree. When respected as living, breathing beings, trees can provide insights into the workings of Nature, cycles, and our own inner essence. Each birth time is associated with a particular kind of tree, the basic qualities of which complement the nature of those born during that time. Appreciate the beauty of your affinity tree and study its nature carefully, for it has a connection with your own nature and lessons to impart.

BEECH ★ Beech is traditionally known as 'Queen of the Forest', because this tree is seen as the female counterpart to the oak, the 'King of the Forest'. The words for 'book' and 'beech' are of the same origin due to the historical use of the tree - closely grained and easily smoothed, beech wood was made for writing tablets. Therefore, it is also connected with ancient wisdom.

HAZEL ★ Magic wands, which were mentioned in ancient Chaldean and Egyptian records, has been one of the main sources of wood for magic for thousands of years. Apollo gave Mercury a hazel wand, which he used to instil good virtues into humankind. In Scandinavia, the hazel was sacred to the god Thor and was used for protection against lightning. Its connection with Thor also associates it with Fire, virility, matters of the heart and childbirth. The nuts, used as charms and love tokens, signified the hazel tree's blessing of fertility, birth and the successful raising of children. And an old saying has it that all your wishes will come true if you carry a twig of hazel as an amulet or charm.

Hazel is said to bring luck, fertility, protection, wisdom and wishes. Celebrated in Celtic folklore as a tree of knowledge, poetry and learning, the hazel tree is reputed to have 'nine hazelnuts of wisdom', which in Celtic legend, fell into a sacred pool or well and were eaten by salmon. According to the story, the fish, called Fintan, imbibed the nine hazelnuts of wisdom and each one consumed became a spot on its scales. Whoever ate the salmon would then receive infinite wisdom.

Hazel wood is pliant and has traditionally been used for divining underground water (Pliny [23 – 79 CE] wrote about the use of hazel rods in water divining). A hazelnut on a string also makes a good dowsing pendulum. Its flexibility also made it a valuable wood for making walking sticks, fishing rods, whip handles and baskets.

Hazel types are usually efficient, highly intelligent and organised. Naturally gifted in academia, you have an ability to recall and retain information with amazing accuracy. You're well-informed and know your facts; generally smart and with an impressive knowledge base, you like things to be ordered, structured, controlled and 'just so', which can sometimes lead to compulsive behaviours. You like rules, although you are typically making them rather than playing by them.

YOUR SACRED CELTIC CALENDAR TREES
★ HAZEL OR VINE (MOON)

HAZEL ★ (5 August - 1 September)
VINE MOON ★ (2 September - 29 September)

The Celts and other ancient peoples had many beliefs and traditions based around the magical lore of trees. The system of Celtic tree astrology was developed out of a natural connection with the Druids' knowledge of Earth cycles and their reverence for the sacred knowledge they believed was held by trees. The Druids had a profound connection with trees and regarded them as vessels of infinite wisdom. Their calendar, being based on a Lunar year of thirteen months, contains a tree for each of these Lunar months, corresponding with (but not exactly) each of the twelve western astrology zodiac signs, which are based on the Solar calendar. Because there are some crossovers, I have included two possible trees for your zodiacal birth period.

HAZEL ★ Please see previous, under 'Your Lucky Woods'.

VINE MOON ★ Three of the 13 Celtic Moon months are governed by plants other than trees. Your birthday, if it falls between 2 September and 29 September, is ruled by the Vine Moon, which is a time to harvest the rewards of all your efforts through the year so far. Vine brings strength, durability and prosperity, and is associated with the fruition of plans as well as symbolising 'bacchanalian' pleasures and joy. In Celtic astrology, the vine is often linked with grapes, although this fruit is not native to the British Isles. Because of this, it is thought that the Druids used the native blackberry or bramble vines in their symbolic mythology instead, connecting the twining of vine plants to their beliefs in the spiralling growth of life energy. Both plants represent forces of vitality and life; and like the grapevine, bramble vines are associated with joy, livelihood, wellbeing and exhilaration, both types providing wine and food. Certainly in colder European climates, the grapevine was reluctant to grow, and its place was taken, spiritually and practically, by the bramble or blackberry; therefore, it is thought by Celtic scholars that the Druids used the blackberry vine rather than the grape one for their Celtic Moon month calendar. The Vine Moon occurs at the Autumnal Equinox and is a time of harmony when days and nights are of equal length, symbolising balance. The Vine Moon is traditionally a time for plans to move into a period of fruition or harvest before the (northern hemisphere) winter sets in. It represents a time of plenty when life's cup is full and the fruits of labour are to be enjoyed.

Vine types, being born within the Autumnal Equinox, are considered to be changeable, indecisive, full of contradictions and unpredictable. It is hard for you to 'pick sides', as you can see all angles equally and can empathise with each. There are aspects of life about which you are really sure, however, and these include good food, wine, art and music. A connoisseur of refinement and quality, you sit easily with luxury and have the Midas touch when it comes to transforming drab into beautiful. Classy, charming and elegant, you win others over with your classic style and poise. Although at times unpredictable, this usually just adds to your mystique.

ESPECIALLY FOR AUSTRALIANS
(OF ALL ZODIAC SIGNS)

If you live in Australia, here are two Australian-based magical woods, for those who prefer to source their woods closer to home and nature. Australia has a less documented history than many European civilisations, but still has no less mythology and legends swirling in its mists of time.

EUCALYPTUS ★ Eucalyptus is very plentiful and has a wonderfully intoxicating, distinctive, clean aroma which is reminiscent of the continent's vast areas of bushland, and has played an important ceremonial and medicinal role in the culture of Australian Aborigines, who have inhabited the nation for 40,000 to 50,000 years. Eucalyptus is a wood of feminine energy whose elemental association is Earth and main origin is Australia. One of the strongest healing woods known, eucalyptus wood has been used for centuries for medicinal as well as ritualistic purposes. Heady and Earthy, the energy of this wood is clean and pure. Eucalyptus is recommended for the promotion of good, robust health, and is also related to luck, especially if regarding knowledge. An excellent tool in divination, particularly when worn as a charm to invoke luck, it brings the wearer or user good fortune when used in rituals seeking positive results.

LEOPARDWOOD (or LACEWOOD) ★ Leopardwood or the Leopard Tree, so named because of its spotted wood, carries the energies of both the masculine and the feminine, Mars (Aries, Scorpio) and Venus (Taurus, Libra), and its main affinity is with the Water element (Cancer, Scorpio, Pisces). Leopardwood is a very useful tool for divination and is associated with positive luck, earning it the label 'gambler's wood'. Overall, its energy is very positive, making it an ideal wood for use in almost any ritual or spell, especially those concerning luck, magic and divination.

THE POWER OF LOVE

Each Sun sign exudes their own love and romance style. This style is an energy unique to that sign, and has the power to magnetise to that person their true, soulful match. Unhappy or unsuccessful relationships are often the result of incompatible Sun signs, personal values, goals, hopes, viewpoints or expectations. I believe everyone has a perfect soul partner (or three!) who is especially for them, and just knowing that special person or persons are out there can illuminate your life's romantic path. In this lifetime, we may not find that person or persons, but can still experience the joys and wonders of many other significant relationships which enrich and add tremendous meaning to our lives. Some partnerships are only fleeting, but the feelings they give us can last a lifetime, while others are more enduring, and the rewards they give us and lessons they teach us can last a lifetime too. Small gestures of love on a frequent basis, consistent nurturing and communication, and making the effort to understand each other, are just four ways to keep the fires of passion and romance burning long after the initially roaring fire has diminished into glowing embers.

Your whole natal chart would need to be examined to form an overall picture of your romantic nature, and although the Sun is a fantastic starting point, it is not the sole consideration. Regarding these other planets, in Carl Jung's studies on psychological astrology, and in traditional synastry (the comparing of two people's natal charts to determine overall compatibility), the harmonious link between the Sun in one person's chart and the Moon in the other's (usually the man's Sun and the woman's Moon) is considered the best indication for a happy and enduring relationship. More specifically, the sextile aspect, an angle of 60 degrees, appeared most frequently between the Sun of one and the Moon of the other in fulfilling relationships. Other positive planetary contacts, such as one person's Moon to another's Venus, or the Mars to the Moon (again, traditional indications of attraction and harmony) also occurred frequently.

The feminine personal planets in a male's chart (Moon and Venus), and the masculine personal planets in a female's chart (Sun and Mars) tell a lot about the inner self and how this is projected onto relationships. However helpful chart analysis is in telling a story about your relationship style and approach, it all depends not on your chart, but on what you do with the resources at your disposal, which your chart can indeed tell you a lot about. Relationships and marriages involving harmonious planetary and zodiacal energies between the two people tend to last longer because they are simply more 'flowing' and easier.

The signs in which the four personal and 'relationship' planets - the Sun, the Moon, Venus and Mars - are placed, coupled with the aspects they make with the other planets in the chart, give important clues into understanding the often unconscious drives within you that shape your relating style, tastes, mannerisms and patterns.

Expanding upon the other planetary considerations is beyond the scope of this book, but it is useful to know, particularly if you are interested in examining the dynamics of a current relationship a bit deeper, or are wishing to attract a new one into your life. But for now, your Sun sign is a wonderful place to start! Your Solar sign is regarded as being at the core of the complex - and very fun - study of relationships! So for now, we will begin this study of love with your essence, your core self, the brightest light shining from within - your Sun sign!

SOME LUCKY-IN-LOVE TIPS
GENERAL HINTS

★ To attract and retain love, the Heart chakra (an energy centre within the body) needs to be balanced and clear from blockages. The Heart chakra is located in the region of the physical heart. Its Sanskrit name is *anahata*, and its symbol is a twelve-petal green lotus flower whose centre contains a green circle and two intersecting triangles making up a six-pointed star representing balance (and also could be said to symbolise six as the number of Venus). Its element is Air and its colour is green. Balance in this chakra is expressed as unconditional love for ourselves and others. Crystals that can be used to cleanse and balance this chakra are mostly green and pink stones.

★ Pink candles (two, representing a couple, or six, representing Venus, is preferable) can be used in love spells.

★ Any 'love-attracting' wishing rituals should be done on a Friday (ruled by Venus) night around the time of the New Moon (signifying the principle of increase and growth).

★ Basil, otherwise known as witch's herb or St Joseph's wort, is said to be the most potent lover herb of all. Basil vibrates to the energy of Mars, which is all about lust and sexual energy, and it is used prolifically in all sorts of love potions and rituals throughout the world.

★ Ginger has a reputation as a potent sexual tonic and aphrodisiac *. Arousing and warm, it can increase sensual vitality, particularly in men. Being warming and spicy, its vibration aligns with Mars. Saffron is also regarded as a potent, albeit expensive, aphrodisiac!

★ Wear red and pink (associated with Mars and Venus respectively), as these colours in all their shades are said to incite passion, lust and romance. Green is also connected with the heart by virtue of its association with the Heart chakra and the planet Venus, and its links with fertility, nature, abundance of all kinds, and new growth.

★ Call upon some higher spiritual help. When working your 'love magic', some planetary influences, goddesses and gods that you can call upon are: Aphrodite, Venus and Eros/Cupid, and other lesser known deities such as Juno Lucina, Demeter, Freya, Ishtar, Circe and Hathor.

★ The planet Venus has developed a rich culture of gods and goddesses associated with her varying levels of love and passion. These include the virgin - Brighid; the fertile woman - Aphrodite, (the Greek goddess); and of course Venus (the Roman equivalent); the mother and provider - Demeter; and desirous or physical love - Eros/Cupid (Venus's son).

★ The pine tree is sacred to Adonis (Venus's lover) and is said to balance the male and female energies. Pine is cleansing and protective and, as an evergreen, symbolises life. Its cones represent fertility.

★ Cardamom is said to have aphrodisiac qualities

★ The three almost universally recognised symbols of love are the goddesses Venus and Aphrodite, and the Cupid. Venus is the patroness of flowers and vegetation, and represents the regenerative cycle of creation, as well as beauty, herbs and physical love. She can be called upon for general love wishes and rituals. The dove, roses, rings, copper, apples, rosemary and the ankh are some of her sacred symbols. Aphrodite is a Greek goddess who has the ability to brings lovers together. Her names mean 'of the sea' as she is believed to have been born of the foam of the ocean. She can be called upon in ceremonies and spells for affection, love, marriage and partnership. Some of her associated symbols are the Flower of Aphrodite, swans, dolphins, frankincense and myrrh. Cupid, the cherubic winged boy with a bow and arrow, is the Roman name, and Eros is the Greek name for the same deity. The son of Venus/Aphrodite, he is an aspect that represents lustful love and desire.

★ Heartsease, another name for the wild pansy, Latin viola tricolour, was one of the most popular additives to the love potions of the ancient Romans and Greeks.

★ In centuries past, when people were more in tune with nature and its cycles, ceremonies, rituals and festivals were held on certain dates or times of year. The following are some examples, and you can reawaken their powers through craft and ceremony: February 2 is Bridhid's Day, or Bride's Day, and represents the white goddess; February 14 is Valentine's Day, traditionally the greatest and most well-known love 'celebration' of the year; March 1 is one of the festival days of Juno Lucina, the light bearer and goddess of women and marriage; the month of April is especially linked to the love goddess Aphrodite; the Summer solstice which falls on or around June 21 is an important time for reconnecting with the spirit of love, fertility and marriage; August 1 is the first of three harvest festivals in the Celtic calendar: The Harvest Festival honours Demeter, the goddess of love, as bountiful mother and faithful wife; the Festival of Lights, Diwali, in October, is sacred to Lakshmi, the Hindu goddess of happiness, love, and good fortune; the Winter solstice which falls on or around December 21, marks the turning point from long dark nights to lengthening days, and is the time of the wheel of love when virgin goddesses gave birth to their children - it is also fittingly symbolised by evergreens such as pine, ivy and holly; in Mexico, December 31, the last night of the year, is traditionally 'wishing night' and is an opportune time to make a wish for a lover in the coming year, using evergreen branches to enhance your request.

* The term 'aphrodisiac' is derived from Aphrodite, the Greek goddess of love, beauty, lust and sensuality

★ GEMSTONES ★

When it comes to calling love into your life using crystals, the general rule is that any of the pink or green stones are closely aligned with matters of the heart and can therefore help you to entice the affections you seek. Although your Sun sign has its very own special gemstones, outlined elsewhere in the book, the following stones can be used by all the signs (except for the first point, which are your own sign's feature stones), as their energies and qualities contain the power to attract and create love in all its forms, from self-love to deeper soulful connections with another, or to increase states of being which open the heart, thus enhancing your abilities to magnetise love.

★ Sapphire, Carnelian, Peridot and Sardonyx ★
Using your Virgoan luckiest crystals is a fabulous start to working on heightening your romantic zest, and making your sensual energy more potent. Emerald is also useful in raising your attracting powers.

★ Rose Quartz is the ultimate love stone. It invites love into your life by helping to open your heart to receive love, and gently reminding you that you are worthy of love. Connected with the Heart chakra, it is the stone of unconditional love, enhancing all forms of it and opening up the heart. It is excellent for increasing self-worth and acceptance. The colour of rose quartz is pink, the colour of Venus, the amorous planet of desire and nurturance. Balancing and calming, it helps to heal emotional pain. Wear this stone, keep some beside your bed, or sleep with some under your pillow to remind you that love it coming your way - and that you whole*heart*edly deserve it!

★ Green Aventurine is considered the 'opportunity and luck stone'. Connected with the Heart chakra, it helps us to recognise opportunities and is said to place us exactly where we need to be for good things to transpire, as energetically it opens our mind and heart to increased perception to recognise lucky elements. It also promotes new growth, optimism, and is an overall attractor of good fortune, adventure and abundance.

★ Jade, on a spiritual level, has an affinity with the Heart chakra. It harmonises relationships, and encourages compassion and the establishment of strong bonds.

★ Emerald is reputedly a stone of constancy in love, and is said to have been brought to Earth from the planet Venus. Because it is green, it also holds deep associations with the Heart chakra.

★ Rhodochrosite can be used to attract one's soul mate. This stone, as with all the pink stones, can be used as an effective love magnet. It encourages you to appreciate yourself by teaching you that you are worthy of love, wholeness and happiness - and so opening you up to receive.

★ Malachite, Citrine, Rhodonite, Moonstone, Morganite, Beryl, Ruby, Mangano Calcite, Garnet, Red and Pink Tourmaline, Tugtupite, Rutilated Quartz, Lodestone, Peridot and Lapis Lazuli are also known for their love properties, and can be used or worn to invite romance into your life, or to bring and retain enduring love.

★ Clear Quartz can be used with any of these listed crystals to amplify their metaphysical properties.

★ Shells: Although shells are not technically a crystal, but rather a natural elemental material, they are associated with love and are sacred to Aphrodite, the Greek love goddess, and are often used in magic talismans to attract romance.

★ ESSENTIAL OILS ★

The following essential oils are known for their aphrodisiac or love-attracting properties also, and can be worn as perfumes on the skin, used in an oil burner or vaporiser, dispersed in a bath, used in spell-casting and wishing rituals, sprinkled on your pillow to imbue your dreams with inspired romantic notions, or in any other creative ways you can think of! **

★ Essential oils, flowers and herbs which contain natural pheromones or like substances, or increase pheromone levels in the body, are: Lavender, Frankincense, Jasmine, Nutmeg, Ylang Ylang, Sandalwood, Patchouli and Asian Agarwood (Oud).

★ The prime love oil, which holds Universal appeal, is rose. Reputedly excellent for both the mind and body, roses are the basis of more than 95 per cent of women's fragrances, and the petals have a long tradition of uplifting the spirits and soothing the soul. *Rosa damascena* is believed to be good for attracting love, while *R. centifolia*, the French rose oil base, is regarded as an aphrodisiac. Rose is traditionally accepted as the all-encompassing Universal fragrance of love, blessed with a reputation for opening up the hearts of all those who come under its spell.

★ Cedarwood oil has been used since ancient times in incense and perfumes. Its deep, woody scent helps to stimulate the Base chakra, increasing sexual passion and desire. Its sedative qualities aid relaxation and encourage openness. In herbal magic, it is also associated with spells for wealth and abundance.

★ Neroli, Geranium, Almond (as a base), Basil, Thyme, Vetiver, Gardenia, Vanilla, Rose Otto, Apple, Cardamom, Lotus, Orange, Ginger, Bergamot, Rosewood and Clary Sage are also exquisitely seductive and sensual, and can be used in any way you like to bring to you that which your heart desires. These oils, when mixed with your own pheromones and magical intentions, will naturally enhance your point of attraction!

** Always research first and use with caution.

VIRGO ★ LOVE STYLE

Most Virgos wear their heart in their heads, not their chests or sleeves. Your willingness to advise, help out and take on responsibilities is your Earthy way of showing love to your partner. Sometimes, in your sincere attempts to improve the life of your loved one, you may be a little critical, picky, prone to worry and pedantic. Even your love life isn't immune to your powers of discernment and analysis. But the rewards for the other person are immense, as you are a devoted, dedicated, considerate and deeply caring lover when your heart has found its home. You are sensual and feeling in romance, but the other person has to be exactly the right fit to suit your fussy tastes and perfectionist nature. Sometimes lacking in warmth and spontaneity, overt displays of attention and affection may unnerve you; and in any case, you would much rather a meeting of the minds than anything else. Once you feel you have mental rapport with your prospective lover, you will willingly be led to the next level - and prove to be a beautifully skilful and sensuous giver of love behind closed doors.

You may be aloof and mistrustful, and you will rarely put your emotional cards on the table or reveal your heart's longings too quickly, but once trust is won, you can unleash a discreet charm and incredible sensuality. You will be attentive and dutiful towards your lover, and if loved in return, provide a stable, organised, solid foundation for the two of you.

Despite your steadfast faithfulness to your relationships, you would rather spend your life alone than opt for second best - and you will choose to remain that way until you find *The One*. Although not known to be extreme, you also don't do things by halves, and give your full heart and soul to any relationship you deem to be worthy. Beware of becoming overly picky and finding fault, for this will only serve to isolate you and ultimately lead to loneliness, anxiety, insecurity, and even despair. Love will burn in the contented Virgo like a steady flame, spreading warmth and delightful reliability and constancy, and you take seriously and solemnly the promise "till death do us part" - rarely, if ever, letting your partner down.

LUCKY IN LOVE? VIRGO ★ COMPATIBILITY

* Please note the following is based on your Sun sign alone. For a whole and integrated approach to relationship compatibility, your whole natal chart would need to be taken into consideration. Synastry (*syn*: acting or considered together, united; *astry*: pertaining to the stars) is a branch of astrology which delves into more complex areas, and is based upon the natal charts of the two people concerned, to determine overall compatibility, potential conflicts and suitability based upon celestial influences. For the purposes of length, the below information is simplified and only refers to Sun sign connections.

Virgo ★ Aries ♍ ♈

Virgo will find much fault with the Aries's carefree and impetuous nature, and Aries will become impatient with Virgo's nit picking and criticism. The Ram's outspoken and direct manner puts Virgo on the defensive, even though Aries's charm and boundless energy initially intrigue the conventional Virgin. Aries and Virgo are different in almost every way, although the two of you could make a great business combination. But in love, this is a potentially difficult and challenging romance, with many clashes. Fire and Earth do not blend well together, and your partnership is a good point in case. High-speed, impulsive Aries is likely to feel frustrated by Virgo's caution, reserve, consideration of all facts before acting, and constant focus on trivial details, while the Virgin could find the Ram a bit pushy, confrontational and impetuous. Fire is volatile and uncontrolled, whereas Earth is practical, stable and controlled, making for a great contrast in characters here. Self-restrained, aloof and cool is the Virgo, and Aries is easily put off by her rather intellectual and detached nature, however her deep sensuality and veiled charm will nonetheless intrigue him. Virgo's nit picking and fussiness may grate on Aries's nerves, and Aries's temperamental and reckless nature will unsettle the orderly, rational and sensible Virgo. Virgo's natural tendency to anxiety and worrying will irk the live-for-the-moment Ram, and he will not understand her obsessiveness and pedantry with what he considers the petty and mundane side of life. Moreover, Aries will not understand the systematic orderliness and lack of spontaneity in the typical Virgin's character, and will either learn to live with it or, more likely, take off and not be seen for dust. If a good mental affinity and rapport can be built despite these differences, these two can make it work - but ultimately, the Aries is too footloose and fancy-free to be tied down by the Virgin's exacting and impossibly high standards.

Overall compatibility rating ★ 5 out of 10
Lucky Romance Tip ★ To attract an Aries, wear the colours red or orange, and use the crystal diamond

Virgo ★ Taurus ♍ ♉

Taurus and Virgo, both being of the Earth element, will enjoy an exquisitely sensual relationship, but you also risk falling into a stifling, dull routine. Virgo enjoys the Bull's Earthy generosity and affection, but resent their stubbornness. Two Earth signs like you speak the same language and have the same sensual approach to love. Remember though that Virgo prefers quality to quantity! Although you are not the most adventurous of pairings, you get on considerably well since you share a need for steadiness, consistency and dependability. You are both practical by nature and prefer routine, but this may lead to a rather mundane existence where one or both of you become stuck in a rut and feel unable to move. Taurus, who is deeply affectionate and in need of physical rapport, may find the Virgo a bit distant and undemonstrative. The Virgin is also aloof and analytical, two traits the Bull doesn't possess, and these could leave Taurus cold. Taurus also likes to possess and feel needed and loved and can therefore smother Virgo, whose feelings are tightly under control. Virgo gives a veiled love, while Taurus exudes a warm, flowing style of love, so you could clash in this area. You are both realistic however, and can usually resolve any issues around intimacy with good old-fashioned problem-solving skills - for both of you are pragmatic, capable and thorough, and you apply these skills to any adverse relationship situations you may encounter. Virgo's intellectuality and emphasis on the mental side of life could also be alien to the more physically-oriented Bull, who couldn't give a hoof about analysing anything. Virgo's fussiness, cleanliness and obsessiveness may unnerve Taurus, who just likes simple comforts and pleasures. Overall though, this is a very promising, albeit sensible, relationship. The bond of your common interests should ensure a strong relationship, which is characterised by faithfulness, reliability and steadfastness.

Overall compatibility rating ★ 8.5 out of 10
Lucky Romance Tip ★ To attract a Taurus, wear the colours pink or green, and use the crystal rose quartz

Virgo ★ Gemini ♍ ♊

The trickster Twins are a little flighty for Virgo's more steady, deliberate nature. Yet Gemini's entertaining and stimulating intellect will lift Virgo's Earthy spirits and keep her guessing, which will continue to intrigue the Virgin. Both ruled by Mercury, the planet of intellect and communication, you will have plenty to discuss and a substantial rapport. Yet Virgo's fussy perfectionism can make the Gemini take flight. Earthy Virgo may not approve of this flightiness, but you are potentially a strong couple and a compelling combination. Overall though, Air and Earth generally don't blend well together, and although you share the ruling planet Mercury, this only emphasises a mental and intellectual affinity between your two very different signs, rather than a deep emotional bond. Virgo's nit picking and fastidiousness will get on Gemini's nerves, and Gemini's fickle and carefree nature will unsettle the orderly, rational and sensible Virgo. The Twins' dispassionate and restless character may resonate with the Virgin's naturally cool and essentially unemotional psyche, but Virgo's natural tendency to anxiety and worrying will irk the much more light-hearted Gemini. Moreover, the Virgin is straight-laced, systematic and pure, while the Twins have an agenda - they are the cunning, manipulative pranksters of the zodiac, which doesn't sit well with the virtuous do-gooder Virgo. Overall, Virgo's pedantic need for logic, detailed analysis and order are the furthest things from the erratic Gemini's mind, and Virgo's meticulous attitudes towards cleanliness and tidiness are not concerns at all for the scatterbrained devil-may-care Gemini. At the end of the romance, the only thing you may find you had in common was your ruling planet, which can very well act as a stimulating catalyst but is just as likely to fizzle out long before it reaches the end of the wire.

Overall compatibility rating ★ 5.5 out of 10
Lucky Romance Tip ★ To attract a Gemini, wear the colours light blue or yellow, and use the crystal citrine

Virgo ★ Cancer ♍ ♋

Cancer's creativity and caring ways may turn Virgo on, however the Crab's emotional dramas and tendency to hoard, whine and cling clashes with Virgo's need for logic, reason and simplicity.

Your two elements Water and Earth blend well together, but the Virgo's incessant nit picking and thoughtless criticism may wear down Cancer's much more fragile feelings. The Virgin is intellect-based and the Crab is emotion-based, so you could be at odds with each other. If the Cancer can learn to cope with the Virgo's naturally cool and aloof façade, you have the potential to make this partnership work, as you are both sensuous, caring, compassionate and devoted. In return for the Virgo's imparting more order and system to the Cancerian's life, the Crab will coax the Virgin out of her emotional reserve and provide a few much-needed lessons in feeling, affection, romance and contentment. Cancer is hyper-sensitive and easily hurt, so the Virgo may need to curb her tendency to criticise and analyse every last detail. Virgo's tendency to be undemonstrative may also upset the needy Crab, who needs hugs, attention and security, while Virgo may lose patience with Cancer's proneness to sulking and moodiness. Both of you are also likely to be anxious and prone to worry some of the time, and you could both become melancholic and unreachable to each other should one or both of you go through a bout of depression. Overall, this is a strong pairing with fair potential, if the Crab can learn to live with the fussy, cool Virgo's pedantry and need for perfection.

Overall compatibility rating ★ 7 out of 10
Lucky Romance Tip ★ To attract a Cancerian, wear the colours silver or white, and use the crystal moonstone

Virgo ★ Leo ♍ ♌

The Lion is often unprepared for the Virgin's fastidious tastes, and Virgo will find Leo too demanding of praise. The Virgin does however appreciate the way these big pussycats will have a go at anything; their bravery and bigness of heart inspires and uplifts the modest and reserved Virgo. The Virgin both frustrates and fascinates Leo. This has the potential to be a love-hate situation, as the Virgo's incessant criticism can wound the Lion's delicate ego. Cool and hot temperaments don't always blend well either. A certain degree of tolerance is called for here, and the Virgin is happy to let the Lion have his time in the Sun without interfering, for she is more than happy to work away in the background. There may not be a big enough degree of intimacy for the sparks to really fly, but if you can respect each other's differences, this has a fair chance of being a sensual, albeit understated union. Virgo's introversion may grate the more extroverted, expressive Leo, and Leo's extravagance and large appetite for life may unsettle the calm, cool and collected Virgo. Leo may also become annoyed by Virgo's obsession with detail and emotional restraint, and her nit picking and criticism may well hurt the Lion's fragile pride. The playful Lion needs love, fun and adventure, while the Virgo needs peace, orderliness and efficient, no-nonsense consistency - the Lion's theatrics and flair for drama will unravel her already frayed nerves. Earthy Virgo is moderate and retiring, while Fiery Leo is dominant and likes to be in control, so the success of this union may be questionable. Leo's ardent emotions will sometimes overwhelm the self-contained Virgo, which could prove their breaking point. The Lion is a social animal who adores praise, the Virgin is a quiet, steady achiever who revels in solitude. This may or may not sit too well with the

Lion, who has a big heart that he loves to share, and he enjoys the thrill of grand romances and demonstrative displays of affection and adoration, which the Virgin is unlikely to provide. That extra spark for passion may well prove elusive between these two.

Overall compatibility rating ★ 5.5 out of 10
Lucky Romance Tip ★ To attract a Leo, wear the colours gold or orange, and use the crystal ruby

Virgo ★ Virgo ♍ ♍

You have the potential to endlessly analyse and improve each other. On the surface you might seem an excessively 'normal' pair, but under the cover or indeed *covers*, some seriously Earthy fireworks may be at work. Each Virgo has their own little way of doing things so the success of your partnership depends on whether your idiosyncrasies are compatible or not. In any case, you will share a caring, sharing and understanding relationship, but things could get a little dull from time to time if you don't loosen up and learn to relax the perfectionist streak you both possess. Generally, you get along well, and are contented and happy. Virgos have a reputation for being critical - and this criticism is most often directed at themselves - but in the case of two Virgos in a relationship together, the harsh inner critic could manifest on the outside as well, being directed at each other and create problems. Although you will rarely make impossible emotional demands on the other, constant fault-finding in each other will erode your confidence, fray your nerves and ultimately give rise to the worry to which you are both so prone. For the most part though, you are on the same wavelength and tend to understand each other's obsessions, compulsions and needs for cleanliness, order and solitude. But therein lies the double-edged sword: the fact that each of you like a practical, organised routine could make it easy for you to get stuck in a rut. You are both analytical and efficient enough to recognise when this occurs and usually find good, workable solutions to get your machine up and running again. More than any other zodiac sign combination, you two must heed the message in the proverb 'familiarity breeds contempt'. Your Mutable, changeable natures should overcome this, but one too many nights on the couch could indeed mean you are stuck in that proverbial rut.

Overall compatibility rating ★ 5 out of 10
Lucky Romance Tip ★ To attract another Virgo, wear the colours white or yellow, and use the crystal sapphire

Virgo ★ Libra ♍ ♎

If Virgo picks holes in Libra or tries to organise him 'into shape', the Scales will drift away on the next fanciful whim, looking elsewhere for stimulation and mental rapport. Libran charm can seem a little wishy-washy to the Virgin, and their indecision can drive the Virgo mad, yet Virgo is also enchanted by Libra's easy grace, natural warmth, wit and sociability. Libra may make demands that seem superfluous to the modest and sensible Virgin, but for talents in mastering life, relationships and love, Virgo can certainly learn something here. The marked contrast usually present in Earth/Air combinations is not so apparent here, as you are both mind-based and not overtly emotional, so won't make excessive demands on the other. You complement each other in many ways and both like to achieve some degree of perfection. Further, you both have a good sense of style, sensuality and discerning tastes. Because Libra seeks, above all else, to achieve harmony, balance, beauty and to keep the peace, he is unlikely to provoke the normally critical, fault-finding Virgo. But socialite Libra may be rather too flighty for the steady Virgo, who strives for consistency and stability, and Libra is dependent on his social contacts whereas Virgo only trusts her own efforts. If Virgo becomes nit-picky of Libra's faults, the Libra will not hesitate to find new company. But overall, this is a graceful, understated union, with both of you being gentle, caring, courteous and considerate of the other at all times.

Overall compatibility rating ★ 7 out of 10
Lucky Romance Tip ★ To attract a Libran, wear the colours pink and blue, and use the crystal opal

Virgo ★ Scorpio ♍ ♏

You two have a lot in common; you both like to analyse and dissect. However, if Virgo dares turn their analysis and criticism upon Scorpio, the Scorpio's affections may vanish without trace. Virgo's affinity with this Watery sign attracts her to the Scorpion's mystery and passion, however the Scorpion may prove too intense for the Virgin in the long run, and if she criticises the fiercely self-protective Scorpio's ego one too many times, she may be stung by Scorpio's infamous tail and never fully recover. Your relationship may well take a little while to get off the ground, but a mutual sensuality will ensure it heats up to a smouldering union. There is likely to be lots of probing, analysis, discernment and considerable sexual chemistry if this partnership does take off, but emotionally you are worlds apart. Scorpio needs a good emotional rapport and Virgo thrives on a substantial mental rapport, so your natures may be vastly at odds too. Scorpio's complexity may be too difficult for the straight-laced, down-to-Earth Virgo to fathom, and the Scorpion's dark moods may unnerve the delicate Virgin, whose feelings are usually more straightforward. Scorpio has strong, passionate feelings, burning desires and is often at the mercy of her own depths, whereas Virgo believes in keeping emotions under firm control and discipline. However, Scorpio demands much of self and others so will appreciate the Virgo's conscientious, dedicated reliability, loyalty and consistency. In any case, you will inevitably share many pleasures together if this relationship takes off - but only if Scorpio can rein in her brooding intensity and Virgo can keep her harsh criticism under control.

Overall compatibility rating ★ 7 out of 10

Lucky Romance Tip ★ To attract a Scorpio, wear the colours red or burgundy, and use the crystal malachite

Virgo ★ Sagittarius ♍ ♐

This is a challenging match, but one that may stimulate both your hungry intellects. Virgo's soothing reliability and cool sensuality can complement the Archer's restlessness - or simply make him want to take flight. At odds by nature, your Earth and Fire combination needs much mutual tolerance to work. The Archer's extravagance and idealistic impracticalities may bring out Virgo's worst, and his playfulness, devil-may-care attitudes, carelessness and flirtiness may also provoke Virgo's critical edge. Your needs may appear very different, but there is substantial potential for a good-natured rapport to develop between you. If anything, your bond could produce a very strong friendship - the Virgo's intellectual mind is highly appealing to the equally mentally-oriented Archer - and you will engage in countless discussions and analyses of anything, all of it, and everything in between. But cracks will soon appear in any romantic relationship you embark upon with each other, as Earthy Virgo is methodical, cautious, analytical and disciplined, whereas the Fiery Archer is impulsive, rash, independent and extravagant. Virgo is mentally equipped to concentrate on one thing at a time, deal with fine details and live in the present, while Sagittarius is wide-angled, hopeful and always looking to the future. Both of you are Mutable signs, which means you are adaptable and have a fondness for change, but these qualities will be expressed in vastly different ways. The tunnel-visioned, plodding, reserved Virgo may grate the broad-minded, far-sighted, optimistic Sagittarian, and the Sagittarian's adventurous, scattered and enthusiastic spirit may be dampened by the Virgo's staid, petty, pedantic, ordered and practical nature. Overall, there could be an initial meeting of the minds here, but it will become apparent over time that your differences outweigh your similarities and the divide could become too wide to conquer - even for Sagittarius.

Overall compatibility rating ★ 6 out of 10
Lucky Romance Tip ★ To attract a Sagittarius, wear the colour deep purple or royal blue, and use the crystal zircon

Virgo ★ Capricorn ♍ ♑

You both share the Earthy need for ambition and to have social respectability and financial security. You can easily empathise, love and respect each other, but beware of playing on each other's over-active conscience. Virgo appreciates the Goat's steadfast approach and devoted nature and can easily relate to Capricorn's needs, being happy to help with Capricorn's lofty ambitions, provided the Virgin doesn't get caught up in the petty details - for the Goat will often have high aims which will not be hindered by anyone. You both belong to the Earth element, so you have your feet firmly on the ground, and you enjoy and appreciate the practical, realistic necessities of life, love and work. Both of you are conscientious, devoted, dedicated and reliable, with a strong sense of duty and responsibility, but these qualities can create a blessing *and* a curse, for you are both prone to falling victim to situations of 'all work and no play'. This, coupled with your serious, cool, aloof natures, can make for a very solemn union. Both of you tend to be workaholics during at least one period in your life, which can strain the relationship and give rise to resentment and cutting remarks. Your ruling planets, wise, self-disciplined Saturn and intellectual Mercury, are well matched for business and practical purposes, but there could be a lack of feelings, warmth, play and romantic zest. Both appreciate each other's systematic, orderly and methodical approaches to life, but when applied to love, these same characteristics may not work so well. You are both industrious and agree on all the essential things, but should ever beware of neglecting life's pleasures. Overall, however, your Earthy, sensual natures are likely to work well together and one thing is guaranteed - you are dedicated to and can depend on each other, sometimes forever.

Overall compatibility rating ★ 6 out of 10
Lucky Romance Tip ★ To attract a Capricorn, wear the colours brown or black, and use the crystal garnet

Virgo ★ Aquarius ♍ ♒

Air and Earth generally don't blend well together, and although your ruling planets, Uranus and Mercury, are similar in nature, this only emphasises a mental and intellectual affinity between your very different signs, rather than a deep emotional bond. The Water Bearer is a difficult yet fascinating creature to the Virgin. The Aquarian's quick inventive flow of ideas will enchant Virgo - until Virgo realises the Water Bearer has left the essential 'nuts and bolts' out of the scheme. The Aquarius's idealistic and unpredictable nature may also irritate Virgo's fragile nerves and make the Virgin more edgy than she already is. Virgo's nit picking and fussiness will get on Aquarius's nerves, and Aquarius's unpredictable, temperamental and unconventional nature will unsettle the orderly, rational and sensible Virgo. The Water Bearer's dispassionate and detached character may resonate somewhat with the Virgin's naturally cool and essentially unemotional psyche, but Virgo's natural tendency to anxiety and worrying will irk the more broad-minded Aquarius. Virgo can't see the forest for the trees, while the Water Bearer can see the entire forest *and* the trees. Overall, Virgo's need for logic and order are the furthest things from the erratic Aquarius's mind, and Virgo's natural, almost obsessive, tendencies towards cleanliness and tidiness are not concerns at all for the free-spirited, vague Aquarius, who has ever wider - and indeed Universal - concerns.

Overall compatibility rating ★ 6 out of 10
Lucky Romance Tip ★ To attract an Aquarian, wear the colours electric blue or turquoise, and use the crystal aquamarine

Virgo ★ Pisces ♍ ♓

Virgo's natural opposite Pisces has many qualities which the Virgin secretly desires, such as the Fish's imagination, compassion and even emotionalism. Yet the Fish's eternal dreams, with no real sense of direction or purpose, can contradict the Virgin's own sense of purpose. Pisces's vagueness and indecisiveness may also irritate Virgo. While you are astrological opposites, you are not necessarily psychological opposites, as your elements, Water and Earth, blend well together. In fact, being cosmic opposites, you have much to teach each other, and each can learn invaluable relationship lessons from the other. Both being Mutable signs, you also share agile minds, and adaptable and flexible natures. These qualities can be used constructively to form a wonderful bond between you, but as with all 'opposites', there will inevitably be clashes and differences. Further, your ruling planets, Neptune and Mercury, operate on different levels and have differing functions. While there may be an Earth/Air affinity between these two very different signs, there won't be much of an emotional bond, and you will tend to 'help' each other more than deeply love each other. Virgo can help the Piscean be more practical, while the Piscean can help the Virgoan 'think' more from their heart rather than their head.

Virgo's nit picking, pessimism and fussiness may inadvertently upset the sensitive and easily hurt Pisces, and Pisces's tendency towards laziness, indecisiveness and daydreaming, will unsettle and test the orderly, rational and sensible Virgo's patience.

The Virgin's naturally cool and essentially unemotional expression, may not sit well with the deeply compassionate and feelings-based Fish, and Virgo's natural tendency to anxiety and worrying will only exacerbate Pisces's tendency towards the same. Although you can complement each other nicely, you both see things through different eyes and each will always be a mystery to the other. Overall, Virgo's need for logic and order are the furthest things from the scattered and dreamy Pisces's mind, and Virgo's natural, almost obsessive, tendencies towards cleanliness and tidiness are not concerns at all for Pisces, who is more concerned about the state of the cosmos than the state of her house. If you two can overcome your many differences, Virgo can bring method to the Pisces's madness, and Pisces will return the favour by adding a bit of ethereal wonder and magic to Virgo's life - keeping the Virgo enchanted by keeping it all just a little out of their reach.

Overall compatibility rating ★ 6 out of 10
Lucky Romance Tip ★ To attract a Pisces, wear the colours mauve or sea green, and use the crystal amethyst

YOUR TAROT CARDS ★ FOR LUCK, MAGIC, ENERGY, ABUNDANCE, QUESTING & MEANING
THE HERMIT, THE MAGICIAN & THE WORLD

Tarot and astrology are inextricably linked. All the cards of the Major Arcana, which comprises 22 of the Tarot's 78 cards, are 'ruled by' or connected with either one of the twelve zodiac signs, the planets and luminaries, or one of the four elements.

The 22 Major Arcana cards contain the richest symbolism of all the cards in the Tarot deck, each carrying a myriad of messages for the reader to decipher. The symbolism contained within these images represents the archetypal aspects of your character. It also describes the path your soul takes through each stage of life, revealing clues through which you can explore different parts of yourself. Each of the cards also represents an aspect of Universal human experience and has a name that either directly conveys the meaning of the card, such as Strength or Justice, or depicts individuals that represent these human archetypes, such as the Hermit or the Empress. The illustrations on each card contain one or more figures and tuning into a card's imagery enables you to grasp its meaning intuitively. Consider the demeanour of the characters, whether it is day or night, the background, any symbols, the buildings, the colours, the vegetation, the weather and the season. Every card has its own story to impart, and through entering that story you can gain deeper insights into the full picture of your journey so far, as well as illuminating your path ahead.

I have outlined three cards here for your sign: The Hermit, The Magician and The World, all of which have links to your zodiac sign itself Virgo, your ruling planet Mercury, and your element of Earth. All three cards will have special meaning for your sign, and can carry powerful messages and lessons for you to reflect upon.

★ THE HERMIT ★
Ruled by Virgo

Keywords ★ Withdrawal, Retreat, Solitude

★ KEY THEMES ★

Introspection ★ Awareness ★ Quiet Contemplation ★ Reflection ★ Solitude ★ Withdrawal ★ Spiritual Learning ★ Self-discovery ★ Soul-searching ★ Good Advice ★ Wisdom ★ Embarking on a Spiritual Quest ★ Re-evaluation of Plans ★ Slow and Profound Evolution ★ Search ★ Discovery ★ Knowledge ★ Discernment ★ Patience

Number ★ 9
Astrological Sign ★ Virgo

"We hear the call of our wild. We play games to end their games ... The play is part of our work of unweaving and of our weaving work. It whirls us into another frame of reference. We use the visitation of demons to come more deeply into touch with our own powers/virtues. Unweaving their deceptions, we name our Truth.

***Mother peace: A Way to the Goddess Through Myth, Art and Tarot*, Vicky Noble, 1983**

THE MESSAGE ★ The Hermit is the archetypal equivalent of the Wise Old Man. He is the wise, Solitary One, a seeker who knows how to call down the power of the Moon, to converse with spirits and work magical spells. The Hermit is telling you that you need to spend some quiet time in meditation. This is a time to reflect, in order to reassess your direction and your commitments. You would benefit from some time alone, listening to your inner voice. Be silent and experience the joy that comes from seeking the truth and path of your own heart. This card is compelling you to learn to feel comfortable in your own company. It indicates a time of spiritual awakening, enlightenment, wisdom-seeking, and journeying to the inner worlds. But it also suggests that perhaps it is time for you to seek out a spiritual guide, teacher, healer or mentor, as sharing wisdom is part of your personal journey.

THE STORY ★ Carrying his luminous but strangely lit lantern, the Hermit walks the enlightened path of wisdom. He walks alone and at night, where both his robe and the dark conceal him, for his teachings are only for those who seek him out. The Hermit's symbolism shows you how to attune to your inner wisdom. He represents a turning away from the external world to focus inwardly. In spite of his reclusiveness, he carries a lantern to light the path ahead, which may be symbolic of his quest for knowledge, and also that introspection is not all about darkness - in fact, one requires the darker recesses of the soul to be illuminated during the 'search'. Sometimes he is accompanied by a serpent, which represents the cycle of death and rebirth.

THE AWAKENING ★ The Hermit is not looking for his way, but rather is showing and lighting the way. He is the master of light, the illuminator, whose lantern represents wakeful consciousness, the eternal soul, vigilance, caution, foresight, perceptiveness and inner light. He is the interpreter of oracles, the bearer of revelations, the inner voice which has been silenced for so long. If this solitary provider of wisdom is followed with reverence, he will shed much light on any problem. Through his urging you to take some time out, he can help you to become more aware of your motivations, your aspirations, your desires, and to give a greater meaning to your life, confronting you with your true path. The Hermit represents the inward self, troubled by deep but enriching and fruitful thoughts, or he could represent the presence of another person in your life, an older one, who has acquired some wisdom or specific knowledge you could benefit from, or perhaps the Hermit simply stands for a solitary, isolated person - which could be you or someone in your close experience. He can also signify a time in your life when you will be on your own, a kind of journey through your own inner 'desert' * landscape.

* Did the creators of the Major Arcana make a glaring spelling error when they wrote 'Hermit' instead of 'Ermit'? No, but it is interesting to note that 'Ermit' is a Latin word of Greek origin whose first meaning was 'desert'; then it came to mean 'he who lives in the desert', in solitude.

SYMBOLISM *★ Nine, the Hermit's number, always symbolises wisdom and a sense of sacred magic. Nine multiplied by any number reduces to nine, making it essentially indestructible. The Hermit is a man whole within himself, an example to all of us of what it means to be *ourselves*. His active inner light shines out to touch others with the knowledge he has gained on his journey.

The Hermit's monk's robe is brown, which is symbolic of the renunciation of worldly pursuits and pleasures in order to disassociate from the world and retreat into the self. It also indicates that he intends to use his spiritual insights in a practical manner. The lantern he carries is symbolic of the guiding light of inner knowing and insight.

The card depicts an old man whose head is bowed down, with a long grey beard and a hunched back who is shrouded in a hooded dark robe of a monk, with only his hands and a tiny portion of his face visible. In one hand he holds a staff to support himself and in his other hand he holds a lit lantern which he shines upon the path before him. His lantern denotes the light he uses to light up his inner world, which, as he grows older, he learns to appreciate. He has an aura of mystery about him, standing alone against a grey horizon; even the Earth's natural richness seems to elude him.

The Hermit is a reflection of age, and represents the wisdom of age, using his lantern to illuminate the path towards self-enlightenment. He is sometimes said to be the Fool midway through his journey, a little wiser, more restrained and less impatient. He warns you to bring all the elements of your life together - action, emotions, finances and morality - to enable you to handle the changes ahead wisely. The Hermit represents re-evaluation, for the Hermit is an old man who looks back on his past and realises that there must be more than this. He knows next to nothing of the 'greater reality' and fears even his own ignorance about wider realms. However, the Hermit *does* show a willingness to remedy that ignorance and offers the patience and discipline required to utilise past experiences and old lessons to make the most out of the future.

This card can be interpreted as standing for caution, old age and experience. The Hermit is not a pessimist, but he has become wary through age and experience; he has learned to be a realist. A prudent attitude is recommended, so sudden courses of action are not the wisest at this time. It is a time for withdrawal from action, towards inner meditation.

The Hermit also signifies the realisation that there is always something new to learn, and serves as a warning against thoughtless actions. The time is ripe for withdrawal from the chaotic outside world in order to enter the peaceful inner one. This is a time for soul-searching and seclusion that is consciously chosen rather than imposed from without; it implies time spent alone for meditation and reflection rather than out of any sense of isolation. This means gently freeing our minds of the external chatter and noise, to allow time and space for our thoughts to clear, and denotes the need for patience and an opportunity to work things out quietly. A degree of solitude is often required and temporary disengagement is allowed. The Hermit enjoys being alone - which isn't the same as being lonely; rather he teaches the lessons of solitude, which is often one of people's great fears. He also teaches us to accept, rather than fight, the passage of time, so the rewards he brings lie in the fostering of patience, tolerance and serenity.

This period of withdrawal is an opportune time to ask oneself if one listens too much to the opinions and advice of others, because often the wisest counsellor of all is the voice of one's inner self. The Hermit teaches the lesson of time, and the inevitability of old age. The truth is, we are always essentially alone, but to face this fact involves wisdom and acceptance, and once we accept it, it becomes far less frightening or threatening. Acceptance, endurance and inner quiet to obtain self-understanding, and timeless wisdom, are the messages learned through our encounter with the wise Hermit. Other divinatory meanings are counsel, knowledge, servitude, solicitude, prudence, discretion, caution, circumspection, vigilance, self-denial, regression, fear of discovery, a tendency to withhold emotions, and annulment.

The Hermit also represents the steadfast courage and determination needed to continue on the 'journey', as he trudges intently onward. Overall, he can be equated with timeless knowledge, making the card a potent reminder that the truth of existence is to be found within ourselves, since we are each part of that Universal truth.

Virgoans are recommended to carry one of these cards with them to illumine their paths, and to magnetise that for which they are asking. Go forth and claim the magic which is yours by using the symbolism of the Hermit as your guide!

★ THE MAGICIAN ★
Ruled by Mercury

Keywords ★ Initiative, Will, Independence

"Dancing in the Fire of Life"

★ KEY THEMES ★
Opportunity ★ Initiative ★ Interesting Prospects ★ Free Will ★ New Ventures ★ Intelligence ★ Apprenticeship ★ Potential Talents or Qualities Shining Through ★ Ability to Convince Others ★ Originality ★ Spontaneity ★ Flexibility ★ Possibilities ★ Skill ★ Adaptability ★ Duplicity ★ Free Spirit ★ Power ★ Influence ★ Cunning

"Whatever you can do or dream you can, begin it.
Boldness has genius, power and magic in it"
Johann Wolfgang von Goethe, Virgo

Number ★ 1
Astrological Signs ★ Aries, Gemini & Virgo

THE STORY ★ The Magician is an effective, powerful man with a strong focus upon goals. He makes plans and then fulfils them. He is a skilled and clever character, who performs occult rituals, pouring energy from his extended hand which erupts into a pillar of living fire. As fire can transform what is added to it, this shaman can transform one thing into another: clay into brick, water into steam, fire into embers. While the Fool before him symbolises the unconscious, untainted mind, the Magician is the embodiment of conscious knowledge, with its ability to know and therefore manipulate the outside physical world. Like the Fool, the Magician wears a pointed hat, the apex of which alludes to the ability to draw down cosmic forces. The image contains a Pentacle, Cup, Sword and Wand, as tokens of his mastery over the four elements. The Magician offers a choice of directions and the opportunity to take one of them; the Cup represents the realm of feeling and relationships; the Sword is connected with the mind and the logical, rational world; the Wand symbolises creativity and imagination; and the Pentacle is associated with the material, the body and the physical world. Opportunities are available in each, or all, of these areas. He represents vigour and talent in any chosen area, which are backed up by a strong urge or pull. Overall, the Magician represents desires made manifest on Earth through the power of thought. He is the mediator between the spiritual and the physical worlds, and with initiative and cunning, he decides which ideas will be made real.

THE LESSON ★ Generally, the Magician signifies fresh beginnings, the start of a new phase or cycle, and a directed sense of purpose. The Magician is a card of potential which points to the importance of a new enterprise. It's time to forget false modesty and to strike out in a new, dynamic, bold direction. Capitalise on your imaginative and creative skills. The fresh start the Magician implies should not be entered into lightly - there's often an element of trickery or doubt surrounding this card, however it is particularly auspicious for business ventures and financial matters because it shows that you have what it takes to succeed; indeed, all the necessary tools are at your disposal.

SYMBOLISM * ★ The Jungian archetype for the Magician is the Trickster, such as the Native American coyote. From the as-yet-untapped potential of the Fool, the Magician emerges as the determination to make things happen. This card therefore denotes confidence, decisiveness and an awareness of one's personal power and effect. You actually have the knowledge, skills and experience at hand but you must now concentrate on using these skills and also on marketing them. There is a suggestion that even if you don't feel confident, you should do your best to appear so, and you may need to use an element of trickery to achieve this - or to get what you want.

Its symbolism is youthful and dynamic, hinting at the vast creative forces being channelled through the body of the Magician with the help of the tools that are laid out before him, using these elements for the manifestation of his desires.

The Wand the Magician is pointing towards the sky symbolises his use of it to access Universal forces in order to amplify the power of his will and intentions.

The Magician's right hand, the symbol of action, points downwards to the four Tarot tools anchoring the energy. The inspiration gained through his spiritual connection with the Universal forces needs Earthly energy, so his body acts as a conduit for these ends.

In most cards he is represented as a travelling entertainer, a 'showman', part mountebank, part wiseman, and possibly also a trickster and illusionist. The Magician, in medieval Europe, lived on the fringes of the law and was regarded with a mixture of fascination and suspicion by the authorities and the people. He is always number One - at centre stage and in the spotlight. This apparent forthrightness can be misleading, for there is always something going on behind the scenes - sometimes even deception. The image exudes originality and confidence, which associates it with positive action, cleverness, cunning, individuality and creativity.

Traditionally the Magician was ruled by Aries, tying in with the fact that both Aries and the Magician are number one in their respective astrological and Tarot sequences. As such, the Magician represents the ego, sitting like the Sun at the centre of the personality, with the Fire of will manifesting his desires into reality through the power of initiative.

The Magician's number is 1, the symbol of a new beginning, and the brim of his hat forms a number 8, the symbol of infinity and eternal life. He is depicted wearing a long robe and standing before a table, upon which lies a Cup, Wand, Sword and Pentacle, representing the four suits of the Minor Arcana, and the elements of Water, Fire, Air and Earth, which in turn stand for feeling, intuition, thought and sensation, the four functions of human consciousness. The four types of divination used that correspond with each element are (respectively): hydromancy, pyromancy, aeromancy, and geomancy. He holds a wand in his hand, and sometimes appears with a serpent coiled around his waist, combined to signify a person of authority with the power to do good. Surrounding him are greenery and flowers. He holds the wand towards the heavens, to symbolise the purity of his higher aspirations, while the other hand points downwards, towards Earth and matter.

The Magician is often dressed in white and red to represent spiritual purity and passion, demonstrating the essential duality of his nature. He is connected with the Greek Hermes, messenger of the Gods; he stands for the link between the gods and men, and this can also be perceived as the link between the conscious and the unconscious mind.

The Magician represents a child, an adolescent, a young boy or girl, a student, a person who is young at heart, open-minded, inquisitive, and dynamic; someone with a youthful temperament or demeanour, whatever their age; somebody who undertakes or achieves something new, or who is starting a period in their life where they can exert their free-spirited essence.

The alchemy of Fire is the Magician's great secret. His activating power changes one thing into another; he represents the toolmaker, the wand-pointer and the shaman. The Magician as shaman demonstrates the channelling of healing heat - the Fire of the Universe coming through the human being. Like any shaman, the Magician is a mediator between two worlds - the inner, spiritual plane and the outer, physical plane.

The Magician symbolises the complex nature of the world, of life and reality. He tells us that the Universe is a formidable cosmic game, and that reality is an illusion, a projection of our consciousness, and not to be trusted without question. He appears wise but he is also artful and cunning; his sideways glance puts us on our guard. In a spiritual context, the Magician shows that it is time to put intuition and psychic abilities to practical use. Indeed, this card stands for the availability of options in many areas, and offers the enthusiasm to follow hunches or one's inner directive. The Magician knows that creative achievement demands a certain diligence, self-discipline, craftiness and wiliness, and that if one wants to manifest something worthwhile, then they need to visualise the goal and work toward it without getting distracted. In the arts of healing and magic, intention is *everything*. 'What you see is what you get' is one way of putting it, so hold the end result in view and get to work. All ideas need a channel to bring them down to Earth, to make them real on the physical plane, otherwise they may fade away into the ethers, unrealised and not manifested. Indeed, you must remember that the Magician works with both forms and the formless, and with the Magician on your side, you should be able to accomplish whatever you set out to achieve.

The Magician stands for a teacher-guide, a person who offers education and enlightenment to all pupils attending the first lesson in the School of Life. The energy embodied in the Magician is that of purpose, action, intention, potential, skill, craftiness, creativity and will. The Magician tells us that we all have the ability to get on with life, as long as we acknowledge and accept there are obstacles to be overcome. He also challenges us not to be deceived by the transient, material world, and to be aware that you are in a position to influence others now *and* in the long-term, but discretion is vital. Your originality and compassion are highlighted here, but beware of being too clever or manipulative.

When working alongside the Magician in your Tarot journey, ask yourself how you can begin to shift your focus in life from external things to your inner self, as by looking inward you can discover even greater treasures than the material world can offer. Its divinatory meanings are originality, individuality, positive action, creativity, self-reliance, imagination, self-confidence, spontaneity, ingenuity, flexibility, self-control, deception and mastery. Generally, he signifies new beginnings, the start of a fresh cycle, a sense of purpose, willpower and initiative. The Magician is a card of potential, showing the importance of a new enterprise. The Magician is ultimately imparting the message that a great reserve of power and energy is available, and it is up to the seeker (you) how it will be used. Powerfully, he shows us that life is a magical act, and our mind the magician. Further, the Magician might well be ageless, which is what most Virgoans aspire to be.

★ THE WORLD/UNIVERSE ★
Ruled by Saturn & the Element of Earth

Keywords ★ Completion, Attainment, Fulfilment

★ KEY THEMES ★
★ Arrival! ★ Completion ★ Fulfilment of Hopes and Dreams ★ Crowning Achievement ★ Total Success ★ Dreams Come True ★ Expansion ★ Aspirations ★ Idealism ★ A Prize or Goal Reached ★ Acclaim ★ Graduation ★ Accomplishment ★ Attainment ★ Joy ★ Contentment ★ Gratitude ★ The Path Toward Enlightenment ★ Perfection ★ Freedom ★ A Move to the Next Level ★ Cosmic Awareness ★ Expanded Consciousness ★ Joy ★ Great Outlook ★

Meditation ★ "I have completed one journey and will now rebirth myself to begin a brand new one. I welcome every chance to grow and learn."

Number ★ 21
Astrological Signs ★ Capricorn, Taurus, Virgo & Aquarius

THE MESSAGE ★ You have arrived at the beginning of the Path to Enlightenment, or could be considerably advanced along it by now. The World card suggests a job well done - you have happily completed something of great significance. Enjoy these feelings of wholeness and completion as your amazing accomplishments have been well-earned. You're now ready to move onto something new. You have grown spiritually and have evolved to a whole new level in your understanding of the Universe and your place in it. As well as this, you have attained complete clarity, cosmic awareness, significant enlightenment, an expanded consciousness and above all, the true freedom that accompanies all this.

THE STORY ★ A statue of a woman has come to life and is dancing, looking back at a leaf she holds in her outstretched hand. Just as the Earth, Divine Mother of us all, evolved from the stars and materialised into reality, so have our physical selves been created out of the same essence so that we may dance the dance of life just as She dances through the cosmos. This dream-like journey is one of going deep within and finding our essential harmony with All There Is. When we arrive at the knowledge of who we really are we gain The World.

THE AWAKENING ★ The World is a symbol of accomplishment, of an end which is also a beginning. The journey is completed! Upon reaching the World your goal is attained and you are suffused with joy and fulfilment. Life is fully and rapturously embraced, and you are free to experience all that it offers. You realise that the end of a journey merely leads to the first step on a new one. By uniting and balancing your long-sought after inner harmony with the skills you have learned in this lifetime so far, you have achieved true success and The World can be yours. Although hard work has been required to attain this, material rewards and inner peace are promised. But overall, you must view your life in the context of the whole of life and All There Is, before you can gain the wisdom you seek. The World imparts the message that each one of us carries a world inside of us, which is neither unattainable, illusory or utopian. It is simply what we are. All the elements are gathered here so that our conscience may awaken and our future will unfold as it is meant to before us.

SYMBOLISM *★ The World card symbolises completion and renewal. It incorporates the wisdom gathered throughout the journey of the previous 21 cards. The World embodies the essence of success, arrival, fulfilment and happiness. It shows a willingness to embrace life fully and to welcome in the new.

The central figure in the World card, hermaphroditic in appearance, symbolises the integration of the masculine and feminine principles to form a complete, unified entity. The wreath is a symbol of triumph, success, rebirth and renewal, while the surrounding creatures embody different aspects of human nature.

One of the most ancient symbols of alchemy is that of Ouroboros, the dragon or serpent which lies in a circle with its tail in its mouth. This sleeping creature must be awoken for its potential to be realised, and its energies released, for us to begin - and achieve - the process of self-transformation. The circle around the dragon, a symbol without end and without beginning, symbolises the fact that one's beginning can also be found in its end, and vice versa. And so the symbol for Ouroboros never loses its meaning, for its meaning is eternity and in a sense the journey is never really completed; each ending is followed by a new beginning. Even if we eventually arrive back at the place where we first began our journey, nothing will be the same; all is transformed.

The World (or Universe), the final card of the Major Arcana, is the supreme symbol of unity and wholeness. It commonly depicts a dancing figure holding the Magician's wand and encircled by a laurel wreath. The wand is symbolic of the magic of self-transformation, while the laurel is the plant of success, victory and high achievement. The circle represents the Ouroboros (a serpent or dragon eating its own tail), a symbol of eternity. In each corner are the four Fixed signs of the zodiac: Taurus the Bull, Leo the Lion, Scorpio the Eagle and Aquarius the Man, which correspond to the four seasons of spring, summer, autumn and winter respectively, the four evangelical qualities of Man: humanity, spirituality, courage and strength, and also the four elements, which the alchemists combined to create a perfect fifth - the 'quintessence', or fifth element. This fifth element is symbolised by the central figure in the card, a genderless hermaphrodite, an image of the reconciliation of opposites, and also of balance. The card's number is twenty-one, the number of completion (three times seven, the two most magically significant numbers). The wreath may also represent zero, the symbol of infinity, with which you started the journey; therefore, the end of one journey is marking the beginning of another.

Astrologically, the World seems to be the most strongly related to the Mid heaven, which is the highest point in the sky at the moment of birth. The World's divinatory meanings are completion, perfection, the rewards of labour, inner satisfaction, the end result of all your efforts, success, synthesis, fulfilment, capability, eternal life, admiration from others, ultimate change, and triumph in all your undertakings. As a symbol of completion, attainment, success and self-knowledge, she suggests that you remind yourself of what you have already achieved, and know that others are aware of you, appreciate and truly admire your past efforts. She tells you that you are now entering an extremely rewarding phase of your life when you will enjoy the benefits of all your hard work.

The World marks the end of a period of time, or the completion of a task, which has its new beginnings as a seed within. It denotes a time of celebration and the wonderful feelings that accompany any occasion during which something is finished, or made whole. It represents a deeply satisfying sense of achievement and fulfilment, suggestive of a peak experience - and expanded horizons ahead. On another level, however, any accomplishment or completion may be followed afterwards by a feeling of emptiness or deflation, as the goal has been realised and the dream made a reality. At this point, the crowned dancing figure who celebrates reaching the finishing mark, suddenly morphs again to embody a foetal-like being, waiting to re-evolve and rebirth itself as the Fool in the never-ending circular journey; in this way, The World symbolises the ending of one cycle and the commencement of another, and indeed The World represents a course that has now come full circle, and suggests you can rest on your laurels for a time before moving onto this next phase, as you have rightly earned it. You now understand your place within that system, and are ready to begin a new phase from the beginning, but this time with an elevated, higher sense of acquired wisdom, spiritual truth and inner knowing.

* Please note that the images described are not found in all Tarot decks. The images in different decks can differ considerably.

THE TAROT'S SUIT OF PENTACLES ★ REPRESENTING THE EARTH ELEMENT

The Pentacle, or five-pointed star, that symbolises Earth in nature magic is often displayed as a central feature on the Suit of Pentacles cards. The Pentacles (known in some old decks as Coins or Discs) represent the Earth element - the energy that keeps us grounded, and the physical or material side of life. They represent the outer manifestation of our spiritual nature, and signify fertility and fecundity in all its forms - sensuality, sensual pleasures, sex and procreation, and the grounding and anchoring of creative energy. The Pentacles tell you about your relationship with the material world, resources, status, tangible assets, and also with your work. Being of the Earth realm, the Pentacles are also associated with prosperity, hard work, financial progress and practical concerns. They can represent the mastery of life's material aspects, or the ambition and striving directed towards achieving them. In essence, the Pentacles are connected with matters that are financial, economic, monetary, or concerning stability. They highlight your attitudes to wealth, work, possessions and success. Dealing with the practicalities of life, they reflect our thinking and actions around earthlier issues, and can inform us of areas where we seek greater stability in our lives. You experience the story of the Pentacles through your relationship with the tangible, physical aspects of yourself - through your attitudes towards your body, sensuality, success, work and worldly goods. A healthy approach towards all of these provides you with a sense of confidence that deepens your perspective on life. Focusing on this suit can help us become more grounded and can reconnect you to life and creativity through linking your Earthy nature to your spiritual essence. The Pentacles provide a solid framework that can be used as a springboard to attainment. Without the foundation of the Pentacles, the effectiveness of the other suits and their elemental correspondences (emotional Water, intellectual Air and enterprising Fire) would be hindered. In a deck of playing cards, the Pentacles correspond to the suit of Diamonds.

THE LUCKY 13 ★ VIRGOAN TIPS FOR INCREASED MAGIC, LUCK & MAGNETISM

1 ★ Incorporate Virgoan symbols into your daily life to remind yourself of your soul's mission.

2 ★ Use the crystal Sapphire in any form in your daily life - wear it, meditate with it, hold it and carry it with you everywhere! Sapphire encourages communication, improves mental focus and clarity, and has a calming and balancing effect on emotions. As it connects mind, body and spirit, it can be used to connect to your spirit guides and teachers, as well as for interdimensional communication. Overall, sapphire encourages you to reach for the stars, speak your truth, stay on your rightful spiritual path, and enhances states of being that will assist in attracting wonderful things to you.

3 ★ Wear or surround yourself with the colours jade green, yellow and brown.

4 ★ Learn the way of the Fish by learning - and practising - the art of daydreaming, spirituality and acceptance. Pisces has much to teach the Virgoan soul. Rise gently above the Earth … Reach for the stars and lose your footing … Abandon Earthly concerns and drift where the wind or tide may take you … Work easier … Develop your spiritual side … Swim with dolphins … Cultivate greater faith in the unseen and intangible … Bathe in the ocean … Dress

up as a mermaid and attend a fantasy-dress party … Indulge in daydreams … Sit in a rock pool and blow bubbles … Stop worrying so much, everything is taken care of … it's *all* within you!

5 ★ Use your lucky numbers 5 and 8, whenever you are needing an extra stroke of luck.

6 ★ Magnify and celebrate your selflessness, diligence, servitude, dignity, humbleness, compassion, inherent sensuality and delightfully practical, helpful nature.

7 ★ Remind yourself of your mission constantly, that is by speaking, breathing and *truly living* your thoughts, ideas and insights - give them form beyond simply analysing them to death! Put the pieces together to form a whole. See? It wasn't that hard!

8 ★ Focus your energies on exploring your inner depths, and transforming yourself through your higher thinking faculties - which are strongly accessible to the acutely intelligent, clever and discerning Virgoan mind. Connect with your deep brainpower and shrewd business sense through any means possible.

9 ★ Use your innate powers of dexterity, discrimination, perceptiveness and pure devotion to a cause, goal or belief, to attune yourself metaphysically and visualise that which you desire, drawing it towards you. If you can develop simple faith in the

positive outcome of events, you can easily use your largely untapped intuition to great creative effect.

10 ★ Tap into and utilise your ability to mentor, advise, heal, empathise with, and transform others through sharing your emotions, spirit and soul. But to do that, you'll need to ease yourself gently off the ground and take a leap of faith into the ether! Your talents could be put to great effect in this other realm.

11 ★ View your discriminatory and perfectionist qualities as strengths and call forth the powers of your dedicated, gifted, unique self. Be who you *really* are, without reservation or apology, and the rest will fall into place.

12 ★ Become the 'Healing Server' of others - and yourself - that you were born to be!

13 ★ Once you have mastered greater spiritual focus and surrendered to the flow of life, learn to share the resulting abundance, insights and knowledge with others so they too can walk the Higher Path!

HAVE YOU PACKED YOUR MAGICAL BAG FOR THE JOURNEY?

If you wish to increase and draw more luck, love and abundance into your life, a power pack is essential. For Virgoans, I would recommend carrying or wearing the following items on you on your travels. Then just sit back and watch as magic pours into your experiences and realities, both inner and outer!

★ One of each of the following gemstones: Sapphire, Carnelian, Peridot, Sardonyx, Emerald
★ Tarot cards The Hermit and The Magician (and the World/Universe card too, if you wish)
★ A bear in any form (use your imagination!)
★ Something made of silver
★ A spider symbol in any form
★ A postcard or image from a cool, dry place (representing your Melancholic disposition). Bon Voyage!
★ A postcard from the future to yourself, proclaiming, 'Wish You Were Here!'

A FINAL WORD ★ TAPPING INTO THE MAGIC OF VIRGO

Blessed with a humble, calm servitude, a delightful lack of ego, a sharp mind, and amazing powers of discernment, you truly are the dutiful helper of the zodiac, affecting everyone around you with your personal integrity and strength of character which is completely devoid of pretension and drama.

Inside anyone who has a strong Virgo influence in their natal chart, is someone who worries too much about imperfection. The Virgo is never satisfied with his or her own standards and this incessant worry can manifest as hidden obsessive-compulsive tendencies. Far from being the worst critic of others, Virgo is their own worst critic, and any criticism directed at others is simple a projection of your own insecurities and doubts about yourself. You may appear to know it all, have everything under strict control and be the hardest worker in the known Universe, but these behaviours hide the fear that you may never be quite 'good enough' - by your own standards of course! Known for your hypochondriac tendencies, you may do this to elicit attention from others, for sometimes you are *yourself* are in need of that care and nurturing you give so freely to others.

Overall, there is something inherently magical about Virgo, the beautiful Maiden. Nothing is distasteful about you. The cosmos has endowed you with the precious and important gifts of decisiveness, orderliness, an eye for detail, responsibility, devotion, practicality, efficiency, perceptiveness, intelligence, cleverness, an enviable purity, self-discipline and impeccable manners. Whether you are fully cognisant of it or not, a magical reservoir of energy is available to you to tap into whenever it is needed.

Finally, to attune yourself to luck, harmony and success, Virgoans should wear, eat, inhale, meditate upon, create, design, and dance with any or all of the suggested luck-enhancers for your Sun sign to receive the most beneficial astral vibrations these 'boosters' can offer you. Wearing, decorating and working with the amazing powers of all your lucky guides, animals, crystals, colours, woods, cards, herbs, foods, places, talismans, planetary influences, charms, numbers, and other magical tips contained within the words of this very book, will bring you greater abundance, love, magic, energy, happiness and personal power, and attract all manner of things to you like bees to sweet flowers. This, my Virgoan friends, I promise you - and Aquarians *never* lie.

> Good luck on the rest of your amazing life journey, and may the LUCK be with you!

Lani is also available for personal Astrology, Numerology, Aura * & Tarot reading consultations, via post, email, Skype and in-person.
Please email lalana76@bigpond.com for more information.

In-person only

Facebook Page ★ Astrology Magic

Other Books in the **Lucky Astrology** Series

Lucky Astrology ★ Aries
Lucky Astrology ★ Taurus
Lucky Astrology ★ Gemini
Lucky Astrology ★ Cancer
Lucky Astrology ★ Leo
Lucky Astrology ★ Libra
Lucky Astrology ★ Scorpio
Lucky Astrology ★ Sagittarius
Lucky Astrology ★ Capricorn
Lucky Astrology ★ Aquarius
Lucky Astrology ★ Pisces

Order your copies now, from White Light Publishing House, at www.whitelightpublishingau.com

www.ingramcontent.com/pod-product-compliance
Lightning Source LLC
Chambersburg PA
CBHW071154300426
44113CB00009B/1205